FEMINISMS OF THE BELLE EPOQUE

Feminisms
OF THE
Belle Epoque
A HISTORICAL AND
LITERARY ANTHOLOGY

Edited by
Jennifer Waelti-Walters
and Steven C. Hause

Texts translated by Jette Kjaer,
Lydia Willis, and
Jennifer Waelti-Walters

University of Nebraska Press
Lincoln and London

© 1994 by the University of Nebraska
Press. All rights reserved.
Manufactured in the United States of America.
The paper in this book meets
the minimum requirements of American National
Standard for Information Sciences—
Permanence of Paper for Printed Library Materials,
ANSI Z39.48–1984.
Library of Congress Cataloging-in-Publication Data
Feminisms of the Belle Epoque :
a historical and literary anthology / edited by
Jennifer Waelti-Walters
and Steven C. Hause ; texts translated by Jette
Kjaer, Lydia Willis
and Jennifer Waelti-Walters. p. cm. Includes
bibliographical references and index.
ISBN 0-8032-4762-1 (cl).–ISBN 0-8032-9748-3 (pb)
1. Feminism–France–
History. 2. Women–France–Social conditions.
3. France–Social conditions–
19th century. I. Waelti-Walters, Jennifer R.
II. Hause, Steven C., 1942–
HQ1613.F396 1994   305.42'-0944–dc20
93-11567 CIP

For Sheila (and Brian too)

and For Kathy

Contents

Acknowledgments

I wish to express my gratitude for funding from the Social Sciences and Humanities Research Council of Canada and the University of Victoria.

Our grateful thanks go to the staff of the Bibliothèque Marguerite Durand, and to Marie-Madeleine Coste in particular, for their thoughtful and enthusiastic help; thanks go also to the staff at the Bibliothèque Nationale and at the Bibliothèque Historique de la Ville de Paris.

This volume would never have existed without the work done by successive teams of student translators and researchers, to all of whom I am indebted for their industry, skill, care, and interest: Marianne Legault, Lucie Léveillé, Johanne Grenier, Jette Kjaer, and Lydia Willis.

Finally, I would like to mention my friends and colleagues Gwladys Downes, Eileen King, and Jean-Pierre Mentha, who have once again helped me enormously by their comments, insights, and attention to the manuscript.

Any errors or omissions are, of course, my responsibility.

Jennifer Waelti-Walters

I wish to thank the National Endowment for the Humanities and the University of Missouri–St. Louis for their financial support of my research. I owe a special debt to the Center for International Studies at UMSL which gives me the time to continue my writing. I greatly appreciate the thorough reading that Karen Offen gave to this manuscript. And I warmly thank Jennifer Waelti-Walters for her invitation to provide the historical side of this collaboration, which she has made go so well. All of my errors were caused by the cat walking across the keyboard.

Steven C. Hause

Editor's Note

To give a sense of each speaker, I have respected, whenever possible, the original sentence structure and punctuation. Changes have been made only when sentences were too long or too repetitive to be easily readable in English. Use of ellipsis points is frequent in these texts and has been maintained. Editor's omissions are therefore indicated by bracketed ellipsis points. Substantial omissions are indicated by bracketed ellipsis points followed by a line space.

Jennifer Waelti-Walters

INTRODUCTION

Many of the roots of modern feminism lie in France. This may surprise readers who are more familiar with feminism than they are with France. After all, the philosophic masterworks of early feminism, from Mary Wollstonecraft's *Vindication of the Rights of Woman* (1792) to John Stuart Mill's *Subjection of Women* (1869), appeared chiefly in the English language. The first large organizations dedicated to seeking women's rights emerged in Britain and the United States, and the first great feminist reforms, the Married Women's Property Acts, were won across America (1839–50) and in Britain (1882) long before France adopted the Schmahl Law of 1907. In the global struggle to win women's suffrage, Australia, New Zealand, and Scandinavia often led in the adoption of feminist reforms, whereas French women did not even win the vote until 1945.

Such facts show that modern feminism reached its first maturity chiefly in Protestant states, where doctrines of individualism flourished. This pattern, however, should not obscure the roots of feminism in late eighteenth- and early nineteenth-century France. Parisian salons, organized and directed by women such as Madame Geoffrin, involved women in the greatest debates of a lively age. The more enlightened philosophers who assembled there, such as the Marquis de Condorcet, advocated women's rights as early as the 1780s. Subsequently, the French Revolution, despite its record of hostility to women's issues, stimulated the growth of feminism by forcing a long European reconsideration of human rights. It produced an eloquent manifesto calling for women's rights in Olympe de Gouges's *Declaration of the Rights of Women* (1791), and it saw the birth of women's political clubs, the precursors of nineteenth-century feminist societies. Indeed, the revolution of 1789 was a profound stimulus to Wollstonecraft, who participated in a radical discussion circle in London and then moved to Paris in 1792, staying in France until 1794. When a European conservative reaction triumphed over French revolutionary ideas in the early nineteenth century, the roots of modern feminism were still to be found in France. French utopian socialism provided an important forum for the continuing discussion of equality and began a tradition of socialist support for women's rights.[1]

Even the word "feminism" came to the English-speaking world with French roots. The first appearance in any language of the word "feminism" (and its cognates) occurred in French, as "*féminisme*" and "*féministe,*" in the late nineteenth century. Some scholars have suggested that the words were first used by French utopian socialists in the 1830s (when parallel "-ism" words, such as "liberalism" and "conservatism," were being coined), but no trace of this has been found in print.[2] The words did appear in France in the 1870s and 1880s, championed by one of the women included in this anthology (see part 5). By the 1890s, both terms were widely used there.[3] The *Oxford English Dictionary* locates the first English usage in 1895; American advocates of women's rights took even longer to adopt the term.[4]

The struggle for women's equality was slow and difficult in France, however; French religious, legal, and political structures created impediments to a women's rights movement more severe than those in Britain and America.[5] Feminism grew more readily in Protestant countries, where individualism and the acceptance of individual rights grew naturally from a religious tradition that emphasized direct, individual access to the Bible, individual interpretation and investigation, and individual conscience as a guide to action. Because 97 percent of its population was nominally Catholic, France lacked the stimulus of such traditions; rather, its religious tradition stressed the importance of obedience to authority.

The French legal system also created severe obstacles. Legal structures were a problem for women in all countries, but they were an unusually formidable impediment in France. Two millenia of Roman legal tradition had reduced all women to the status of being permanent minors, without direct rights of their own. Napoleon's codification of French civil law in 1804 reiterated this status and even worsened it. Married women were reduced to a form of servitude: Article 213 of the Napoleonic Code legally required wives to obey their husbands. Other portions of the code made women powerless to control their public or private lives, their bodies, or their offspring.[6] French laws inhibited the birth of a movement to protest such inequality by limiting the rights of association, assembly, and the press.

The political structure of nineteenth-century France also caused that nation's women's rights movement to lag behind Britain's and America's. The conservative Catholic monarchy of the Bourbon Restoration (1815–30) and Napoleon III's authoritarian Second Empire (1852–70), were less responsive to social innovation, fundamental reform, or the extension of individual rights than were republican America or liberal England. Even when the French finally created an enduring and democratic state, the Third Republic (1871–1940), French politics limited progress toward women's rights. Many of the republican feminists (who dominated the movement in the late nineteenth century) limited their demands and restricted their behavior for fear of adding to the instability of an apparently shaky regime. Many of the democratic men who founded the Third Republic hesitated to give full rights to women for fear that they would use those rights to aid the conservative enemies of the republic. The republican slogan–"Liberty! Equality! Fraternity!"–meant exactly what it says, gender specificity included.

As the nineteenth century passed, French women did win some minor advances, such as the Pelet Law of June 1836, which facilitated the creation of elementary schools for girls and led to a significant increase in the literacy rate among women. What little was achieved, however, had to be won within the misogynistic atmosphere of a society where even a progressive thinker (the anarchist-socialist Pierre-Joseph Proudhon) could insist that women were suited to be only "housewives or harlots," providing for the comfort or pleasure of men.[7] The model of the socially acceptable choice in this dichotomy was the passive and self-sacrificing bourgeois wife; the ideal woman was held by the cultural norm, as well as the law, to be subservient to men.[8] This polarized view of women persisted throughout the century and found many cultural expressions. As feminism grew, for example, artists increasingly depicted women as sinners and temptresses who led men to perdition. Woman was either the "idol of perversity" or the "new woman," both of which were a threat to men's happiness, or even to their very survival.[9] Indeed, according to the male-dominated press of that era, the "new women" were man-hating, man-imitating, cigarette-smoking shrews who refused their "natural" roles while fighting for rights that no real woman either wanted or needed.

Thus, during the belle époque at the end of the nineteenth century,

French men could celebrate the centennial of the revolution that had established their basic human rights. French women could not. Victor Hugo predicted that whereas the eighteenth century had proclaimed the Rights of Man, the nineteenth would proclaim the Rights of Woman, but this did not prove true.[10] Instead, French women of the belle époque were still developing their first large feminist organizations and just beginning to educate the French nation about feminist grievances. Indeed, even today, two hundred years after the French Revolution, many of the issues raised by the feminists in this anthology are still at the heart of debates.

The feminist movement of the belle époque was not a homogeneous, monolithic phenomenon: then, as today, there were many varieties of feminism, many feminisms.[11] More than a dozen associations for political action were active by the turn of the century, and they represented a wide range of opinion (see table 1). The older organizations (dating from the 1870s and 1880s) were strongly republican in their political philosophy, reflecting the French struggle to create the Third Republic during the 1870s. Their leadership, and most of their membership, came from the educated, urban (overwhelmingly Parisian) middle classes. Groups such as Léon Richer's *Ligue française pour le droit des femmes* (the LFDF: the French League for Women's Rights), Maria Deraismes's *Société pour l'amélioration du sort de la femme* (Society for the Improvement of Woman's Condition), and Hubertine Auclert's *Droit des femmes* (Women's Rights) and *Suffrage des femmes* (Women's Suffrage) supported republican France and sought to win the civil and political equality of women within it. They disagreed on priorities, such as seeking the vote, but they typically cooperated well (see the discussion of political rights as a divisive issue in part 7).[12]

By the turn of the century, however, a variety of different women's organizations had appeared. Catholic women had begun to organize groups that would later become the largest women's organizations in France.[13] Even the most explicitly feminist of the Catholic women's groups, Marie Maugeret's *Féminisme chrétien* (Christian Feminism), had doubts about the republic (which was actively anticlerical) and the program of republican feminism. Maugeret's Catholic feminists demanded many civil rights for women, including the vote (which few Catholic women accepted then), but vigorously disputed much of the feminist program: divorce, birth control, and abortion were utterly unacceptable (compare Countess Lecointre's summary of the program of *Féminisme chrétien* in part 1 with the militant feminist demands of Nelly Roussel and Madeleine Pelletier in part 6). These and

Table 1. Principal Women's Rights Organizations in France, 1900–1901

Group	Founded	Leader(s)	Associated Publications	Estimated Membership
Republican Feminists				
(Militant Suffragists)				
Suffrage des femmes	1876	H. Auclert	"Le Féminisme"	under 100
Egalité	1888	E. Vincent	Pamphlet series	under 100
Solidarité	1891	C. Kauffmann	(none in 1900)	under 100
(Moderate Suffragists)				
Amélioration	1876	A. Feresse-Deraismes	*Bulletin*	100–150
LFDF	1882	M. Pognon (pres.)	(none in 1900)	under 200
		M. Bonnevial (sec.-genl.)		
(Moderate and Conservative)				
Conférence de Versailles	1892	S. Monod	*La Femme*	350–400
Avant-Courrière	1893	J. Schmahl	Pamphlet series	approx. 200
Etudes	1898	J. Oddo-Deflou	*Bulletin*	approx. 100
CNFF	1901	S. Monod (pres.)	*La Femme*	21,000
		A. de Sainte-Croix (sec.-genl.)		
UFF	1901	"Marbel"	(none in 1901)	under 100
Union de pensée féminine	1901	L. Martial	(none in 1901)	under 100
(Provincial)				
Comité féministe républicain	1889	E. Darnaud	"Courrière féministe"	approx. 25
Société d'education et d'action féministe	1897	O. Laguerre	Pamphlet series	under 100
Catholic				
Féminisme chrétien	1897	M. Maugeret	*Le Féminisme chrétien*	under 100
Action sociale de la femme	1900	J. Chenu	*Action sociale*	under 200
Devoir des femmes françaises	1901	F. Dorive	*Le Devoir des femmes*	under 100
Socialist				
Groupe féministe socialiste	1899	E. Renaud	*La Femme socialiste*	under 100
		L. Saumoneau		

Source: Steven C. Hause with Anne R. Kenney, *Women's Suffrage and Social Politics in the French Third Republic* (Princeton, 1984), 41–42. Table reproduced with the permission of Princeton University Press.

many other disputes kept many Catholic women outside of the women's movement of the belle époque. Indeed, the majority of accepted, acceptable, and accepting French women remained untouched by the struggle to improve their lot.

Althought Protestants formed only 2 percent of France's population, Protestant women founded and led the largest women's rights organization of the belle époque. The *Conseil national des femmes françaises* (the CNFF: the National Council of French Women) was actually an umbrella organization that brought together a broad coalition of women's groups ranging from philanthropic societies to trade unions. The CNFF offered a middle ground between the militant feminist societies and the conservative Catholic women's groups. Most of its leaders preferred less controversial programs, focusing on greater educational opportunities, for example, or on moral issues such as the campaign against legalized prostitution (see CNFF leader Avril de Sainte-Croix on prostitution in part 4).

Yet another form of feminism grew from the differing interests of working-class women. Socialist feminism, in organizations such as the *Groupe féministe socialiste* (the GFS: the Socialist Feminist Group), usually criticized both the republican government of France and the middle-class feminist agenda for reforming it. The majority of working-class women devoted their political energies to trade unionism ("syndicalism" was the French term) and to socialism, rather than to feminism, because they expected greater improvements in their lives from radical economic changes (see Hélène Brion on this subject in part 3). Socialist feminists (most notably Madeleine Pelletier) sometimes cooperated closely with militant bourgeois feminists, but the relationship between feminism and socialism was not always comfortable.[14]

Taken together, these diverse groups brought more than 20,000 members to the campaign for women's rights at the beginning of the twentieth century. When World War I brought the belle époque to a close, French feminist groups claimed more than 100,000 active members.[15] They were far more active than older accounts of French history or Anglo-American–centered histories of feminism suggest. Between the centennial of the French Revolution and the turn of the century (1889–1900), they organized seven international congresses in Paris to discuss and publicize issues relating to the status of women; three more followed in 1907, 1908, and 1913. The most influential of these was the LFDF-organized *Congrès international de la condition et du droit des femmes* (the International Congress on the Condition and the Rights of Women), which presented a comprehen-

sive feminist program in September 1900 and received extensive press coverage (see Harlor on education in part 2 and Marie Bonnevial on work in
part 3 for excerpts from this congress).

Another index of French feminist activity during the belle époque was
the growth of the feminist press. Led by Marguerite Durand's feminist daily
newspaper published entirely by women, *La Fronde* (1897–1905), more
than forty newspapers and journals supporting women's rights were founded during this period.[16] Many of them had short lives and small subscriber
lists, but they effectively shared feminist ideas within the movement and
brought feminist issues before the public eye (see appendix 1).

This anthology samples the feminist writings of this energetic era. Other
anthologies have translated works of French feminism from different periods.[17] In addition, some general anthologies have provided a glimpse of
France during the belle époque (see the list of translations in appendix 2).[18]
Noting these previous translations helps to indicate the movement's scope,
but it is not possible to provide comprehensive coverage of feminist
thought during the belle époque within a volume of practical size. Instead,
this volume offers a broadly based sample of the feminisms of the era. In doing so, it must regrettably omit some important feminists. Students of socialist feminism could ask for the inclusion of a legion of women such as
Paule Minck, Léonie Rouzade, Eugénie Potonié-Pierre, Elisabeth Renaud,
and Louise Saumonneau.[19] Those interested in male feminism might miss
Léon Richer, Ferdinand Buisson, or René Viviani. Some will wish that the
chapter on education included Pauline Kergomard. Others may want an excerpted article from the Protestant social feminism of Sarah Monod or the
Catholic feminism of Marie Maugeret. And dozens of important feminists
who wrote on women's suffrage, such as Maria Martin and Jeanne Schmahl,
are missing from this anthology.[20] We would have loved to include them all.
Instead of lamenting the shortage of space, however, we have concluded
that, if it does nothing else positive, the list of omissions demonstrates the
vitality of feminist thought in belle époque France.

Another important feature of this anthology is its mixture of historical
and literary sources. Historians typically understand a movement by relying
on "primary evidence" such as that in part 1: a lecture, a pamphlet, or a journal article produced by members of the movement. Fewer historians use evidence such as the three novels excerpted in part 2; some historians even dis-
miss fiction as having no place in the discovery of objective truths about the
past. Similarly, some literary critics have insisted on excluding all materials
outside of the covers of a novel. They confine their interpretations entirely

to "the text" of the work under consideration, shunning contemporary sources such as the lectures and journal articles offered here.

We created this anthology in the belief that the two disciplines enrich each other. It encourages historians of feminism to explore the rich evidence found in novels, and it urges literary critics to view their feminist texts in the context of the contemporary women's rights movement. The belle époque provides a good model for this combination. In 1897, Jacques Flach offered the first course on the condition and rights of women at the *Collège de France*. Flach entitled his course "The History of the Condition of Women in France according to Legal Documents and Literary Works."[21]

Historians of feminism should realize how frequently women have turned to the writing of fiction to express the difficulties in their lives. Mary Wollstonecraft, for example, wrote more than just *A Vindication of the Rights of Woman*. She had previously published *Mary: A Fiction* (1788), a semi-autobiographical novel that contributes significantly to an understanding of both her life and her feminism. Students of feminism should note that several prominent belle époque feminists wrote similarly revealing novels. Two of the militants represented in this volume did so: Madeleine Pelletier's *La Femme vierge* came out in 1933, and Nelly Roussel's *Ma forêt* in 1920. Some of the novels excerpted here were written by women who were active in the feminist movement, such as Louise Compain (see part 3). Conversely, some of the feminists mentioned in this volume (such as Paul and Victor Margueritte) were better known to their contemporaries as novelists. Historians who are aware of such connections thus can use the novels excerpted here to understand the woman question of the belle époque.[22]

Students of literature can profit similarly from this perspective drawn from two disciplines. In nineteenth-century French literary and linguistic usage, for example, the feeling any woman had for her man was "love," whether the precise feeling was desire, adoration, affection, respect, or fear. How such an all-encompassing expectation of self-sacrifice could be reconciled with any sense of independent self-worth, however modest, was one of the primary problems of emancipation and one that had to be addressed before there could be any hope of a mass movement of women in France. If reconciliation proved impossible, then the concept of love would have to be redefined within the culture so as to enable new relations between men, women, and children.

As feminist fiction of the belle époque shows, one of the main pillars of French culture at the turn of the century was this concept of love in both the private and the public spheres.[23] This concept manifested itself in a social structure that rigorously separated roles by gender; consequently, women were obliged to work for autonomy and emancipation within the confines of femininity and marriage. Such conditions led to what has been called "relational feminism."[24] Its program of reform necessarily created priorities different from those of the Anglo-American model, wherein individualistic feminists demanded rights identical to those of men. Relational feminists demanded equivalent rights, not identical ones. Viewed in this context, feminist novelists were trying to reconceptualize the relations between women and men, while the activists normally studied by historians were pushing for social reforms. The concerns of the former can be clarified by learning about the latter.

Whatever interests the reader brings to this volume, we hope that it makes audible the voices and makes visible the issues of the women's movement in France during the belle époque. Those voices have been organized here into seven topics. They begin with an overview of the situation of women and the feminist movement at the turn of the century. The introductory voices in part 1 include the passionate speech of a militant feminist (Nelly Roussel) arguing that women are "always sacrificed," an analytical pamphlet by a conservative feminist (Countess Lecointre) comparing the programs of the various feminisms, and a journalist's (Thérèse Pottecher) article surveying the state of public opinion on the woman question. These readings, and those in the following sections, are organized chronologically, to suggest the development of thinking over time.

The next sections examine a variety of subjects that concerned the women's movement of the belle époque. They begin, following the order of a young woman's life, with the subject of education. The documents in part 2 include visions of the ideal education for women from both a novelist (Marcelle Tinayre) and a militant feminist (Madeleine Pelletier), plus several other feminist concerns, such as the plight of educated women and the life of women teachers.

Part 3 moves to the next stage in life for some women (or the stage that replaced education for others): work. Excerpts here range from feminist discussions of paternalistic attitudes about "protecting" working women (Clotilde Dissard) and of their rights as working women (Marie Bonnevial) to a comparison of socialist and feminist efforts on behalf of women (Hélène Brion). Part 4 examines a tragic corollary to this subject that greatly concerned feminists: the huge numbers of women who were driven to prostitution by economic desperation. Avril de Sainte-Croix presents a feminist view of these "female serfs," a series of case histories illustrates the life of prostitution, and Madeleine Pelletier appeals for a single standard of morality for both sexes.

Parts 5 and 6 shift the focus to women's personal relationships. The first examines male-female relations and marriage during the belle époque, under the Napoleonic Code. Part 5 thus includes an attack on the condition of marriage in the 1880s (Hubertine Auclert), discussions of male-female equality in relationships and marriage (Léopold Lacour and Louise-Marie Compain), and a novelist's (Colette Yver) depiction of the double standard. Part 6 follows questions of a woman's life into the most personal (and yet most controversial) area of all, the issues involved in maternity. Excerpts here deal with such subjects as the treatment of an unmarried mother (Marcelle Tinayre), rape (Lucie Delarus-Mardrus), birth control (Nelly Roussel), and abortion (Madeleine Pelletier).

The survey concludes by returning to public life and the issue of political rights for women. Part 7 presents the appeal of the French suffragette Hubertine Auclert, who called for the vote in the 1870s. Many feminists were slower to join the battle for political rights, but a generation spent confronting the treatment of women in education, work, and marriage led most feminists to suffragism by the end of the belle époque. The anthology thus closes, as it opened, with a speech by Nelly Roussel. This time, Roussel was addressing a great suffrage campaign in 1914 with the argument that, instead of being "sacrificed," women must become citizens with full political rights.

Many of these discussions by feminists of the belle époque will have a startling familiarity to readers a century later. Both eras witnessed a mounting interest in, and political pressures over, women's issues; concomitantly they both saw the proliferation of conferences on the status and rights of women, the publication of increasing numbers of women's journals of all kinds, and the opening of more professions to women. Both periods also experienced a vigorous antifeminist backlash, with passionate appeals to restore and protect the traditional roles of women as wives and mothers in the home. There seems, for example, to be very little difference between the demands of conservative, religious feminists described by Léopold Lacour in *Humanisme intégral* in 1897 and the movement of reactionary women in North America today. Both groups worked to change the circumstances of women's lives, but the traditionalists sought more security in dependence (e.g., taking the risk of desertion out of marriage), whereas others sought more independence and autonomy. These poles of opposition have not shifted in the last hundred years.

Neither has the basic situation of far too many women. Women are still the poorest members of society, earning lower wages than their male counterparts; they still experience the tension between work and home, where they are still judged by social expectations based in the values and assumptions of the bourgeois nuclear family; and they are still insufficiently protected from violent, abusive, or alcoholic partners or from the harassment of co-workers. Some of the feminist campaigns of the belle époque seen in this volume succeeded in improving women's situation. The conditions for single mothers are better, fewer women stay in unhappy marriages, education for girls has improved, and there are more professional women. Even given such improvement, however, women today still confront many of the problems of their predecessors. Doctors, teachers, and lawyers today confront problems strikingly similar to those described in Colette Yver's early novels. The debate over who has the right to control women's bodies is strikingly similar to the debate Nelly Roussel and Madeleine Pelletier knew.

The battle of belle époque feminists against androcentric values and behavior thus remains remarkably pertinent to the discussion of women's issues in the western world today. And these writers certainly do not deserve to be untranslated, undiscussed, and out of print, which they have been for a century. World War I ended the belle époque and curtailed the apparent feminist progress that its generation had achieved. It is a sad irony of our historical memory that we recall the war and its warriors far better than the reformers whom it silenced. Thus, in closing, it seems only fair to honor the memory of the feminists translated in this volume with the famous lines written to remember the men of 1914:

> They will not grow old as we that are left grow old
> Age will not weary them nor the years condemn
> At the going down of the sun and in the morning
> We will remember them.

Notes

1. The bibliography for this volume lists only works published during the belle époque and later works about that period. The footnotes will add brief introductions to the woman question in earlier periods. A good starting place for such background is Claire G. Moses, *French Feminism,* or Maïté Albistur and Daniel Armogathe, *Histoire du féminisme français.*

2. For example, in the essay on women in his Oxford history of modern France, Theodore Zeldin stated that "Fourier invented the word" (*France, 1848–1945,* 2 vols. [Oxford, 1973–77], 1:345) but gave no citation. Karen Offen has undertaken a careful study of this claim and found it in some French dictionaries and even in the writings of French feminists in the 1890s, but none of these claims has provided a verifiable usage in the writings of Fourier; see Offen's "Sur l'origine des mots 'féminisme' et 'féministe' "; "On the Origins of the Word 'Feminist' and 'Feminism' "; and "Defining Feminism: a Comparative Historical Approach." *Signs.* Claire Moses has also concluded that Fourier did not coin the terms; see her article "Debating the Present."

3. See Offen's study of this evolution and the claims made by Hubertine Auclert in part 5. For Auclert's role in popularizing the terms, see Steven C. Hause, *Hubertine Auclert.*

4. The supplement to the first edition of the OED acknowledges the French origin of "feminism" and cites *Athenaeum* magazine, April 27, 1895, as the earliest English usage. For American usage of the terms, see Nancy F. Cott, *The Grounding of Modern Feminism* (New Haven, 1987).

5. For a fuller discussion of these impediments, see Steven C. Hause with Anne R. Kenney, *Women's Suffrage,* 18–27 and esp. 254–81.

6. The legal treatment of French women as inferiors can be found throughout the original text of the Napoleonic Code, but it is most clear in the eight chapters of Title Five, "On Marriage" (Articles 144–228). The original text of Article 213, promulgated on March 17, 1803, stated simply: "The husband owes protection to his wife, the woman obedience to her husband." That text remained unchanged until Léon Blum's Popular Front government began reconsideration in the mid-1930s, resulting in the law of February 18, 1938. The expanded Article 213 of 1938 still identified the husband as "head of the family" and gave him specific powers, such as the choice of the family residence. The Vichy government of Marshal Pétain rewrote Article 213 in the law of September 22, 1942, asserting a traditional vision of the family in which the father was empowered to act "in the common interest." That text remained the law in France until the new feminist movement won a revision in the law of June 4, 1970 (currently in force), stating that "The spouses together assure the moral and material direction of the family."

7. Proudhon (1809–65) was one of the most important founders of anarchist thought and a leading influence on the shape of socialism in France. He was vehemently opposed to the emancipation of women, as he showed in this oft-quoted line from his electoral program of 1848. For further translations of Proudhon's pronouncements on the woman question, see Susan Groag Bell and Karen M. Offen,

eds., *Women, the Family, and Freedom,* 1:190–92 and 1:280–81; see also the comments of Hélène Brion in part 3. For further discussion of Proudhon, see Moses, *French Feminism,* and the works of Marilyn J. Boxer on socialism and feminism.

8. For an introduction to such cultural attitudes in the mid-nineteenth century, see Anne Martin-Fugier, *La Bourgeoise* (Paris, 1983).

9. For a discussion of women as "idols of perversity" in the arts, see Bram Dijkstra, *Idols of Perversity: Fantasies of Feminine Evil in Fin-de-siècle Culture* (Oxford, 1986). For a discussion of the "new women" in literature, see Jennifer Waelti-Walters, *Feminist Novelists of the Belle Epoque.*

10. Hugo (1802–85) supported the feminist movement. In 1853 he delivered a eulogy for Louise Julien that included the following: "Friends, in future times, in that beautiful and peaceful fraternal and social republic of the future, the role of women will be great. . . . The eighteenth century proclaimed the rights of man; the nineteenth century will proclaim the rights of woman" (*Oeuvres complètes* [Paris, 1968], 7:872); see Nelly Roussel's discussion of Hugo in part 1. For more on Hugo and feminism, see Moses, *French Feminism,* esp. 149; Patrick Bidelman, *Pariahs Stand Up!,* 10; and Hause, *Hubertine Auclert,* esp. 19–20.

11. The plural form, "feminisms," was used in a variety of ways during the belle époque. It appears, for example, in the title of one contemporary essay found in our bibliography, Jeanne Laloe's "Les Deux féminismes"; it is discussed, as the title shows, in Jean Rabaut's *Histoire des féminismes français* (Paris, 1978); and it survives in the title of an anthology from present-day France, Marks and Courtivron's *New French Feminisms: An Anthology* (Amhearst, 1980). For current usage of the plural form, see Jane Jensen, *"Ce n'est pas un hasard:* The Varieties of French Feminism," in Jolyon Howorth and George Ross, eds., *Contemporary France: A Review of Interdisciplinary Studies* 3 (1989): 114–43.

12. For an introduction to the range of the women's movement at the turn of the century, see Hause with Kenney, *Women's Suffrage;* Moses, *French Feminism;* Bidelman, *Pariahs Stand Up!;* Albistur and Armogathe, *Histoire du féminisme français;* and Laurence Klejman and Florence Rochefort, *L'Egalité en marche.*

13. For the emergence of the Catholic movement, see Steven C. Hause and Anne R. Kenney, "The Development of the Catholic Women's Suffrage Movement." The best study of the activity of conservative Catholic women is Odile Sarti, *The Ligue patriotique.*

14. This subject has attracted a great deal of scholarly attention; see the works of Charles Sowerwine listed in the bibliography, especially his *Sisters or Citizens?,* and the works of Marilyn Boxer, especially her article, "Socialism Faces Feminism." Subsequent footnotes provide detailed references.

15. See the comparable membership chart for 1914 in Hause with Kenney, *Women's Suffrage*, 134–35.

16. For Marguerite Durand and *La Fronde*, see Sue H. Goliber, "The Life and Times of Marguerite Durand."

17. Anthologies already exist for the era of the late eighteenth century and the late twentieth century; see Darline G. Levy, Harriet B. Applewhite, and Mary D. Johnson, eds., *Women in Revolutionary Paris, 1789–1795: Selected Documents* (Urbana, 1979), and Elaine Marks and Isabelle de Courtivron, *New French Feminisms*.

18. The most valuable is the two-volume anthology edited by Bell and Offen, *Women, the Family, and Freedom*. This collection covers the entire modern era, from 1750 to 1950, and provides sources from all of Europe and the United States. Other helpful anthologies include Erna O. Hellerstein, Leslie P. Hume, and Karen M. Offen, eds., *Victorian Women*, and Eleanor S. Riemer and John C. Fout, eds., *European Women*. See appendix 2 for a list of translations from the belle époque in these volumes.

19. See Sowerwine, *Sisters or Citizens*, for more on these women. Some of their works are listed in the bibliography; others are to be found in socialist periodicals such as those included in appendix 1.

20. Most of these prominent figures of the belle époque are mentioned in following sections and in the notes. For more on them, see Klejman and Rochefort, *L'Egalité en marche*, Albistur and Armogathe, *Histoire du féminisme français*, or Hause with Kenney, *Women's Suffrage*.

21. Klejman and Rochefort, *L'Egalité en marche*, 123 n.3.

22. See, for example, the use made of novels by Jo Margadant in *Madame le Professeur*. Margadant uses novels such as Gabrielle Reval's semiautobiographical accounts (see part 3) to portray the women teachers of the early Third Republic. Bonnie Smith has also used novels to understand the era. Bell and Offen include excerpts from short stories, novels, and plays in *Women, the Family, and Freedom;* see especially their presentation of Marcel Prévost's novel *Les Vierges fortes* [*The Stout Virgins*] (2:47, 51–56); of Emile Zola's *Fécondité* [*Fruitfulness*] (2:129–32); and of Eugène Brieux's play *Maternity* (2:130, 132–34).

23. This theme is developed at length in Jennifer Waelti-Walters, *Feminist Novelists*.

24. See Karen Offen, "Defining Feminism." Offen has opened an important debate among feminist scholars with this essay and the concept of "relational feminism." Responses to her advocate a narrower definition of feminism and the strict historical limitation of the term to those who used it to describe themselves; see Moses, "Debating the Present," and the works she discusses.

I

THE SITUATION OF
WOMEN

NELLY ROUSSEL

Nelly Roussel[1] (1878–1922) was born into the Parisian middle class and married into the bohemian artistic world. She and her husband, a struggling sculptor named Henri Godet, participated together in freethinking, socialist, and feminist organizations at the turn of the century. Roussel preferred the moderate feminist movement and chiefly worked with groups such as the National Council of French Women (CNFF) and the Fraternal Union of Women (UFF). These associations articulated programs that were clearly feminist, yet restrained. Roussel soon developed ideas more advanced than her colleagues' (especially on questions of sexuality, birth control, and abortion), but she never broke from her moderate friends, choosing instead to try to enlarge their feminism.

Roussel and Godet had three children, and she spoke often and proudly of her role as a mother. She usually placed these discussions in the context of a broad "integral feminism" that had room for both motherhood and militancy. In both contexts, Roussel stressed women's right to make decisions concerning their bodies. Her sense of autonomy for women linked the campaign for legal rights with personal arguments about each woman's right to control her own life and to make her own decisions.

Nelly Roussel was trained as a diction teacher and had some experience as an actress. These qualifications, plus an amiable and extroverted personality that won friends quickly, made Roussel the most admired feminist orator of the belle époque. She began a series of public lectures in 1901 and took these talks on an annual lecture tour of provincial France (with a long list of sponsors) between 1903 and 1913. Roussel gave 236 speeches during those years, including "She Who Is Always Sacrificed," the text of which is translated here in its entirety. She gave it for the first time on January 18, 1905, in Paris, and she repeated it on some fifty occasions in 1905 and 1906 alone. It is the least specialized of her addresses and thus serves admirably to introduce feminist thought in the generation before World War I.

She Who Is Always Sacrificed

Ladies, Gentlemen, dear Comrades,

If there is a universal question par excellence, a question that interests, almost to the same degree, not only all women of all classes and of all countries, but all humans without distinction of sex or even of opinion, who are not completely indifferent to the social conditions of the circles in which they evolve, it is the question we are going to discuss today.

Only a few young nations, those newborn states, like certain states of Australia,[2] for example, which, not having had our struggle against secular prejudices and ancestral traditions, were immediately and easily able to recognize the principle of the equality of sexes within their constitutions. We can say that on the whole surface of the globe, from the Orient to the Occident and from the pole to the equator, one half of humanity, and precisely the one that is the most interesting because it is the one that suffers most, has been and still is more or less oppressed and bruised by laws and customs!

This is, Ladies and Gentlemen, not only *unjust* but also *illogical*; it is with this lack of logic that I should like to begin.

When human beings abandoned the primitive nomadic state to be constituted into societies, they had and could only have had one objective: *to improve the conditions of their existence*. They hoped through the *union* and *organization* of their efforts to thwart nature's plots. Too often this nature is not the tender mother exalted by the poets but a blind and cruel stepmother against whom we always have the *right* and sometimes the *obligation* to fight. In other words, when we left nature, it was obviously with the intention of doing better than she does!

We must admit that this initial intention has sadly degenerated; because,

Source: Albistur and Armpgathe, eds., *Nelly Roussel: l'éternelle sacrifiée* (Paris, 1979), 31–25. Trans. Jette Kjaer and Jennifer Waelti-Walters.

setting aside its only reason for existence, the social organization we had high hopes for soon became a new source of sufferings and dangers instead. Treacherously, it became the *accomplice* of the nature it had the mission to fight; it aggravated its laws instead of alleviating them; it accentuated its errors instead of correcting them.

Illogical until the end, it preferred to hound the half of humanity that had more claims to its solicitude, since an unkind nature had already reserved for this half the most painful and most dangerous task: the task of reproduction, which unique goal it pursues unceasingly! (Applause.)

The miserable destiny of woman, who is the sorrowful and unacknowledged generating force, has been perfectly summed up by the great philosopher Diderot: "The cruelty of civil laws combine with the cruelty of nature against woman."[3]

All the doctrines of liberation that today attempt to reform this social organization to make it what it should always have been: a *cordial understanding* between humans, which attempts to give everyone the greatest amount of happiness possible by suppressing useless pain and by proportioning equitably rights and duties, satisfactions and needs, compensations and sorrow; all doctrines of liberation, however they may be labeled and whoever the men who are associated with them, must include *feminism* as one of their top priorities. In order to avoid all ambiguity I believe it necessary here, Ladies and Gentlemen, to define precisely the meaning of the word "feminism," which our adversaries have taken pleasure in distorting. At first they tried destroying the most serious and poignant issues with ridicule by representing the "feminist," the woman who "makes demands," as a grotesque, disagreeable, extravagant, and half-deranged creature who, despising and repudiating all the attributes of her sex, replaces them with some of the masculine vices and defects.

Fortunately, public opinion has been quick to judge such crude stupidity and evident bad faith. It understood that a doctrine that tried to "masculinize" woman could not be "feminism." Feminism, on the contrary, could be defined as a "blossoming of *femininity.*"

When our detractors realized that they were on the wrong track, they changed tactics; and falling into the opposite error, they pretended to see in "feminism" a declaration of war on *man,* on all men!

The shortest account of our theories will suffice to demonstrate decisively the inanity of such an accusation.

If there is a "war" between man and woman, it is not we, the women, who have declared it! We limit ourselves to a *defense* against everything in the world that infringes on our rights, hampers and hurts us! We desire nothing more ardently than *an end to these hostilities,* and this depends *only on you,* Gentlemen. We are not, and we have never been, your *adversaries,* and we ask only to stretch out our hands in a fraternal gesture toward you! But you, at least *some of you,* became ours by violently blocking our path when we started our march toward the conquest of our freedom!

It is not really our fault if there are men similar to church congregations that declare themselves *persecuted* when their *privileges* are touched upon and cry out, *"our rights are interfered with,"* as soon as one begins to oblige them to *respect other people's rights!* (Applause.)

Alas! The war between the sexes has existed since the day man assumed an illogical and unjustified power over woman! There is no agreement possible between the master and the slave. And this war will end the day that, thanks to our efforts, justice and liberty for all finally reign!

No, the war between the sexes was not born of feminism; however, it must end with it! So, relax Gentlemen, we do not dream of *vengeance,* and we shall not return the evil that you have, perhaps unconsciously, inflicted upon us; we do not dream of substituting our tyranny for yours; we want the suppression of *all* tyrannies.

To sum it up in a few words, "feminism" is simply the doctrine of *natural equivalence* and *social equality* of the sexes.

Fortunately, there are men with enlightened minds who fight whole-heartedly alongside us[4] because they have understood that our claims deal not only with the issue of *justice,* toward which their upright nature and generosity cannot remain indifferent, but also with an issue of *general interests;* for the liberation of woman, the flowering of the feminine soul, which has been proscribed, chained, and unappreciated for such a long time, will open up a new era of peace, love, and beauty for the whole of humanity!

Ladies, Gentlemen, my dear Comrades,

When we look at the position of woman within the family and society, the first question that arises, that demands our attention, is an economic one; a question of bread, a question of life! If we desire *economic independence* above all, it is because we have understood that this independence is the natural source of all others. It is because we have understood that work, carried out under good conditions, of course, that is, under conditions that are very different from those that obtain at present, is the only way for every human creature to live in freedom and dignity. It is because we have understood that what creates slavery for a woman is not so much the odious articles of the Civil Code that establish her civil inferiority and class her with the mad, with children, and with criminals (Ladies take a bow); not so much the legal chains, it is more material necessity that, nine times out of ten, forces a woman to fall back on the man who keeps her or helps her in some way, a man who, most often, takes advantage of such a situation to enslave and humiliate her!

Let us not have any illusions; let us look coldly at things as they are.

The middle-class young woman who marries, or rather *allows herself to be married,* to a gentleman she hardly knows and perhaps never will love, in order to "have a position"; the working woman who takes a lover because her meager earnings do not enable her to live on her own; and the unhappy creature who picks up the first passerby in the street in order to eat, all three are making more or less the same gesture, for which our laws and customs almost inevitably condemn them. *They are giving their bodies to men in exchange for daily bread!* (Applause.)

And when love slips in between a man and a woman (which fortunately does happen), it is by *chance* and *exception*. It is almost never the *sole* and *essential* basis of the union!

This is what displeases us and causes our revolt. This is why we ask for entry into *all* careers, admission to *all* professions, and that in each of these professions and in each of these jobs, we receive pay equal to that of men for equal work.[5] In short, this means we have the possibility of providing all our needs ourselves, and can wait, free and proud, until our heart speaks, so that we then *give ourselves out of love,* and do not *sell ourselves out of necessity!* (Applause.)

This is only one reason, Ladies and Gentlemen, and there are many more militating in favor of woman's work; I mean professional and paid work. It is sufficient to look around in order to see the number of unmarried women, abandoned women, and widows who, if they do not want to die of starvation, are obliged to earn their own living; in order to understand how stupid and cruel it is to make this courageously accepted task more difficult for them by creating thousands of obstacles, by closing a large number of doors for them and by paying pathetically low wages for their work in the few areas left open to them! But the most virulent *antifeminists* among you,[6] Gentlemen, those most opposed to woman's work, should at least consider their own mortality, and that they themselves could one day be lost to their families!

It is necessary to develop the question to consider it in all its importance. Even if work were not a *necessity* for us, Ladies and Gentlemen, it would remain a *right,* a strict and *absolute* right.

Those who pronounce with so much assurance on the "role of woman," on what is suitable or not suitable for "woman," etc., do they by chance imagine that all women are *identical* creatures and that there do not exist between them physical and moral *differences* as profound and as essential as are the differences existing among the individuals of the other sex?

Everyday experience shows that they are mistaken.

Will they uphold that what suits one of us must *necessarily* be suitable for others? This would be simply absurd!

Then, in the name of which right, which principle, is each one of us refused the liberty to follow our vocation, obey our natural tendencies, choose ourselves the kind of occupation suitable for us? In the name of what right is the field of our activities restricted and a predetermined path, the same for everyone, imposed on us?

Take notice, Ladies and Gentlemen, that it is not necessary to defend the *principle of woman's work.* This principle does not count a single adversary, since the same people who scoff at or are indignant at hearing about *female lawyers, female physicians, woman magistrates, woman civil servants, or newspaper women*[7] find it natural and even *necessary* that *laundresses, seamstresses, linen maids, female cooks, housemaids,* etc., should exist. Moreover, I do not believe that the occupations of laundress, seamstress, linen maid, female cook, housemaid, and many others such as the *female bread carrier* or *vegetable vendor* or *streetsweeper,* the *female farm worker* in the country, or the *saleswoman* in the cities can be considered less tiring, more in conformity with the female constitution, or more compatible with the tasks of motherhood than any liberal profession.

Without looking any further, why cannot we acknowledge that simple *household chores* represent as considerable an amount of effort and fatigue as many masculine occupations? Nevertheless, as you know, Ladies, this type of work, housework, almost always falls on the woman alone! It is true that this is *not paid* work, and that this type of work has always been considered by men as particularly suitable for women!

But no one seems to understand that it is precisely this lack of appreciation for housework that has pushed many women, who are eager for independence, to abandon the home for the factory or the workshop; this means exchanging *unpaid work* for *paid work.* By paying for the housework that the woman accomplishes at home according to its worth and by likening house-work to a true *occupation* that must, like the others, receive a wage, it may be possible to keep a large number of spouses at home, in the place where, un-der the pretext that it is the men *who bring the money into the home,* their hus-bands now despise and humiliate them in spite of the services they render.

Let us go on. How does one explain the mentality of those who are not indignant at seeing a woman's charm wither and her health deteriorate in painful manual labor, and who also want to prohibit her access to certain ca-reers where her intellectual faculties could be used so happily? The mentality of these people is very simple. Respectful of the traditions of the past, they blindly accept without question all that *existed before them,* all they have been accustomed to seeing since birth. "Novelty" and "change" induce an in-stinctive, irrational fear in them. They do not seem to understand that all *re-alities* started as *utopias,* and that all things that appear to be the most simple, the most natural, the most legitimate, even the most necessary, were initially received exactly as they are receiving the innovations presented to them to-day. Their objections do not rest on any serious base and cannot be taken into consideration. They are absolutely illogical and incoherent.

If there really are occupations that are ill-suited for women, or rather, for certain women, then that is for women to decide. We do not ask for any-thing except *freedom of choice.* We maintain that any given individuals, who-ever they may be, *know better than anybody else what is suitable for them.* No-body has the right to tell another person: "This is the path you have to follow; I shall not allow you ever to leave it."

Look around you! Our society is full of those unfortunates who were *mis-led,* who perform indifferently and with repugnance a task they were not made for when they could have led happy lives by following their inclina-tions and tendencies freely!

I do not want to leave this question of woman's work without insisting on an essential point that has been badly neglected thus far.

If the lack of appreciation and the fact that *housework* is unpaid constitute a mistake as well as an injustice, then the injustice and the mistake become even more revolting if *mothers'* work is not appreciated either.

Well, a mother's work, this noble and painful work, this most sacred work that should, like other work, and even more than other work, ensure the independence and the well-being of all who perform it, has so far been only a source of slavery and inferiority! . . .

Of all social functions, the first, the most magnificent, the most painful, and the most necessary is the only one that has never received wages.

A society that supports the soldier, the bringer of death, has for the mother, the bringer of life, nothing but indifference and contempt! Indifference! What do I say? Rather, *hostility,* for this ungrateful society is not only content to *forget* mothers, but it also *oppresses* and *humiliates* them. The function of the mother, this terrible and sublime function, which among bees causes the *female* to be treated as *queen,* has been used in our society as a pretext for enslavement!

When, in the name of our duties, in the name even of our pain, we dare to claim our rights, we are told with a shrug of the shoulders: "Rights? What would you do with them, woman? Do you need to have rights? . . . Do not grumble, get on with the only task suitable for you, the task that is your only reason for existence. Bear citizens and soldiers for us; produce, produce children without respite; let your charm wither, and wear out your health in continual pregnancies.[8] Go! Suffer and struggle, weep and moan; bear your martyr's lot; but do not expect to be appreciated; do not expect any reward; you are made to give and not to receive." Married, . . . your child will remain the *property of his father,* the fortunate father whose task in the common effort was limited to a few moments of pleasure; and you, the suffering and wounded creator, who has paid for that child with your blood and your tears, you do not exist; you do not count! In marriage, annihilated as a *woman,* you must also be annihilated as a *mother.* Furthermore, as an unmarried mother you will be left alone to carry the burden of what bourgeois hypocrisy will scornfully call your "fault." And it will not be enough to expiate it through the physical tortures that represent for you, woman, a sort of ransom for love; it will not be enough that you, poor girl, should have suffered the "sacred torture" of motherhood all alone in your garret, without help, without care, without a consoling word of love and without a comforting touch of the hand! . . . No! . . . Society, the keeper of morality, will add all its refinements! The better to punish you, it reserves for you abandonment, contempt, and misery; the impossibility to re-create a happy and free life through work, even the impossibility of obtaining any kind of assistance; and finally, the necessity of making your sad choice between *suicide* and *prostitution!* . . . If then, terrified, desperate, weary of suffering, you kill the little child that you wanted so much to love, society will find judges who will condemn you to solitary confinement, to live out your miserable pariah's existence! (Applause.)

This is the way, Ladies and Gentlemen, that a society *that asks for children* treats *mothers* within marriage and outside marriage!

And you are surprised that we rebel? Our rebellions will continue to grow! The ill-paid worker refuses to work; nowadays, the right to strike is not contested any longer. We, women and mothers, *are the worst paid of the workers;* and there could not be any more legitimate *strike* than ours!

This word "strike" should not make anyone smile. Indeed, this *strike* has already been declared within the as yet confined circle of those who think and who understand; but it will expand continuously; the apostles of freedom will preach it in the four corners of the earth!

Understand me well, Ladies and Gentlemen; let there be no ambiguity. We do not rise up against *love,* because if we rose up against love, we should rise up against *man,* and I want to repeat that we feel hatred only for society! We know that love, in conscious beings, is the vivifying source for the replenishment and the exaltation of all energies and enthusiasms. We do not want to be deprived of this force; we do not want to be deprived of this joy. But, thanks to the progress of science, we know that it is possible to *separate love* from its natural consequence: *procreation.* We maintain that we want to *protect ourselves against procreation* only so long as our suffering wombs must bring forth sons who despise us or daughters who suffer like us; as long as an ungrateful society responds to our aspirations and to our desire for a *complete life* and for freedom and light only by shrugging its shoulders or by sniggering contemptuously!

We, who are mothers, maintain that motherhood, with its pain and fatigue, with all its requirements of devotion and courage, represents more than *the amount of work that each individual owes the community, and in exchange for which he is entitled to support.*[9] It would therefore be just that this community, whatever its form or organization, be considered the *debtor* of any woman who gives birth, and that what this woman has given of her energy and her life to the community should be returned to her not only in *respect, veneration,* and *moral satisfaction,* but also in *security* and *material well-being.* In a word, it would be just that maternity be considered a true *social function,* the most honored and the best rewarded of all. Only under such terms would all women be completely and truly *independent,* even those who for some reason cannot or do not want to take on another lucrative occupation besides their maternal function!

Ladies and Gentlemen, this contention that maternity is a *"social function"* does not contradict at all the *right* of women to *engage in professional work,* which I claimed for them a little while ago; I believe it necessary to insist on this point in order to avoid ambiguity.

If it seems inadmissible to me that a woman should be a prisoner in her home, condemned to be always and exclusively *spouse and mother,* when her tastes, her aptitudes, her tendencies, and her vocation urge her to be elsewhere, I find it equally unjust *that she should not be able to stay at home if she so desires.* Material necessity should not force her to leave the home when she prefers to stay there.

What we want is very simple and can satisfy everyone. We want for *all* men and women the *right* and the *possibility* to live a *complete life,* to follow their chosen path freely, to pursue their own happiness, whatever this happiness means to them and to march toward an ideal *whatever it may be.* My neighbor's ideal, although different from mine, does not seem less respectable to me.

Thus, Gentlemen and dear Comrades, it must be repeated again and again, *feminism* means not only emancipation of woman *outside the home,* but also and especially the raising of her status *inside the home.* And those who declare themselves the most ardent supporters of woman in the home, the most ardent adversaries of outside occupations for her—there are probably some of them here, and I am addressing them in particular—even they, if logical, should be the first to support us when we ask for the reorganization of the family home on a new basis that is more equitable and conforms more nearly with the legitimate aspirations of today's woman.

If woman's place is in the home and only in the home, this place should be made attractive enough that she would desire no other. But when one impartially and cold-bloodedly examines the true position that most of them endure in the homes, is it any wonder that many women, disgusted by their homes, seek to create an interesting and worthwhile existence elsewhere?

Come now, Gentlemen, I am speaking to you here in all sincerity, do you believe that an intelligent woman, a woman who reflects and comprehends, who knows what she commits herself to in getting married, a truly *conscious* woman concerned about her dignity, can accept the position that your laws have given her in a legal union? If you were in her place would you accept it? . . . (Reply: No!) I am certain that at the bottom of your hearts, all of you, without exception, would say no. If you would not accept this because of your *human dignity,* can you be surprised that we, who, with all due deference, are human, thinking beings to the same degree as you, should also refuse it? . . .

For my part, I never attend a marriage, be it civil or religious, without experiencing a very painful feeling. At an epoch when it is maintained that slavery has been abolished, in a *republic* based on *liberty* and *equality*, how can this oath of *obedience* sworn in public by a human creature be permitted! In order to justify this *obedience,* imposed on woman by the law, it would be necessary to prove that the husband is *always* and in *all things the more capable of the two spouses.* But you know as well as I that this is not always the case. You know as well as I that in most cases, for the *administration of property,* if there is any, the *management of the house,* the *education of the children,* and a thousand other things, the woman is the equal of the man and sometimes even his superior.

We have seen enough husbands mistreating and ruining their families on the one hand, and on the other enough women managing perfectly under the most trying circumstances, to know what to conclude on this point. And thus the systematic legal inferiority of the woman is not only an *injustice* and an *insult to human dignity,* it is also a *hindrance to domestic and social prosperity,* since it deprives the family and society of one indispensable component, *feminine initiative.*

Perhaps I shall be told that this famous oath of obedience, against which I am protesting, very often constitutes only a vain formality and that most women accept only as much as they are prepared to take. Far be it from me to deny that there are good marriages. I know of some of these "good marriages"; I know of perfect and charming unions where love alone reigns supreme, and dictates their mutual rights and duties to the couple. Those couples have already achieved in our present society the ideal that we dream of for the future! . . . But one must be very blind or lacking in good faith to recognize that such unions are at present very rare exceptions! . . . We feminists are not thinking about happy and beloved women; they do not need us; we are not concerned with them. However, we know that there are others, an immense throng of others for whom the "law of man" has retained all its harshness! We do not think that the privileged woman accomplishes her duty by remaining egoistically enclosed in her own happiness without concern for the tears shed around her! I know of nothing more odious, more revolting, than a woman who, when one talks to her of feminism, replies: "I'm not interested in feminism; I have no need for it!"

No, Gentlemen, it is not at all sure that the famous oath of obedience nearly always represents a "vain formality." First of all, if this were true, I could ask why you insist so much on keeping it, and what inconvenience there would be in eliminating it? We do not usually hang on to useless things. You see, Citizens, we have met too many of those supposed *Republicans, Socialists,* even *Libertarians* who, after having held forth in all public meetings on *equality, liberty,* and *fraternity,* forget all their beautiful theories when they return home; they talk as masters, are served by, oppress, and humiliate the members of their families, totally forgetting that families *are the cell that make up the body politic,* and a *republic* will never be made up of little *kingdoms!* (Applause.)

But, and this is our vengeance, Ladies, those men will never know the infinite sweetness of the ideal union based on the harmony of souls and the communion of spirits! Those poor fools who believe in happiness for men based on women's tears are much mistaken!

Later, in a very long time perhaps, when humanity knows true civilization, when men are loyal and good, when women are independent and respected, our descendants will ponder all the complications that we have voluntarily imposed on our existence and all the stupid and cruel chains that we have forged for ourselves. What will they who love each other simply, freely, and with dignity, without hierarchy, ulterior motives, or petty considerations of propriety or interest, think of marriage with its ridiculous formalities, its barbarian rules, and its shameful trafficking![10]

While you are waiting for this happy day, all you who are listening to me, wives, mothers, and the young girls who are the wives of tomorrow, be it in a free union or in legal marriage, do not agree to *obey;* repudiate this ignominious word! Certainly, be loving, be devoted, be good and be tender, but always and in everything remain *proud!* . . . Your devotion must be *voluntary,* it must not be *compulsory;* accomplish your duties, but demand your *rights.* Demand your rightful place in that family which is your domain (you have heard often enough that the family is your *domain!*) and whose center and soul you are. Do not ever agree to play a secondary, inferior, and humiliating role in it. Tell yourself that your character *is as good as that of another;* and keep your head up high, conscious of your value and of your dignity.

But talking is not enough, we must act. Wishing for a transformation will not do; we must work to make it a reality.

Revolutions are made first *in the brain;* and as long as they are not made there, do not hope to make them anywhere else! . . . Educational reform is the first chapter of all the social issues. Now, and we must not refuse to see it, present-day education, education as it is still understood in our time, although claiming to be enlightened and free, has in fact no sense to it.

The education that has a double role—*the development of the individual* and *his preparation for life within the community*—whose first task, I should say its sole purpose, is *to favor the happy blossoming of all human faculties,* is, only too often, a *damper* and a *yoke,* especially for women.

I say "especially for women," for indeed there is a great difference between the sexes in this respect. The young man is more or less free; family supervision is less heavy for him; he may *read;* he may *go out;* he may use his leisure time more or less as he pleases. But the young girl is a prisoner of *prejudice* and of *"proprieties."* A young girl *is not allowed* to read everything; a young girl may not go out *on her own.* Moreover, in families of modest means, she is needed to help her mother with the household duties. It would not occur to a mother to ask her son for help and even less her husband! Household work does not concern men! . . . And it is in the name of these principles that in far too many families we see the woman exhausting herself looking after and serving the man when both of them return in the evening, equally tired from a meeting, festivity, walk, or job. It is repeated in many different ways that woman is the "weaker vessel"; one finds her alleged *weakness* used as an excuse to refuse her certain rights, as though the "rights" of an individual were measured by the strength of his muscles! But there is no fear of imposing on this "weaker vessel" all the unpleasant and rough tasks that the *stronger* vessel refuses to perform . . . (Applause.)

Workers demand an eight-hour day.[11] In my opinion, they are perfectly right; even eight hours is too much . . . *But when will there be an eight-hour day for women?* . . . When will there be *eight hours of rest* and *eight hours of leisure time* for housewives and mothers? . . . This is, certainly, one of the most interesting and most important questions for the future of humanity and one many sociologists have never considered.

And yet something could be done. It would not be impossible to find a practical solution to this problem. At a time when everything is being grouped and *industrialized* little by little, and when everything is being perfected by simplification, when the machine is replacing hands by working better and faster, is it not extraordinary that household tasks are *the only ones* that have remained almost exactly as they were a hundred years ago?

Let us hope the day will come when rational and scientific methods will be applied to *everything* and, for example, will do for the kitchen, for the mending, and perhaps even for the housecleaning what has already been done satisfactorily for quite some time for laundry, bread baking, and the manufacture of garments. Whereas all these used to be done at home, they are now done by *professionals* in special workshops.

While awaiting this profound transformation, which we must call for with all our hearts and spur on with all our efforts, would it not be just and logical in hardworking families where *each* has *an occupation* that upon returning home *each* took a part in sharing the additional tasks, since each will profit from the well-being resulting from their perfect completion?

Let us leave this and come back to the subject that preoccupies us, namely, *the education of young girls*.[12] While the young girl is completely in the power of her parents, she can learn only *what they make her learn;* generally, however, parents do not make her learn what she *should know*.

A young girl's education is now a very simple thing that can be summed up in a few words: anything that forms her *character, anything that might make her different from the conventional type that is held up as a model,* is *a fault* and must disappear.

The idea is to make her not a *conscious* and *free* being, but rather a docile *instrument* in the hands of the man who will be her master. She is not prepared for *life's struggle* but only for *husband hunting*. She is brought up not for *herself* or for *her personal happiness,* but to satisfy the desires, caprices, and will of the male! . . . She is destined to become not *somebody* but simply *the wife of somebody*. This is why naïveté, modesty, and resignation are her most beautiful virtues. There is no effort to develop her critical faculties; that would be dangerous. That is, of course, why she is left to ignore anything about life and anything that could constitute a danger for her. Yet the best means of protecting her against the dangerous impulses of passion is to let her know what risks she incurs when she yields to them!

When, in a family, a girl shows signs of an above-average intelligence, the parents sigh: "What a shame she is not a boy!" Yes, what a shame, firstly for her and secondly for humanity, because if she were a boy no sacrifice would be too great for the parents to cultivate her growing intelligence to the full and give her a free and magnificent start; they would be proud of their boy and would like to make something of him, but she is a girl! What is the use of intelligence in a girl? Intelligence is not necessary to look after a home or practice the art of suffering in silence. All that is wanted and all that is sought is perfect adaptation to the traditional mold.

How dare they speak of woman's alleged intellectual inferiority!

What is strange about such a system is that not all women become completely stunted under it and that some of them even succeed in freeing themselves, becoming assertive, and liberating their personalities. It is amazing that the nineteenth century was able to produce women like George Sand,

Clémence Royer, Rosa Bonheur, and Louise Michel, and that they were able to succeed.[13]

Do you understand how much courage, daring, and tenacious willpower it takes for a woman, even the most gifted, to make a place in the sun for herself and to conquer her part of life?

Can you imagine, as a parallel, what treasures of art, of science, and of poetry happy and respected women will create for the world?

Our work would be incomplete, Ladies and Gentlemen, if we insisted upon reforming only feminine education, since masculine education, although different, is not better. Moreover, the bigger fault of the two educations, the masculine and the feminine, is precisely their dissimilarity. The children of both sexes are taught principles that are false, narrow, and stupid. There is, therefore, no jealousy possible between them. But those narrow, false, and stupid principles are not the same; there are two sets of morals, one for men and one for women. The same words do not have the same meaning, depending on whether one applies them to one sex or the other. Take, for example, the word "honest." An honest woman is one who has not had a lover, but a man is honest in spite of the worst debaucheries, so long as he has not committed any too obvious fraud. A woman's honor resides only in her virginity when she is unmarried; in her fidelity when she is married. The deepest, the purest, the most sincere love is no exception to what is commonly called a "fault." But he, the man, has nothing to fear: the most craven actions, the abandonment of a bastard and then a mistress, do not taint his honor in any measure. Both crimes have the same source, and the consequences should be similar; it is the height of absurdity that the abandoned mistress be held up to ridicule and contempt!

Do we not see every day that public opinion judges differently the same actions, carried out in the same circumstances, depending on which of the sexes is involved, and judges more severely the same crimes and offences when they are committed by a woman! I know very well that in the recent court case of the antimilitarists this was not the case;[14] but if, instead of signing a petition, the woman had had an abortion or if she had shot the lover who was about to abandon her, or her guilty husband, then she would have been very severely punished, while a man would have been acquitted. One is led to believe that a woman's life is less precious than a man's. The truth is that magistrates and jurors have remained profoundly impregnated with the old Roman tradition stipulating that a woman belonged to her husband, who had the right of life and death over his family circle!

I find the difference between the two moralities and the two educations in everything: we are always reminded of duties, while you, Gentlemen, are insufficiently reminded of them. We are taught only sacrifice, the abdication of all pride, of all our natural rights, and of our most legitimate desires, while a man is told only about his freedom, his power, his greatness, and his virility; even in his games his brutality, his egoism, and his arrogance are flattered!

He is made to feel ashamed of any kind of delicacy of sentiment, which is considered a proof of weakness and, as they say, good only for women. But you need an elite soul, Gentlemen, to resist the education given to you, to remain just and good in spite of it. Certainly, we want to perfect woman, but we have seen too many women, too many feminine, sublime, and charming souls, misunderstood, despised, and hurt to fail to understand the necessity of extending our need for perfection to man. From infancy onward, the war of the sexes is declared by the parent-educators. The little male child, just starting to wear trousers, when made to stand in a corner because he has misbehaved, feels that the biggest insult inflicted on him, a mere boy of three years of age, is to tell him: "You look like a girl," or "Let go of this, it is good only for girls." As for the little girl, she is encouraged to avoid boys, "those devils, those bad boys who are all the same." A little bit later, on the school benches and in the schoolyards, they are separated with the greatest care, just when working and playing together would be so useful; for because of their differences, they would perfect each other. They would grow up side by side, nourished by the same truth; they would learn to know and understand each other better and would be better prepared to unite and love each other.

Coeducation, or the education of boys and girls together, has produced enough dependable results everywhere that we should adopt it from now on.

In America—the country of practical innovations—coeducation exists at all levels, both in practice and within the curriculum; it is so well established that no one is surprised any more!

In England and in Holland it is practiced on a less important scale. In France, need I say, coeducation practiced at the orphanage of Cempuis provoked, in 1898, violent controversies led by all the clerical and reactionary factions. But Paul Robin, principal and founder of the Prévost orphanage at Cempuis, has carried on his work, which is still alive and remains one of the most admirable pedagogical models for the whole of France.[15] (Applause.)

I can talk to you about this since I have had the pleasure of meeting several former pupils, men and women, from the orphanage. "What characterizes good pupils at Cempuis," the young wife of one of them said to me, "is precisely their respect for women." This is certainly not the utterly superficial respect made up of politeness and condescension that is used in the world, but a profound and sincere respect expressed by one human individual for another.

It is not so in the family; and yet it would be so simple, so natural! It is because people are afraid of trying out the coeducation of the sexes that sisters and brothers remain strangers to each other.

All too often they do not have the same likes and dislikes; families give their sons preferences and privileges; they train the girls to serve the boys. If forced to show a preference for the loss of one of them, they would more readily sacrifice the girl. You all know, Gentlemen, much better than I, that a boy is accustomed to seeing in a woman a different being, of a species different from himself, of lesser importance, destined to serve him and at the same time used for his pleasure. He sees in her something unique, a sex about which he knows nothing other than what he reads in those infamous magazines, which taint and debase many of our adolescents by their titillating accounts.

If, while waiting for coeducation, and Mothers, it is you to whom I am speaking, you could become the confidantes, the counselors, the friends of your sons; if brothers were the comrades of their sisters, how many things would be changed! Alas, both sexes arrive at adulthood, at marriage, and at communal life in total ignorance of each other. Men despise women, women are afraid of men, and it is under these conditions that one talks of creating a harmonious world.

The task of the separation of the sexes, which is begun so well in school and within the family, continues in society. Woman does not exist socially, and her legal nonexistence within society is obviously the cause of her inferiority within the family. This law that has been made *against* her has been made *without* her. What we ask for today is the admission of women into all careers including the civil service, equality of pay for men and women, equality of instruction and education, the necessary remuneration for housework and motherhood, coeducation, the suppression of all articles of the Civil Code that establish inequality, and the raising of woman's status as spouse and mother within marriage. Without exception, all these reforms are necessary! But one should not expect too much from masculine generosity. As long as we are poorly defended, as long as we have no active part in the management and the constitution of human societies, we must expect to be neglected, despised, or forgotten by these societies. At present, participation in social organization manifests itself by the electoral process, eligibility, and universal suffrage. I do not want to discuss here the advantages and disadvantages of this system, which has its partisans and its detractors. So-called *universal* suffrage exists; as long as it exists it will be used against us; therefore we demand our part in it. We see in the granting of political rights not the final objective, but a simple means to improve our society, one that you, Citizens, did not disclaim.

M. Viviani, a former deputy, who has been in the thick of things and knows how they work, said: "Legislators make laws for those who make legislators."[16] It is impossible to express more frankly and sincerely that anybody who is not a voter does not count in the eyes of the elected!

It is true that once the election campaign of flatteries, promises, and lies is over, voters do not count any longer! There is a lot of truth in all this, but one should not exaggerate, because I think that if only employers put their ballots into the ballot boxes, the situation of the workers would be even worse. (Applause.)

It must be pointed out to you, Gentlemen, that it is not only the interest of our sex, but also the general interest of society, that demands our participation in your organization.

The more one contends that man and woman are different and destined to complete each other, the more we shall see that logically they cannot do without each other; that no undertaking is lasting and perfect without a close and continual accord between the two elements of humanity!

Wanting to organize human society, or create a movement of opinion without the participation of the two elements, masculine and feminine, is as false, as chimerical, and as impossible as pretending to create a child without the participation of both a mother and a father!

It is in the name of these principles, ignored for too long, that we demand our place; that we want the feminine spirit to blossom freely and be officially emancipated. The whole of feminism is contained in these few words.

And what is extraordinary, Ladies and Gentlemen, is that feminism has not yet become unnecessary! It is extraordinary that this simple idea, which is so logical and so elementary, the idea that the sexes are equal and should participate in all things, is not accepted and proclaimed by all avant-garde men, and all men of common sense; that emancipated spirits, or at least spirits who consider themselves emancipated, seem unable to free themselves from the old sexual prejudices stemming from religious beliefs; and that these prejudices outlive the beliefs by so long!

How many of the so-called freethinkers, and you know them all, Ladies and Gentlemen, those freethinkers one unfortunately meets everywhere, still reason like the Bible or the Diaconales when it concerns women only.[17] Those men advocate removing us from the domination of the priests in order to be able to strengthen their own domination as husbands; they do not like strangers taking a part of their "authority." Those so-called freethinkers are amazed by the attachment of women to religion. What have they done to detach them from it?

How do you dare reproach women for searching for a refuge under the shadow of the church, since church doors are the only ones open to them? You have chased them from everywhere else . . . They have no other distraction, no other nourishment for their natural needs, but the ceremonies of the religious cults.

It is you, Citizens, who are really the guilty ones; it is your indifference, your egoism, and your contempt for women that have filled the churches.

Be sure that the day women are not kept at a distance and relegated to the second rank, the day when they find a home where they are not despised and can enjoy the happiness, respect, and tenderness to which they are entitled, the day you, Citizens, will be able to prove by your exemplary conduct the superiority of this secular morality that you demand, the day women take an active part in all social events to the same degree and with the same rights as other citizens, on this day the churches will be empty. Then, if you so wish, Gentlemen, on this very day we shall work together to empty the cabarets, because, do not harbor any illusions, Gentlemen, the cabaret is for a man what the church is for a woman: a place of stupefaction and perversion. If you tell me, as it has been said, that pious churchgoers are not ripe for emancipation, I shall reply that drunken cabaret-goers are not any more suitable! (Applause.)

Ladies and Gentlemen, dear Comrades, I have tried to show you, as rapidly and as completely as possible, the whole of what is called *feminism*. I hope I have shown you the wisdom and the importance of it sufficiently for many of you to feel the need to reflect on it, to discuss it among yourselves, to become interested in what does concern you, and to propagate ideas that are just.

We can say today that if the material progress of feminism is now starting to be felt, its moral progress is already immense.

This *idea* is getting through to the masses; right-thinking people are flocking to us from all sides; propaganda is being actively spread with the objective of "defending and winning rights for women"; existing groups are adding feminist demands to their programs. All circles, whether in bourgeois drawing rooms or the most humble meetings, are talking about it. Our theaters, our novels, and our lectures deal with it. The daily press is no longer uninterested and the very frankness of our adversaries shows plainly that they are taking us seriously. They feel that the moment of profound transformation has come. One cannot stop revolutions! Conservatives are beaten in advance.

Recently, congresses of freethinkers and the secular school system have included feminine emancipation in their programs, and a number of sizable specialized feminist international congresses have met with real success in certain capital cities. The Berlin Congress in 1904 brought together 4,000 women from all countries.[18] The Paris Congress in 1900, during the World Exposition, was reported by eminent journalists of our large daily newspapers.[19]

In one of those congresses an eminent man shouted: "What a country of savages we must live in that such a revolution must be fought for so many times!"

A special, grateful homage must be paid to work that contributed to the progress I am referring to, that of *La Fronde,* directed for the last five years by Mme Marguerite Durand, who has sacrificed her peace and her fortune to it. *La Fronde,* a daily newspaper directed, administered, typeset, and printed exclusively by women, focuses on feminism without neglecting other issues and has since the time of the Dreyfus affair been in the first rank of the daily press.

It shows what feminine initiative and willpower can do. Today *La Fronde* has become a monthly paper, without losing any of its interest. Now another great daily newspaper, *L'Action,* has taken up the fight independently against the influence of the clergy. *L'Action* has resumed the interrupted task and opens its columns to our demands and to our revolt because it has understood, according to the profound statement of Charles Letourneau, that no social progress is possible if woman does not participate in it.[20]

I must add in haste that *L'Action* and *La Fronde* are not the only French feminist newspapers; there is *Le Journal des femmes* and others, too.[21]

To conclude along the same lines, I should like to point out an interesting innovation. An important group, (the Union for the Protection of Women) [*l'Union protectrice des femmes*], has just published a small almanac for 1906 that provides, in a limited form, an excellent summary of the issues and a source of documentation for all those interested.

So much effort cannot be useless; those "savages" mentioned by the journalists will finally become civilized. The struggle may be long and painful, but the victory will be the more deserved, more lasting, and more magnificent. We have against us centuries of ignorance, slavery, and barbarism, coupled with two evil forces: routine and prejudice; but our apostolic ardor cannot be hindered by obstacles! We shall continue the struggle without ceasing. Whatever Jesus may have preached, it is not in resignation that we shall find freedom. There is only one means to shake off oppression, and that is revolt.

I should like to quote the words of Victor Hugo from a memorable speech:

> The eighteenth century proclaimed the rights of man.
> The nineteenth century will proclaim those of woman.

If the nineteenth century has not entirely completed this task, it has at least prepared it in principle. It is up to our twentieth century to gain the crown of glory for achieving it. We must hope that it will succeed!

Notes

1. There is no full-length biography of Nelly Roussel. The longest sketch of her life can be found in the introduction by Maité Albistur and Daniel Armogathe to their edition of the French text of this lecture, *L'Eternelle sacrifiée*, 7–25.

2. Five states of Australia had already granted some form of women's suffrage when Roussel spoke: New South Wales (1867), Victoria (1869), West Australia (1871), South Australia (1880), and Tasmania (1884). For lists of states granting women's suffrage, see tables 1 and 14 in Hause with Kenney, *Women's Suffrage*, 19 and 253.

3. In Diderot's response to Antoine Léonard Thomas's "Essai sur le caractère, les moeurs et l'esprit des femmes dans les différents siècles" (Essay on the Dispositions, the Customs, and the Attitudes of Mind of Women in Past Centuries) [1772], reprinted in *Oeuvres de Diderot* (Paris, 1951), 187–90.

4. Roussel knew and respected a number of male feminists, including Henri Béranger, Paul Bert, Ferdinand Buisson, Colonel Converset, Emile Darnaud, Sébastien Faure, Judge Magnaud, Paul Robin, Frédéric Stackleberg, René Viviani, and her husband, Henri Godet. See Armogathe and Albistur's comments in *L'Eternelle sacrifiée*, 40. For an example of male feminist thinking, see the excerpt from Léopold La-

cour's book in part 5. For other feminist thinking on the subject of male feminism, see Madeleine Pelletier's argument (in part 2) that "the men who are feminists are a lot more feminist than the women." For further illustrations of male feminism of the belle époque, see the works of Buisson, Jean du Breuil de Saint-Germain, Charles Gide, Lacour, Paul and Victor Margueritte, Léon Richer, and Viviani, as listed in the bibliography. For a discussion of these men, see Klejman and Rochefort, *L'Egalité en marche,* 117–26. For a case study of male feminism, see Karen Offen, "Ernest Legouvé."

5. In March 1907, Marguerite Durand organized *Le Congrès du travail féminin* (Congress of Women's Work) to draw attention to these questions. Equal pay was finally mandated by the Ministry of Labor on July 30, 1946.

6. Candid and articulate antifeminism was common in the belle époque. The best known antifeminist of the era was a prize-winning sociologist, Théodore Joran, who built a cottage industry in publishing attacks on feminism, which he considered a "revolt against the great law of humanity" (*Le Féminisme à l'heure actuelle,* 5) Joran produced eight books between 1905 and 1913, beginning with *Le Mensonge féministe (The Feminist Lie)* and ending with *Le Suffrage des femmes (Women's Suffrage).* He was awarded a prize by the *Académie des sciences morales et politique* (the 1913 *Prix du budget*) for the latter title, which asserted that the feminist argument "is only a tissue of errors, ravings, and sophisms" (viii).

7. Women in these occupations in France were recent developments when Roussel spoke, and opportunities for women remained very limited. Madeleine Brès began medical studies in 1875 and became the first woman physician in France (feminists used the term *doctoresse*). The legal professions were slower to admit women. In 1892 Jeanne Chauvin became the first woman to complete legal training in France, but opposition to her was so strong that a riot halted the examination of her thesis. The French bar remained closed, even to women with Chauvin's training, until 1901. Women were restricted in publishing newspapers until the Press Law of 1881. The first daily newspaper edited and published by women, Durand's *La Fronde,* appeared in 1897.

8. The duty of women to bear children was the subject of a heated debate during the belle époque. This derived from widespread French concern about a falling birthrate that threatened the "depopulation" of France; see the discussion of this (including Roussel's opinions) in part 6. For more on depopulation, see Joseph P. Spengler, *France Faces Depopulation* (Durham, 1938), and John C. Hunter, "The Problem of the French Birth Rate." The feminist implications of this debate have been analyzed by Karen Offen in "Depopulation."

9. See Roussel's further discussion of this in her speech on "The Freedom of Motherhood," translated in part 6.

10. Unmarried couples living in *union libre* were an important issue in 1906. To take but two examples of that year alone, Paul and Victor Margueritte published *Marriage–Divorce–Union Libre* and Madeleine Vernet published *L'Amour libre* (Epone, n.d. [1906]). Public discussion of *union libre* became even more intense in the following year when a future premier of France, Léon Blum, advocated trial marriage in *Du mariage*.

11. The eight-hour day remained a distant dream in 1906; twelve-hour days and sixty-five-hour weeks were more common. The eight-hour day appeared in socialist and syndicalist programs in the 1880s, but even these radical claims often accepted a six-day, forty-eight-hour work week. When Roussel spoke, a unified socialist party (the SFIO, or the French Section of the International Workers) had just been founded (1905), reiterating this demand. The eight-hour day was adopted in France by Blum's Popular Front government in 1936.

12. See the excerpts in part 2 especially those by Thiébaux, Harlor, and Pelletier.

13. George Sand (Amandine Aurore Dupin, Baroness Dudevant, 1804–76) was a French novelist who outraged middle-class opinion by leaving her husband, living on her own in Paris, dressing in trousers and smoking cigars, having multiple lovers, and claiming the right to passion for women. Clémence Royer (1830–1902) was a philosopher and scientist; she translated Darwin into French and became the first women to hold a university chair (Lausanne, 1859). When Roussel spoke, Royer's recent death had made her a prominent intellectual figure often cited by French feminists. Rosa Bonheur (1822–99) was a French artist, especially famous for her painting *Labourage nivernais,* which presently hangs in the Musée d'Orsay in Paris. Louise Michel (1830–1905) was a revolutionary and an anarchist. She had been exiled for her role in the Paris Commune of 1871 (see her account, *La Commune,* published in 1878), and returned to celebration as an elder stateswoman of revolutionary politics.

14. Roussel refers here to the trial, on December 27, 1905, of Felicia Numietzka, Léon Clément, and Gustave Hervé for antimilitaristic activities. Roussel can state "I know very very well" because she was a witness on their behalf at the trial.

15. Paul Robin (1837–1912) was a notorious figure of the belle époque as the leading French advocate of birth control, which was how Roussel met him (see part 6). He decided to advocate birth control after his experiences as the founder of the Prévost orphanage (1883). Robin introduced many educational innovations at the orphanage, including coeducation and holistic education (*"l'éducation intégrale"*). For more on Robin, see Angus McLaren, *Sexuality and Social Order,* 93–109.

16. René Viviani (1863–1925) was a prominent moderate socialist politician and the premier of France at the beginning of World War I. He was elected to the Chamber of Deputies in 1893 and rapidly rose to its leadership. Viviani served as France's first Minister of Labor when the ministry was created in 1906, holding that post for four years and supporting feminist aspirations on several occasions. He had participated in Léon Richer's *Ligue française pour le droit des femmes* (LFDF) from the 1890s. He addressed the 1900 feminist congress and vigorously urged moderate feminists to work for the vote; Roussel is quoting his speech to that congress (see Marguerite Durand, *Congrès international,* 290–91). Viviani was probably Durand's secret lover (see Hause with Kenney, *Women's Suffrage,* 289 n.20).

17. The Diaconals are the final lessons given to a deacon (*diacre*) before ordination. They concern moral theology and the question of sexuality.

18. The congress was the regular quinquennial meeting of an international organization of moderate feminists, the International Council of Women. An American suffragist had been working since 1899 to use the Berlin congress to found a similar group devoted to winning the vote, the International Woman Suffrage Alliance (IWSA). Many of Roussel's friends participated in the two meetings. See Hause with Kenney, *Women's Suffrage,* 74–75.

19. There were actually three important feminine/feminist congresses held in Paris in conjunction with the World's Fair of 1900. The first, a meeting of Catholic women, was conservative but contained a small group of Christian (i.e., Catholic) feminists led by Marie Maugeret. The second congress brought together the moderate women who founded the French branch of the International Council of Women. The third (and most militant) congress, the *Congrès international de la condition et des droits des femmes,* was a regular assembly organized by the LFDF. This was the congress to which Viviani delivered the speech that Roussel quoted (see n.17). Roussel participated in both the second and third congresses and became an active member of the organization founded by the second congress, the French Council of Women (CNFF); see Hause with Kenney, *Women's Suffrage,* 29–31, and Klejman and Rochefort, *L'Egalité en marche,* 137–47.

20. *L'Action* was a leftist republican daily newspaper. When Durand's *La Fronde* folded in 1905, it technically merged with *L'Action,* and Durand continued to write for that newspaper. The paper had a strongly profeminist tone and was one of the few Parisian dailies to endorse women's suffrage vigorously. Roussel also had personal reasons to be fond of the newspaper: it was one of the cosponsors of her provincial speaking tours.

Charles Létourneau (1831–1902) was an anthropologist famous for his political approach to ethnography.

21. For the size and scope of the feminist press during the belle époque, see appendix 2. For an introduction to these publications see Albistur and Armogathe, *Histoire du féminisme français,* 368–73. *Le Journal des femmes,* which Roussel cites, was a militant monthly (1891–1911) published by Maria Martin, and the successor of Hubertine Auclert's *La Citoyenne* (1881–91), which Martin edited during its final months; see Hause, *Hubertine Auclert,* 143–48.

COUNTESS
PIERRE LECOINTRE

The feminist movement of the belle époque overwhelmingly drew its leadership from the educated women of the urban middle class, such as Nelly Roussel.[1] The women who founded feminist organizations, and the officers who led those groups, chiefly came from the middle class. The women who published the periodicals and who organized or delivered the lectures also came from that background. A significant number of women from working-class origins certainly participated in the feminist movement,[2] however, these were often women who had won an education or a career that moved them into the middle class, such as Dr. Madeleine Pelletier, who is represented further on in this anthology. Politically active working women turned in much greater numbers to the socialist and syndicalist movements.

Few women of the aristocracy participated in the feminist movement, although there were important exceptions, such as the Duchess d'Uzès.[3] More aristocratic women participated in the Catholic women's movement, joining the League of French Women or similar groups. This women's movement had a conservative focus on issues such as the family and the church, but it gradually developed feminist interests on its agenda.[4]

Seen in this context, Countess Pierre Lecointre is an interesting individual who illustrates the variety of feminisms during the belle époque.[5] Coming from the Catholic aristocracy, she took a very different attitude to female emancipation from that of left-wing feminists like Roussel and Pelletier. Lecointre opposed (and spoke out publicly against) contraception, abortion, and women's suffrage, but she favored the improvement of conditions for women as perceived by religious women brought up to do good works. Because she declined to join the feminist organizations of the era (she occasionally participated in Catholic groups such as Maugeret's *Congrès Jeanne d'Arc*), little is known about Countess Lecointre's life. It is noteworthy, however, that she was well educated and known for her work in paleontology.

Lecointre's *State of the Feminist Question in France in 1907* is a twenty-four-page brochure published in Paris in 1907. After giving a brief introduction on the status of French women under the Ancien Régime—that is, before the revolution of 1789—the author demonstrates "the state of the feminist question" through simple lists. She provides a chronology of changes in the laws regarding women, a list of laws proposed but not yet adopted in 1907, and the programs of several feminist groups. This translation omits a list covering earlier eras, a listing of the situation in foreign countries, and a tribute to individual feminists such as Hubertine Auclert; it also slightly abridges the programs of various groups to eliminate repetitiveness. The text provides a valuable reference document that shows concisely and clearly the legal issues of concern to feminists at the turn of the century.

The State of the Feminist Question in France in 1907

III. The Situation of Women in the Nineteenth Century

1803: Napoleon's civil code. *Women lose their rights*. Confirmation of the Divorce Law.[6]

1808: Napoleon organizes the Labor Relation Boards without including women, either as voters or as candidates.[7]

1816, May 8: The Divorce Law is repealed.

The Charters of Rights of 1815 and 1830, the laws of July 29, 1820, and April 19, 1831, give and confirm Women's indirect right to a political vote by proxy. The tax contribution of a married woman goes toward that of her husband—and if she is a widow, to her son, son-in-law, grandson, and grand-daughter's husband to complete the amount of tax required by the electoral tax assessment. Women lost that right in 1848.

Source: Countess Pierre Lecointre, *Etat de la question féministe en France en 1907* (Paris, 1907), secs. 3–5, 7. Trans. Jette Kjaer and Jennifer Waelti-Walters.

–Fourier states the principle of absolute equality of the sexes.

–Saint-Simon preaches women's emancipation.[8]

–The municipal law of 1837 (July 18) gives the husband of a woman married under the regime of community property the right to represent her in the municipal assemblies, as a "co-taxee"; a provision maintained by the law of July 24, 1867, and abolished by the law of April 6, 1882.

1851: Pierre Leroux proposes to give Women the right to administrative suffrage.

1869: The countercouncil of Freemasons, opened in Naples on December 8, had the following written in its program: "Women must be freed from those ties that the Church and Legislation have created in order to prevent their full development, and thus must be emancipated totally."[9]

Women are left with the rather vague right to take part in communal referenda at the discretion of the mayor. The general referendum, which is often used in Switzerland and the United States, is not considered legal in France, even for male voters on the electoral role; it is only tolerated, and that rarely. We have examples of Women taking part in some of them: in Fougère, (Ille-et-Vilaine) Bagnols, (Gard) Ferrière-en-Gâtinais, (Loiret) Asnière, (Seine) in 1906, Beauvais, (Oise). The women are consulted every year in Argenteuil, Neuilly-sur-Seine, etc.

In 1898, M. Argeliès, a member of parliament, drafted a bill that would have made the communal referendum legal, but he did not include Women in this draft, which would take away the precisely defined right remaining to them, that of taking part in *commodo* and *incommodo* inquiries in their community.

IV. Recent Changes in the French Legislation Concerning Women

May 15, 1850, and	
April 10, 1867	Organization of primary education for girls.[10]
1862	Organization of professional education for Women.
1868	Women are admitted to take courses in the state's University Faculties.
May and	
December 1874	Law on the protection of female minors in factories and workshops.[11]
	Law on the protection of girls employed in the itinerant professions.

August 31, 1878	Decree regulating conditions of women owning land in the colonies.
February 27, 1880	Voting and candidature of Women in the Board of Education.
December 21, 1880	Organization of the Secondary Education for girls.
April 9, 1881	Law giving Women the right to have personal savings accounts and to take out the money deposited without their husbands' assistance.
June 16, 1881	Law on the creation of free instruction at the primary level.
July 27, 1881	Law on the foundation of Normal schools.
January 3, 1882	Creation of scholarships in the Elementary Establishments of Education.
January 14, 1882	Decree on the organization of Secondary Education for girls: bachelor's degree, opening of courses of law, medicine, pharmacy, etc., to Women.
January 17, 1882	Order of the Prefect of Seine admitting Women into the competitive examinations for hospital internships in Paris.
March 28, 1882	Law making Primary Instruction compulsory.
April 5, 1882	Law suppressing the "co-taxee" in local communities.
July 27, 1882	Decree organizing courses for the female directors of kindergartens.
July 28, 1882	Decree regulating the granting of scholarships in high schools and colleges for girls.
December 30, 1882	Decree relative to the inspection of classes of girls.
March 21, 1884	Law authorizing Women employees in industries to form unions or employers' associations.
July 27, 1884	Law establishing divorce and fixing the same penalties for adultery for the two sexes.
July 20, 1886	Law constituting a national pension plan for old people.
October 30, 1886	Decree declaring Women voters and eligible candidates for primary school councils.
November 11, 1888	Decree concerning teachers of needlework in high schools and colleges.

July 24, 1889	Law on the protection of morally abandoned children, loss of parental rights, guardianship, etc.
March 9, 1891	Law giving to the surviving spouse the lifelong interest on the estate of the predeceased.
November 2, 1892	Law modifying Women's working conditions, regulation of work inspectors.
November 30, 1892	Law on the exercising of medicine (midwives, etc.).
January 20, 1893	Law modifying *unfavorably* that of 1881 on savings bank accounts for Women.
February 6, 1893	Law granting the Woman legally separated from her husband legal competency in civil matters and the right to separate households.
May 13, 1893	Decree concerning Women's work.
June 12, 1893	Law concerning hygiene and security for workers.
July 25, 1893	Decree concerning Women's work. This decree sets the weights that can be carried by apprentices and young working women.
March 10, 1894	Decree on the application to Women of the law of June 12, 1893.
November 15, 1895	Decree giving Women the right to be administrators of the Welfare and Public Assistance offices in Paris.
June 20, 1896	Law giving Women the right to authorize the marriage of their children, despite the refusal of the husband, if a legal separation has been pronounced in their favor.
August 17, 1897	Law modifying Articles 45, 49, 70, 76, and 331 of the Civil Code (marriage formalities, legitimating children, etc.).
December 7, 1897	Law allowing Women to be witnesses to civil actions or deeds.
January 23, 1898	Law giving Women the vote in the Courts of Commercial litigation.
April 1, 1898	Law giving married Women the right to be a part of Mutual Societies, and even to establish them without the authorization of their husbands.
April 19, 1898	Law for the suppression of child abuse.

December 17, 1899	Decree giving Women the vote in the Board of Labor.
1900	Women are admitted to the School of Fine Arts.
1900	Ruling on the classes of the National Conservatory of Music.
March 30, 1900	Law modifying the law of November 2, 1892, on child labor, female minors, and Women in industry.
October 1, 1900	Memo from (his honor) the Minister of War canceling all dowries for officers' Wives, but maintaining the principle of preliminary enquiry and authorization.
November 7, 1900	Memo from the Minister of War canceling all dowries for noncommissioned officers' Wives.
December 1, 1900	Law, the object of which is to permit Women with a degree in law to be sworn in as lawyers and practice this profession.
December 29, 1900	Goirand law called "about seats" in shops, stores, etc.[12]
January 2, 1900	Decree modifying that of September 1, 1899, and giving Women candidates rights in Labor Relation Board elections.
March 14, 1904	Law on the employment offices.
December 15, 1904	Law repealing Article 298 of the Civil Code and permitting marriage with the accomplice of an adulterer.
December 9, 1905	Law on the Separation of Church and State. This law gives the right to take part in the administration of the material possessions of the Church by belonging to cultural associations. [...]

Article 386 of the Civil Code was modified during the year of 1906 in the following direction: as long as the divorce has been pronounced in their favor, widows or divorced women will from now on, even in the case of remarriage, keep the use of interest on their children's estates until they have reached eighteen years of age or become independent. [...]

v. Laws Proposed but Not Adopted in the Two Assemblies

Bill giving Women the right to vote and stand as candidates for the Labor Relation Boards.

The text passed by the House was modified by the Senate (March 15, 1906), which accorded the right to vote but not to be a candidate.

Bill, the object of which is to ensure married Women free disposal of their earnings (Prop. Goirand).

Bill to protect Women against certain abuses of marital rights (Prop. Jourdan).

These two propositions were united in the report of the Commission voted on in the House on February 27, 1896.

Bill protecting married Women's profits and salaries (Prop. Grosjean, February 27, 1905).

Bill on the protection and assistance of mothers and nurselings (Prop. Strauss in the Senate, adopted December 3, 1903).

Bill modifying legislation on the duration of Women's work (Prop. Suchetet, June 2, 1902).

Bill with the same object as above (Prop. Rudelle, June 26, 1902).

Bill with the same object as above (Prop. Waddington, senator, adopted in the Senate on March 26, 1904).

Bill on the determination of paternity (Prop. Rivet and Béranger in the Senate, January 28, 1905).[13]

Bill giving Women the right to vote in the election for municipal councils, city district councils, and provincial councils (Prop. Dussaussoy, June 1906).

Bill concerning a married Woman's salary and giving her free disposal of it (Prop. Gourju, June 26, 1906, in the Senate).

Bill concerning Workers' consultation boards. Women would be voters and eligible candidates just like men (Prop. in June 1906, voted in the Senate).

Bill for the repeal of Article 340 of the Civil Code, determination of paternity (Prop. Viviani in the Chamber, August 1906).

Bill for the simplification of certain marriage formalities (Prop. by Abbot Lemire, report to the Senate by M. Catalogne, December 1906).

Bill that it be a right that separation should become divorce at the end of three years (Prop. Violette, January 1907). [. . .]

VII. Programs of the Four French Feminist Groups

CHRISTIAN FEMINISM[14]

Mlle Maugeret, Mme Duglos, Mlle de Grandpré, Mme Fournet, etc.

PROPOSALS MADE AT THE JOAN OF ARC CONGRESS IN 1904[15]

To adhere to the League of Senator Béranger against license in the streets.

For Women to increase propaganda against freemasonry.

That society Women will not encourage "starvation pay" by buying below the going rate.

For a more demanding and more scientific education for girls.

For the founding of social support for working Women, help for employed Women, etc.

For an increase in workers' gardens, horticulture, and home economics.

For the distribution of morally acceptable publications by society Women.

That French Women may be moved by the same spirit of tolerance that unites Protestants and Catholics in the United States in their work.

For young Women and former nuns to enter nursing schools.

For Women to acquire broader rights of guardianship.

PROPOSALS MADE AT THE JOAN OF ARC CONGRESS IN 1906 (SELECTIONS)

For the formation of mutual aid societies.

That the Froebel method be adopted in the free kindergartens.

That the school of home economics fight the use of brandy in cooking.

For the Catholics to join actively in the fight against alcohol and to sign the petition against absinthe.

To vow that a newspaper delivery be organized in the suburbs.

To vow for the fight against freemasonry to be pursued on all grounds and by every means, in order to safeguard children's souls.

For the mothers to try by every means in their power to instill an ardent love for France in their children.

To get the vote for women in the Municipal and Provincial Assemblies (adopted unanimously).

To get the direct political vote for Women (adopted by a small majority).

The National Council of French Women[16]

Mmes Isabelle Bogelot, Sarah Monod, Maria Pognon, J. Siegfried, Avril de Sainte-Croix, d'Abbadie-d'Arrast.

PROPOSALS MADE IN 1903

To fight tuberculosis by disinfecting contaminated rooms; disinfecting free for the poor.

For unification of the school curriculum for both sexes.

That financial compensation be given by the man to the seduced Woman and the child born out of wedlock.

To allow determination of paternity, by the child, its mother, or its guardian.

To raise salaries of working Women by the suppression of intermediates and the creation of cooperatives.

To ask the Government of the Republic that it ask the International Tribunal of the Hague for assistance in resolving international conflicts.

To congratulate the Director of Public Assistance and the Prefect of the Seine for their poster against alcoholism.

Equal justice, liberty, morality, and rights for both sexes.

To ask that birth certificates sent to individuals bear no mention of illegitimacy.

To protest the use of the words "house of ill repute" in legal statements and request the abolition of state brothels.

To request that Women be regional delegates.

To work toward the suppression of obscene publications in the streets.

That ample place be made for Women in the medical stations in offices.

An address to the Queen of Spain requesting that one of the Women of Fez's Harem, who is a refugee in Spain, not be turned over to the Moroccan authorities.

PROPOSALS MADE IN 1905

That Women be able to be guardians of foreign children, court appointed guardians, legal guardians, members of family councils, guardianship councils, judicial councils, etc.

For the maintenance of "loyal commissions" for the protection of younger children, as well as children who are in temporary or permanent public care.

For the material betterment of the condition of Female school teachers.

For the enlargement of Women's rights and first of all that they have free disposal of their salary.

For the reorganization of apprenticeships.

For the development of professional schools: home economics, dairying, agriculture, and horticulture.

This group has just founded a section for the study of complete political voting rights for Women.

THE FRENCH GROUP OF FEMINIST STUDIES[17]

Mme Oddo-Deflou, Brunet, Fournet, C. and H. Belilon, M-E. Bolleter.

Since its foundation in 1898, this group has demanded political suffrage for Women.

PROPOSALS MADE IN 1904—1905—1906

That paternal power, which today is concentrated in the hands of the father, be distributed equally between the father and mother.

Equality between the spouses must replace the power of the husband.

Legal incompetence of Women must be abolished and replaced by the principle of competence.

The legal regime of separate property must replace the present regime of community property.

Determination of paternity must be allowed.

Acceptance of Women as guardians, members of family councils, and such.

Equal pay for equal work.

Participation of Women in public affairs: in their community, district, or region.

CONGRESS ON THE CONDITION AND RIGHTS OF WOMEN[18]

Mme Clémence Royer, Féresse-Deraisme [*sic*], Maria Pognon, Bonnevial, Vincent, Marguerite Durand, Hubertine Auclert.

PROPOSALS OF THE CONGRESS OF 1900

Economic, Moral, and Social Issues

1. That the principle "equal work, equal pay" be adopted.
2. That the female work inspectors be elected by the Women's unions.

3. That the workday be shortened.

4. That the duration of work be set at eight hours.

5. Law called "about seats" in the stores (since adopted in the Chamber).

6. That the work of servants be considered along with that of Women in factories.

7. That Women's work in their homes be evaluated and paid.

8. For the protection of apprentices.

9. To vow for the protection of pregnant Women.

10. For the protection of working Women in their homes.

11. That employees, working Women, and servants be under the jurisdiction of the Labor Relations Boards.

12. That female servants who are underage be inspected, especially in regard to their hours of work.

13. That young female servants be given special rooms to sleep in alone.

14. That there be a free employment bureau in the town halls.

15. That special shelters be created all over France for Women at the end of their pregnancy.

Education

1. Integral education that is free, compulsory, and similar for both sexes. The same for secondary instruction, with an entrance examination.

2. That professional training be given to all, so that everyone has a manual trade.

3. That history be taught in order to instill admiration for benefactors of the human race and hatred of war.

4. That an encyclopedic curriculum be adopted, giving everyone a wide range of knowledge.

5. That the trade schools be increased.

6. That there be no more dogmatism in the schools.

7. That all girls in high schools take the baccalaureate examination.

8. That all young Women, rich or poor, be obliged to learn a trade.

9. That complimentary instruction be created for young Women including child care, child psychology, elementary medicine, etc.

10. That some legal knowledge be provided in all schools.

11. That nurseries be annexed to the girls' high schools so that the girls can learn how to care for children.

12. That a considerable time be spent on agriculture in primary schools, schools of home economics, etc.

13. That children of both sexes be taught together.
14. Coeducation.
15. That mixed schools give preference to Women teachers.
16. That end-of-apprenticeship examinations be instituted.
17. That a civic spirit and sense of solidarity be developed.
18. That an incapable student be stopped at the end of a school year.
19. That institutions be founded for the rational education of children.
20. That all levels of university education be open to Women.

Legislation and Private Rights

1. That lawyers, etc., cease to use their ancient and ridiculous phraseology.

2. That a Woman can keep her nationality by making a declaration on her wedding day.

3. That all laws imposing obedience to her husband on a Woman be abolished.

4. That divorce by mutual consent be authorized.

5. That the murder of an adulterous Woman and her accomplice no longer be considered "excusable."

6. That the article forbidding marriage between accomplices in adultery be repealed.

7. That insanity should give a right to divorce.

8. That the regime of separate estates at marriage and communal acquisition thereafter become legally and generally accepted.

9. That a Woman should enjoy the right to her salary.

10. That a deserted Woman can attach her husband's salary.

11. That a married Woman be authorized to live apart from her husband.

12. That the courts pronounce in cases of conflict in the exercise of marital power.

13. That a Woman be free to initiate legislation.

14. That the determination of paternity be authorized for the woman, the child, and the guardian.

15. That the term "paternal power" be replaced by the term "paternal protection."

16. That children be free to marry at twenty-one years of age.

17. That a Woman can be a guardian and member of a family council.

18. That contracts for the hiring out of children be controlled more closely.

19. That the salary of a minor cannot be seized.

20. That minors be considered independent at the age of eighteen if they have means of subsistence.

21. That a substantial part of a minor's earnings be deposited for him in a savings account.

22. That all public and administrative functions be open to Women.

23. That divorce be authorized in the States where it does not exist.

24. That divorce requested by only one of the parties be authorized.

25. That legal separation be abolished.

26. That special legislation concerning adultery be abolished.

27. That a Woman who marries keep her maiden name and not take that of her husband.

28. That Maternity benefits be created.

29. That natural children have the same rights as legitimate children.

Notes

1. For the development and importance of this fact, see the discussion in Hause and Kenney, "The Limits of Suffragist Behavior"; and Hause with Kenney, *Women's Suffrage,* 114–24. For a different view of middle-class women during the belle époque, see Smith, *Ladies of the Leisure Class,* and Anne Martin-Fugier, *La Bourgeoise* (Paris, 1983).

2. The role of working-class women in both feminism and socialism has attracted a great deal of scholarly attention. See the many works of Charles Sowerwine listed in the bibliography, especially his *Sisters or Citizens?;* the works of Marilyn Boxer, the fullest of which is her doctoral dissertation, which is more accessible in her summary, "Socialism Faces Feminism"; and Hilden, *Working Women.* There is also a large French literature on this subject. See the work of Michelle Perrot, especially her bibliographic essay "De la nourrice"; of Madeleine Guibert, especially her *Les Femmes;* and of Marie-Hélène Zylberberg-Hocquart, especially her *Femmes et féminisme.*

3. D'Uzès was one of the richest women in France and the head of one of its oldest noble families. She worked with Jeanne Schmahl in *L'Avant-Courrière* to win the legal right of women to control their own wages (the Schmahl Law of 1907, which Lecointre labeled the Gourju Bill after its sponsor, Senator Antonin Gourju) and in the foundation of the French Union for Women's Suffrage (UFSF); see her *Souvenirs* (Paris, 1930). For an introduction to her feminism, see Hause with Kenney, *Women's Suffrage,* especially 110–15.

4. For an introduction to the Catholic women's movement, see Hause and Kenney, "The Development of the Catholic Women's Suffrage Movement."

5. Little is known about the life of Countess Pierre Lecointre. Not only is there no full biography of her, but no contemporary sketch appeared in the feminist periodicals of the belle époque.

6. Divorce was legalized in France by the revolutionary Legislative Assembly in September 1792. The Napoleonic Code reaffirmed that right, but it was abolished under the monarchical restoration of 1815. For the history of divorce, see Roderick Phillips, *Putting Asunder*, esp. 405–12 and 422–28.

7. These Labor Relations Boards (*Conseils des prud'hommes*) provided arbitrators in work disputes. Women won partial rights in these boards (as Lecointre notes later on) in 1899. They won fuller rights in 1907, shortly after the publication of Lecointre's pamphlet, as one of the first feminist benefits of Viviani's organization of the Ministry of Labor.

8. The utopian socialism of Charles Fourier (1772–1837), Count Henri de Saint-Simon (1760–1825), and their followers was one of the most important forces in the early development of French feminism. See the works of Claire Moses, especially *French Feminism* which devotes an entire chapter to the Saint-Simonians; "Saint-Simonian Men/Saint-Simonian Women: the Transformation of Feminist Thought in 1830s France," *Journal of Modern History* 54 (1982): 240–67; and "Difference in Historical Perspective: Saint-Simonian Feminism," in Moses and Leslie W. Rabine, *The Word and the Act: French Feminism in the Age of Romanticism* (Bloomington: 1992). See also the work of S. Joan Moon, notably "The Saint-Simonian Association of Working Class Women," *Proceedings of the Western Society for French History* 5 (1977): 274–81. Older French sources include Marguerite Thibert, *Le Féminisme dans le socialisme français de 1830 à 1850* (Paris, 1926), and Charles Thiébaux, *Le Féminisme et les socialistes*.

9. Freemasonry had a mixed record on women's rights, and the literature on the Masons is enormous. For the radicalism of French masonry at the start of the Third Republic, see Philip Nord, "Republicanism and Utopian Vision: French Freemasonry in the 1860s and 1870s," *Journal of Modern History* 63 (1991): 213–29. For masonry and feminism during the belle époque, a good starting point is the works of Madeleine Pelletier, who was very active in the Masons; see her "Admission des femmes à la franc-maçonnerie," *Acacia* May 1905, and "L'Idéal maçonique," *Acacia* May 1906. See the analysis of Pelletier in Gordon, *The Integral Feminist*.

10. Educational rights constituted one of the first and foremost claims of the women's movement from its beginnings. The roots of modern primary education for boys date from the Guizot Law of 1833; only part of these benefits were given to

girls in the parallel Pelet Law of 1836. For the text of these and subsequent educational laws, see P. Chevallier and B. Grosperrin, eds., *L'Enseignement français de la révolution à nos jours,* 2 vols. (Paris, 1971), vol.2. The education of women has attracted great scholarly attention. See the works of Linda Clark, especially "The Primary Education of French Girls," and *Schooling the Daughters of Marianne;* the works of Françoise Mayeur, especially her *L'Enseignement secondaire;* Offen, "The Second Sex"; Quartararo, "The Ecoles normales primaires"; Moch, "Government Policy"; and Margadant, *Madame le Professeur.*

11. For the question of working women and protective labor legislation, see Stewart, *Women, Work, and the French State,* and Boxer, "Protective Legislation."

12. Lecointre's brief description may leave the impression that the Goirand Law was obscure or trivial, but it was neither. The law required department stores to provide seats for salesclerks to rest during their long (often twelve hours) workdays.

13. The right of unmarried women to file paternity suits (called *recherche en paternité* in contemporary feminist literature) against men who impregnated and abandoned them was one of the most ardently sought rights of the era. Article 340 of the Napoleonic Code explicitly prohibited paternity suits. They were legalized in 1912, a result of the Viviani Bill of 1906, which Lecointre mentions.

14. The term "Christian Feminism" was used during the belle époque to denote "Catholic Feminism." It derives from the title of a monthly periodical, *Le Féminisme chrétien,* founded in 1896 by Marie Maugeret. Maugeret created an organization with the same name in 1897 and used it to draw Catholic women's groups into portions of the feminist program; see Hause and Kenney, "The Development of the Catholic Women's Suffrage Movement"; Klejman and Rochefort, *Egalité en marche,* 110–12; and Sarti, *The Ligue patriotique.*

15. Maugeret founded the Joan of Arc Congress in 1904 to provide an annual meeting of the entire Catholic women's movement. The congress was therefore more Catholic and conservative than feminist.

16. The National Council of French Women was the French branch of the International Council of Women, founded in 1900–1901. Most of its leaders, such as Julie Siegfried and Sarah Monod (who were both pastors' daughters), were from the French Protestant elite; see Hause with Kenney, *Women's Suffrage,* 36–40, and Klejman and Rochefort, *Egalité en marche,* 149–58.

17. This organization, often referred to as *Etudes* (Studies), was organized in 1898 and led by Jeanne Oddo-Deflou, a member of many feminist leagues. The group focused its energies on reforming the Civil Code; see Hause with Kenney, *Women's Suffrage,* 57, and Klejman and Rochefort, *Egalité en marche,* 149–58.

18. The Congress on the Condition and Rights of Women in 1900 was organized

by France's oldest feminist league, Richer's LFDF, which was then led by Maria Pog-non (the president) and Marie Bonnevial (the secretary-general, who is represented in part 3 of this anthology). For sketches of the LFDF, the 1900 congress, and the women who led them, see Hause with Kenney, *Women's Suffrage,* and Klejman and Rochefort, *Egalité en marche.*

THÉRÈSE POTTECHER

Nelly Roussel's militancy and the Countess Lecointre's conservatism drew on two different feminisms. Thérèse Pottecher[1] offers a third perspective. Pottecher was not active in the women's movement, although she demonstrates clear sympathies to it. She was a journalist who published a lengthy survey of French feminism in the respected monthly *La Grande Revue*. This periodical had an editorial policy supportive of feminism and had earlier published René Viviani's essay on women's rights entitled "La Femme" (Woman).

Pottecher's essay originally appeared in three long segments. The first discussed the historical background, and the second discussed current feminist groups and activities. The final section, translated here, explored French public opinion about feminism in 1910.

The Feminist Movement in France: Public Opinion

In a democratic country, political parties must repeatedly appeal to the great force of public opinion if they wish to exert effective pressure on those in power and break down their resistance. Can feminism count on this force in France? Not yet. Nevertheless, the adversaries of feminism are no longer joking, and the question of female suffrage is now being discussed seriously. In a country where laughter kills, that is a first victory. Feminism has two kinds of enemies: professed enemies and the indifferent. As always, the latter are worse.

The Adversaries

Lawyers and sociologists, who belong to the first group, represent a tradition that is hostile to women.[2] Others invoke arguments against women drawn from their history of physical weakness, as M. Th. Reinach, for example: "Can reform that goes against one of the oldest specializations, the best set forth by nature and the most reinforced by history, be called progress?" (response to the UFSF Survey, the *Revue*, July 9, 1910).[3] A dangerous approach, for it is easy to use the verbal weapons of our adversaries against them. Feminist doctrine has its historical reasons too, since it has been established that under feudalism women were occasionally ranked as lords, having the right to suffrage, justice, etc. Whereas the argument drawn from female physiology is a rather poor one. Women may be the weaker sex, but does physical strength really justify superiority and legitimate rights? Are the strongest and most muscular people better adapted? The fact that the dinosaurs were defeated and died out completely is enough proof against this. It is not clear just how the maternal specialization of women, which is only temporary, lasting fifteen to twenty years at most, could constitute any incapacity or inferiority whatsoever. Besides, the old argument of the precedence of the sexes is increasingly being abandoned. What weight could it carry in a society of so-called universal suffrage, where Mme Curie can teach at the Sorbonne but is unable to vote,[4] while some incorrigible drunkard staggers to the ballot box to place his vote.

Source: Thérèse Pottecher, "Le Mouvement féministe en France," *Grande Revue,* January 1911: 598–601. Trans. Jette Kjaer and Jennifer Waelti-Walters.

Others put forward the social order and the necessity of a family hierarchy to justify the exclusion of women from political rights. M. Duverger (*De la condition civile et politique des femmes*) and M. Deherme (*La Démocratie vivante*), for example;[5] these men are bent on confining women to the home. "Emancipated women," writes M. Deherme, "want to be independent of men, when it is the very condition of family members to be closely dependent on one another. And mutual dependence of families is the condition of all societies." So be it; but is not M. Deherme confusing dependence, that is, solidarity among family members, with subjection? Is it not in the name of solidarity itself that we have an interest in raising the condition of women and allowing them to be true partners with their husbands, as well as substitutes when the latter are away? Another person will say sincerely: "A woman's happiness lies in being a slave." Perhaps, if we are talking about a woman who is passionately in love. But shall it be maintained that the order that exists when it comes to passion is in keeping with that in marriage and with social interest? Does the man who brings a slave into his household not risk finding in her a rebel or silent enemy? How many times has marriage not shown the danger of such a notion! Some people take a moral stance (M. Joran, for one: *La Trouée féministe*), assigning women a destiny on purely moral grounds without considering the transformations taking place in the modern world. These changes cannot be attributed to feminism but to the social and economic evolution alone.[6] For a writer such as M. Joran, feminism is the same as anarchy, because he considers only the advanced factions of feminism, with their anarchistic and socialistic members. Countless others are hostile to the political emancipation of women out of contempt for political action. Perhaps there is an excess of idealism here. This attitude is very common among a number of intellectuals.

Furthermore, people object that women are not prepared to play a political role. Fair enough; but such an education cannot be purely theoretical. It can be taught only by exercising the vote; at first carefully restricted to municipal functions, if need be.

Let us mention above all that many cultivated women are sometimes openly hostile to female emancipation, or else completely indifferent to it. This attitude is found particularly in those who have gained a prominent position in the literary or art world . . . As Mme Auclert has remarked: "Women who have succeeded think they no longer belong to the female sex." This type of sentiment is quite common in upstarts of all sorts.[7]

Many politicians, by party interest, are also opposed to female suffrage.

Quite a large number declare themselves in favor of feminism in principle, but are hostile when it comes to practicing it. For they fear women's reactionary spirit, so they say . . . This reservation, and even defiance, is certainly shared in large part by the radical majority in power. And yet the Catholic majority, except for some liberal-minded and perceptive individuals, does not seem ready to back the effort of female emancipation either. Thus Pius X, in an interview published by *Fémina,* urgently prophesies: "Women will never be voters or members of parliament!"[8]

Finally, let us mention among the adversaries of feminism that immense herd of people who, although they do not reflect, nevertheless allow themselves to express their opinion on every topic. They are the ones who always bring up the argument about the socks that need mending or the homefires, and who enjoy laughing loudly when we speak about female suffrage. But their assurance, their self-importance alone, has an influence on the ignorant and timid who belong to the masses.

The Indifferent

Above all, it is the large majority of French women who, by their lack of concern and the dead weight of their inertia, raise the greatest obstacle against feminist progress. This is where we must make more effort to spread publicity. Lacking education, many of our best women do not know how to rise above the very limited interests of the family unit, for they do not see that this unit is dependent on the entire nation. They are deficient in public spirit.

The Partisans

Quite an important fraction of public opinion adheres, perhaps rather easily, to the idea of a vote reserved for unmarried women and accepts a female franchise, though not eligibility for office. Others wish that the experiment of feminine suffrage not take place unless the electoral system be reformed. The UFSF Survey, the results of which have been published in the *Revue* (June/July 1910), is very revealing in this respect. But the majority of the responses attracted by the poll favor the vote for women without any restrictions whatsoever.

The Press

Last year as well as this year, a number of articles sympathetic to the feminist cause appeared in the press. Let us mention those of M. Paul Margueritte in the *Journal*, M. Ginisty in the *Petit Parisien* (dealing with female candidates), and the articles from *Le Rappel*.[9]

Finally, let us not forget that feminism has several ardent defenders in the Chamber of Deputies and, by its program alone, has gained the support of the whole unified socialist party. The head of State, M. Fallières, declared himself a partisan of women's rights (speech at the *Ligue de l'enseignement* in October 1909).[10]

Therefore, one can say, keeping in mind the many expressions of sympathy and approval it has received lately, that feminism has gained sincere ground in public opinion. Yet this success is little in face of the conquests that still need to be made over the spirit of our nation.

Notes

1. The editors have found no biographies or contemporary sketches of Thérèse Pottecher.

2. Author's note: Cf. Ch[arles] Gide, *Etude sur la condition privée des femmes,* quoted by Turgeon, *Le Féminisme français* (Paris, 1907).

3. Théodore Reinach (1860–1928) was a distinguished historian whose writings won him election to the *Institut de France*. Reinach's words were in response to a survey of cultural leaders, entitled "Should Women Vote?" This survey had been organized by Jeanne Schmahl, the founder of the French Union for Women's Suffrage (UFSF), and conducted by members of the UFSF during 1910. The results of the survey were published in *La Grande Revue*.

4. Marie Curie (1867–1934) had already won her first Nobel Prize when Pottecher wrote this line. Curie, her husband, Pierre Curie, and Henri Becquerel shared the 1903 prize for physics (the third awarded) for their pioneering work on radiation and radioactivity. A few months after Pottecher's article appeared, Marie Curie won the 1911 Nobel Prize for chemistry, for her discovery of the elements radium and polonium. This made her the first person to win two Nobel Prizes, not to mention winning in two different fields; however, she still could not vote in France.

5. Alexander Duverger (1870–1937), the author of *De la condition civile et politique des femmes* (Paris, 1872), and Georges Deherme (1870–1937), the author of *La Démocratie vivante* (Paris, 1909), were two of the respondants to the UFSF survey.

6. Théodore Joran was a prominent sociologist and antifeminist; see note 6 for Nelly Roussel's speech in part 1.

7. Feminist writings by Hubertine Auclert (1848–1914) are included in parts 5 and 7; see the introduction to her there. Auclert knew from personal experience that women gave little support to the women's movement at this time. See her article, "L'Avarice des femmes," *La Citoyenne*, April 1884, and her speech to the LFDF, "Les Plus grands ennemis des femmes sont les femmes," contained in her dossier at the Bibliothèque Marguerite Durand; see also the discussion in Hause, *Hubertine Auclert*, 167–70.

8. *Fémina*, June 1906; 241. For a discussion of papal opposition to women's suffrage, see Hause and Kenney, "The Development of the Catholic Women's Suffrage Movement."

9. All three newspapers mentioned had important connections with French feminism. The *Petit Parisien* had supported the campaigns of Léon Richer in the 1870s; *Le Rappel* had supported Auclert's early suffragism; and *Le Journal* led the suffragist campaign on the eve of World War I. See the survey of the press in Hause with Kenney, *Women's Suffrage*, 153. Paul Margueritte (1860–1918) and Paul Ginisty (1855–1932) were novelists who published numerous essays in newspapers. Margueritte frequently supported women's rights; see, for example, his *L'Enlargissement du divorce*.

10. Armand Fallières (1841–1931) was the president of France—a position of relatively little political power—from 1906 to 1913. The *Ligue de l'enseignement* (the Education League) was founded by Jean Macé in 1866 and played an important role in the creation of the French public school system during the 1870s and 1880s. Fallières told the league, "I have always thought that women must have the same rights in society as men have," but this opinion did not lead him to play an active political role on behalf of feminism.

2

EDUCATION

MARCELLE TINAYRE

Marcelle Tinayre (1877–1948) was born Marguerite-Suzanne-Marcelle Chasteau.[1] She completed her education through the level of the *bacca-lauréat,* the university entrance examination that concludes French second-ary education.[2] Chasteau did not complete a university education, however, choosing instead to marry Julien Tinayre, a painter and engraver, just two weeks after she passed her final examinations. She turned to literature early in her marriage and published two novels, *Vive les vacances* (Hooray for Hol-idays [1895]) and *L'Enfant gaulois* (The Gallic Child [1897]), under the pseudonym of Charles Marcel. Tinayre soon began earning her living from her writing and used her own name for her novels and journalism for the re-mainder of her life.

Tinayre contributed regularly to a wide variety of newspapers and peri-odicals, such as *La Mode pratique, La Vie heureuse,* and *Le Temps.* She wrote the first serial story published in Marguerite Durand's *La Fronde* and through that connection made her first contacts in the world of French fem-inism. The novels she wrote before 1914 were concerned with the psychol-ogy of love and how male-female relations governed the situation of most women. She increasingly became a proponent of feminism and the indepen-dence of women. This led her to an interest in women usually considered marginal to society and to literature; she created, for example, several admi-rable and respected spinsters, perhaps the first in French literature.

In 1908 Tinayre was named to receive the Legion of Honor (chevalier), but she wrote a satirical piece on the award before she received it; conse-quently, her name was removed from the honors list. In 1939 she received the Barthou Prize from the French academy.

The novel *Hellé* (1899) is central to Tinayre's systematic study of the psychology of love. Hellé, the heroine, is set up as the measure against whom all other female protagonists must be judged. She is provided with the ideal education to strengthen her judgment, she lives in circumstances that develop her self-esteem, and she inherits enough money to be totally independent. Because Hellé has no immediate family, there are no father-daughter conflicts and no one for whom she must sacrifice herself. Hellé's situation, in short, is ideal. She then meets, loves, and chooses between a dashing young poet and a dour humanitarian sociologist. After some wry and ironic scenes where Hellé's independent spirit clashes with the traditionalist ego of the poet, she comes to appreciate the stalwart character of her other suitor and works with him for the improvement of society.

The following extract from *Hellé* gives Tinayre's portrait of an ideal education for women in 1900.

Hellé's Education

Eight years of my life had been lived unconsciously, without mishap, and almost without memories. No illness had weakened my vigorous constitution at all, or aroused the unhealthy excitability that turns precocious children into little pests. I had the happy and free spirit of a young fawn set loose in nature where all instincts could be satisfied. I could climb right up to the fork in the fig tree without effort and jump across ditches, and I used to run bareheaded for hours under the burning sun. My shoulders were broad, my eyes gray, shaded with emerald. There were gold lights in the chestnut silk of my hair. Wherever I went, people looked at me with the pleasure the sight of a fresh and robust child arouses. But, ignorant of the pretty manners taught to well-brought-up girls, I knew neither how to smile, nor reply, nor show off my intelligence by reciting sentences learned by heart beforehand. I was little credit to my aunt, and the Countesses d'Escarbagnas blamed her slightly for that fact.

I came to experience my second birth quite suddenly, and it was an unforgettable initiation. Books expanded my universe, revealing to me the world

Source: Marcelle Tinayre, *Hellé* (Paris, 1899), 14–21. Trans. Jette Kjaer. Reproduced by permission of the Société des Gens de Lettres de France.

of dreams. Even words, by the way they fell together, came to life in a way I had not imagined. They were color, music, fragrance. Being already sensitive to the rhythm of verse and the echo of rhyme, I sensed an unknown beauty extraneous to the meaning of the sentences I read. Some appeared so sweet to me, with their liquid vowels and feminine syllables, that I repeated them aloud in delight. I had discovered in the attic an old volume of the *Odyssey* and one of Lamartine's poems that bore, on their red covers, the inscription "X High School . . . ," surrounded by an almost-faded laurel wreath. The translation was mediocre, full of platitudes and false elegance, but the divine charm of old Homer still lingered in the stories, as naïve as a nanny's bedtime stories, and in the repetition of wonderful adjectives that came to haunt my imagination. I knew no history or geography and was not even sure whether Greece existed or had ever done so. Nevertheless, I used to travel through this land, creating fabulous cities, caves, beaches, and seas where I situated my familiar heroes. Today I can hardly imitate the spontaneous, effortless way I used my intellect as a child.

For a whole year I did nothing but reread these two books, write, and scribble a few drawings. Sometimes, using by instinct a form of chant, I entertained myself by reciting aloud verses that pleased me most, those long lamartinian lines that I liked for their dignified rhythm and melancholy tones. Little by little I modified the poems, adapting them to the feelings of a child. Without knowing it, I was repeating humanity's first rhythmical sounds to express the joyful effect nature had on me. How long ago they seem, those bright, azure afternoons, when the only limits to my world were the walls of an immense garden, full of flowers and vermilion fruits, a unique decor whose eternal theme lives on in my farthest imaginings. Under a velvet-leafed fig tree between the enormous burdocks and the wild borage, with blue stars on its thick, wide, silver, downlike stems, little Hellé appears in my memory pouring out her inarticulate soul . . .

That was where my uncle surprised me one day. Remaining hidden in the lower foliage below me, he listened to me for a long time, and when I ran away, upset, he picked up the book I had forgotten.

That evening after dinner, he asked:

"Who gave you this book, Hellé?"

"No one, Uncle. I found it, a long time ago."

"Have you read it?"

"Yes, Uncle."

"Can you tell me what you've read?"

I confused the Sirens with the Cyclops, Nausica with Circe, and the good king of the Phaeacians with Penelope's wicked suitors. My uncle listened to me closely. Encouraged, I boldly recited the first stanza of *Vallon* for him. He appeared disconcerted.

"It's really extraordinary!" he told Aunt Angélie, who was dreading a fatherly admonition. "This little one has a feeling for poetry. I heard her singing by herself. Her children's songs showed assonance, measure, and an attempt at rhyme. How can she enjoy repeating verses that she cannot understand? And notice how she chose the most characteristic episodes from Homer's epic!"

After two or three similar experiments, Uncle Sylvain announced that he would be taking charge of my education.

For M. de Riveyrac, my childhood represented exactly that of humanity itself. Instead of tiring my supple and obedient memory with dates, axioms, and useless details, he took a natural approach. He taught me a clever series of lessons about various things, and then used legends, poetry, and song.

My hours of work—reading, writing, arithmetic, and drawing—were few. My uncle never let me despair over disheartening difficulties, and, without giving me the solution or explanation I was looking for, he put me skillfully on the right track. Most of the time I would take my book with me into the garden, but on cold or rainy days I was allowed to curl up in a corner of the library. I can still see the vast room where books, books, and more books covered the brown paneled walls. I could not forget its particular atmosphere, the smell of the old bindings, the dust that had accumulated on the plaster moldings. On either side of the fireplace were two plaster busts with hollow eye sockets, representing Homer and Plato. A fragment of the Parthenon frieze and a large photograph of Raphael's fresco *The School of Athens* were framed by the medallions of Goethe and Schiller on the panel. Between the two windows a small terracotta Pallas from the excavations of Olympia stood protected in a display cabinet.

My uncle was standing in front of his desk, writing. A reflection from the window lit up, from behind, his Roman profile. The points of his high collar were done up tightly with a black tie, his gray hair brushed into a tuft on the top of his head. As soon as four o'clock struck, he put down his pen. I put on my straw hat, and as we went across the fields or out into the garden, by the espaliers loaded with their treasures, I told my teacher what I had read and he made comments.

Uncle Sylvain hated the purely bookish education found in schools, which substitutes mnemonic processes for reflection, reasoning, and experience. For him, the child's first educator was nature, which, by revealing its laws, accustoms us at an early age honestly and peacefully to ponder life and death. The wonders of the plant, its structure and renewal through seeds and fruit, were to prepare me for studying animals and man. In this way, through analogies that I gradually discovered, I was easily able to learn about human and animal functions. The false modesty, semi-ignorance, suppressed curiosity, and studied naïveté of young girls, proudly cultivated by families and teachers, appeared ridiculous and contemptible to M. de Riveyrac. He did not believe it was ever good to make a mystery, which inevitably is impure, out of naturally pure things, for pure things are degraded by the base view one has of them.

To the study of nature, my uncle added history. He divided into three periods the years he spent on my instruction, measuring the quality of intellectual nourishment to the strength of my intelligence. He compared himself to a mother who gradually replaces her infant's milk diet with vegetables, and then meats to strengthen and provide energy. First I studied the cycle of legends, delighted by the naïve stories from the Bible, Herodotus, *The Odyssey,* and *The Education of Cyrus*. I was permitted to read Plutarch next, and works of actual historians, and toward the end of my adolescence, Uncle Sylvain taught me the main systems of philosophy and the evolution of religious dogmas.

To complete my moral education, which had begun with the revelation of determined natural laws, Uncle Sylvain practiced the Socratic method to develop and rectify my judgment. He endeavored to unite permanently the idea of Beauty to that of Virtue. He did not say, "That is bad," but "That is ugly," certain that Goodness, like Beauty, is a form of harmony. But he despised conventional morals, social lies, and prejudice. He considered himself an old philosopher, beloved of Athena, goddess of reason and measure. It was to her that he was dedicating a healthy and wise virgin, instructed by his care.

Such an education did not comprise smaller talents or niceties. It even seemed, by disciplining my imagination, to restrain my sensitivity. When I was about fifteen, my aunt was very sad to discover that I had neither excessive emotionality nor softheartedness, qualities she associated with a poetic nature. M. de Riveyrac did not deign to explain to her that to hurry thus the development of feelings, provoked by religiosity and the first growing pains in precocious adolescents of our time, was in no way normal or healthy. He repressed the exaltation that would have altered the lines of the statue he was slowly carving in imitation of his ideal. The day he found me with a *Life of St. Catherine,* lent to me by my aunt, he flew into a rage that made us tremble:

"I don't want to see any more of these barbaric monstrosities here!" he cried, throwing the book out of the window. "That's all we need, Hellé carrying scapulars, saying the rosary, and believing in demons. A girl I've raised as my own son! You want to make an artful woman out of her, a halfwit, a prey to the confessional!"

My aunt did not dare fight with my dear and terrible teacher over me. But, knowing I had not had my first Communion, the "Countesses d'Escarbagnas" no longer came to see us.

The years slipped by, all identical. I was sixteen when my aunt died.

Notes

1. No biography of Tinayre has yet been published. For a study of her writing, see Jennifer Waelti-Walters, *Feminist Novelists,* 31–53.

2. For the subject of women and the *baccalauréat* during the belle époque, see Mayeur, *L'Enseignement secondaire des jeunes filles,* and Offen, "The Second Sex and the Baccalauréat."

HARLOR

Harlor was the pseudonym of Jeanne-Fernande-Clothilde-Désirée Perrot (1871–1970).[1] She grew up in a comfortable and well-educated middle-class family. Her mother, Amélie Hammer (*née* de Bettignies), had been an early feminist, attracted to the women's movement in the 1870s by Léon Richer. Amélie Hammer became the vice president of Richer's LFDF in 1882, and she later served as the president of Lydie Martial's moderate feminist society, the *Union fraternelle des femmes* (UFF), whose members included Nelly Roussel. Harlor's stepfather was a noted violist and composer, Richard Hammer; she prepared for a musical career under his tutelage and was a noted pianist in her youth.

At age twenty-six, however, Harlor decided on a career as a writer. She began in journalism, joining the staff of *La Fronde* when it was founded in 1897 by her lifelong friend Marguerite Durand.[2] She subsequently wrote for an enormous range of publications, including Maria Martin's militant *Le Journal des femmes*, Jane Misme's moderate *La Française, Le Figaro, La Revue socialiste, La Grande revue, La Revue d'art dramatique, La Revue de Paris, La Gazette des beaux-arts, Le Mercure de France*, and *Le Larousse illustré*. Harlor also produced a number of novels, including *Tu es femme, Les Ardents*, and *Arielle, fille des champs*, these works won her the Grand Prix George Sand in 1930.

At *La Fronde*, Harlor became increasingly active in the feminist movement, and she participated in the women's rights congresses of 1900. The *Congrès des oeuvres et institutions féminines* led her to join the *Conseil national des femmes françaises* (CNFF), which resulted from its deliberations. At the

Congrès international de la condition et des droits des femmes, Harlor delivered
the report on education; the following document is the text of her speech.
Shortly thereafter, Harlor joined the UFF and later succeeded her mother as
president of that group. At the beginning of World War I she joined a prominent male feminist, Léopold Lacour (see part 5), in founding a patriotic society, *Droit et Liberté* (Rights and Freedom), to rally French women to the
war effort.

Harlor later joined Durand in creating the Library of Feminist Documentation in 1932. After Durand's death in 1936, the library became the Bibliothèque Marguerite Durand, and Harlor was its first director (1937–48).

The Education of Women's Will

Ladies and Gentlemen,

For the last ten years education of the will has been widely discussed. Literary people have recently exalted Napoleon as the great professor of energy. And just as in 1830 the passion of love was proclaimed superior to all
morality, likewise today certain circles are inclined to sacrifice to the beauty
of energy, as an end in itself and its own unique ideal. This thesis, I may say,
contains nothing very new, because this glorification of energy was the leading idea in the works of Stendhal and Balzac, both of them having been di-
rectly influenced by the same Napoleonic epic. And their renewed admiration for it has naturally created a new morality or rather a new religion of
the "I."

But, first of all, one must recognize that at the present time the theory in
its extreme form is legitimated by the regrettable French tendency of finding
effort distasteful. It is only too true: young French people think only of es-
caping life's difficulties. The ambition of their youth is neither to act nor to
be free. They aspire to easy and regular work, a monotonous and safe existence free from struggles, and especially, responsibilities.

What is also true is that our pedagogical system is to a certain extent
guilty of this moral collapse. The dreadful error of this system is that chil-

Source: Harlor (pseudo.), "L'Education de la volonté chez la femme," *La Revue socialiste* 31,
no.184 (1900). Trans. Lydia Willis and Jennifer Waelti-Walters.

dren or adolescents are never left to be responsible for themselves, nor are they inculcated with the taste and practice of freedom, and so they are rendered inept in taking initiative.

But it is strange, or rather all too natural, that those who theorize about effort are men, and that women are totally absent from their discussions. It would seem that the masculine half of a people is all its people, and that this half could give its maximum of energy while the will of women would remain half-paralyzed.

Male antifeminism is usually so profound, even among the elite, that it is, one might say, ingenuous: the most distinguished spirits eliminate quite naïvely from their human and national preoccupations feminine humanity and the female nation. And if one pointed it out to them, their antifeminism would not be affected: it would pass from the unconscious to the conscious, and we should be compelled not only to take note of it but to counter their arguments.

Well! What would those arguments be?

We are prepared to assume that the intellectuals we are talking about would not quite dare to take on themselves the ancient balderdash illustrated by Molière in *L'Ecole des femmes* [The School for Wives] and in *Les Femmes savantes* [The Learned Women]; they would blush to convert into modern prose the famous catechism by Arnolphe to his Agnès:

> Although society is divided into two halves,
> these two halves, nevertheless, are not equal:
> the one is the upper half and the other lower;
> the one is in subjection in everything to the other,
> which governs. The obedience that the well-drilled
> soldier shows to the chief who leads him, the valet
> to his master, a child to his father, the novice
> among monks to his superior is not even to be
> compared with the docility, obedience, humility, and
> profound respect that the wife should show toward
> her husband, her chief, her lord, and her master.

However, with some tact, some concessions, and a certain verbal delicacy, their thoughts would basically reveal themselves as hardly any different from those of the comic tutor. Rather, those men who would be audacious enough to grant us a certain right to intellectual culture, who would be willing to believe us capable of a certain cerebral development, who would even find it desirable—for men—that women should have some knowledge of many things, should be intelligent and moderately educated, those men would still not accept an equal development of women's wills. They would choose to split the female "ego," because they cannot help believing that a woman is really intended to gravitate toward the man-king; that she is a satellite; that this is a law of nature; and that it would consequently be madness, foolishness, and social disaster indeed to propose for the *second sex*, as it is called, men's famous teaching of energy.

Did not Michelet, for example, consider himself a feminist by preaching that man—the husband—should become the educator of his wife, not to emancipate her, to raise her to self-governance and autonomy, but gently to make her like himself, to convert her precisely into a satellite whose complete happiness would be found in her harmonious gravitation around the delighted master.[3]

But this alleged feminism condemns itself. It is illogical. From the moment one looks at a woman as capable of developing her thoughts, it is absurd to consider her incapable of developing her character. One can divide human nature only artificially. In reality, the human being is a single being. Either total antifeminism or total feminism is right.

Up to now the education given to women has been oppressive. And the age of the system endows it in some way with the dignity of a natural law. Indeed, when one proposes to change feminine education in a more liberal direction, the large majority, one could say almost everybody, is sincerely appalled, as though one had proposed something that was against nature. This is because they are confusing the effect with the cause. They say that a limited education is suitable for women's limited energies. That, on the contrary, those energies have been diminished by education does not occur to them. They do not allow women the excuse of having been forced for centuries into a position of moral and intellectual inferiority: they believe them inferior by nature.

And how does the "ego" of a being that is taught not to have any intrinsic value develop? Because, even today, is not the object of the education given to a woman to make her obedient? From her youngest years she is taught to sacrifice her individuality. As a little girl she must be silent and without spirit, displaying gentle manners and a timid soul. As she grows up, a more rigorous surveillance surrounds her. And all this so that she will not acquire a taste for independence. She is never allowed to make any decisions or assume responsibility for her person. It is a training in immobility of thought, in patience, and in love of detail and insignificant objects. Generally, when the vision has been concentrated too often on little things, it no longer has enough strength to embrace larger horizons.

Nevertheless, how much progress has been made, at least in the field of education!

Only a few years ago one wanted a woman to remain without any general knowledge. Only very light nourishment was offered to her spirit: a strictly essential dose of elementary knowledge. And since to survey her and to keep her ignorant was not a sufficient guarantee against revolt and the curiosity of her spirit, religious teachings served to curb her soul definitively. If her conscience awoke for an instant, this was a sign of diabolic pride. Man's severity and God's wrath were immediately brought to bear on her. How could she hold her head up high when to the weight of social laws was added the terrible weight of divine laws? Alone, she was unable to triumph over unanimous blame and soon was forced to capitulate and, vanquished, return into humility.

But it was nevertheless necessary that the humble creature have some interest in life. She was given the right to resort to guile. Moralists tolerate, even advise her to use, crafty manipulation and ingenious lies such as the slave uses to bend his master's authority. But even when he dominates, the slave keeps his power by pretending to ignore it; his attitude remains modest and his voice frightened. The gestures of servility constantly remind him of his condition and that obedience is merely a new pleasure for the master. And in this way the woman spends the best part of her existence imagining coquetries that would raise her to the role of slave-queen. Unless totally indigent by nature, she should not even have the strength of craft, but allow herself to be placidly led.

Sometimes she is less narrowly brought up. Especially in large cities she is less subject to religious observances that stunt the spirit. Nevertheless, the principles of the old education subsist.

The modified pedagogical methods and an extended curriculum are not sufficient to form character. The stutterings of intellectual life do not trouble the torpor of moral life. The proof is that even though woman has been slightly emancipated on an intellectual level, she nevertheless continues to be kept under the traditional yoke. To tell the truth, her new knowledge is but decoration, fashionable finery that must not change her passive attitude toward man in any way. He is still designated as her supreme educator, guide, and natural master.

A woman does not have to choose a social position. There is only one for her: marriage. It is her career, a career with many duties and few rights, since according to law and custom marriage is an association for life where the two partners have unequal rights. And parents in their bourgeois wisdom understand it thus when they talk of *establishing* their daughter.

That a woman should sign such a contract without considering it an insolent injustice shows that her reason and her dignity must be asleep. To know how to reason and to be proud of it is superfluous for anyone who has only to obey. It would be a weapon given to the person directed for use against the director.

The act of reasoning is the liberator of consciences. When thought often comes back on itself, when it analyzes itself, it acquires the habit of discernment, and when, knowing its own strength, it aspires to using that strength, there is no more guardianship possible. Creatures of reason want to be the mistresses of their own destinies.

The principle is to lead the woman to marriage and not to prepare her for life. She makes the most serious commitment of her life with a puerile soul. Indeed, the ideal is that she should ignore the principal conditions of that commitment. Yet, if she deviates from the obligations that she has unconsciously shouldered, it is clearly pointed out to her that she is held responsible.

However, this is but an apparent illogicality. She is made to promise obedience: she has therefore been warned that she is divesting herself of her own will.

To make the law of suffocation of feminine individuality quasi-absolute and untouchable, it has been inscribed in the Moral Code. If it had been left with the value of a purely social law, it would have become very relative and much less respectable.

But one should not see in the constraint imposed on women merely a masculine egoism. Another reason for it is the idea that two equal wills cannot coexist in one family. The family as it is still conceived of nowadays is a hierarchy. It represents the principle of authority dear to the guardians of social order.

For this reason these guardians are of an unshakable antifeminism: they see in the feminist doctrine a revolutionary threat.

But how can they avoid the transformation they so fear? Their very abuses are what precipitate it.

In the matter of marriage, for example, a woman used to promise to obey, but it was understood that a man would take her under his absolute protection. She did not bring any dowry and did not earn a living: the husband guaranteed it for her. In exchange, she gave up her freedom. In a way the deal was equitable. Now, man accepts and generally asks that his wife bring him a dowry or that she be capable of earning a living. The conditions of the matrimonial contract are no longer the same.

Whatever the causes of these changes, they are a sign that the time has come when a woman must be able to be self-reliant. And whether one deplores it or not, she has been forced into acts of independence. Whether single or married, she is facing the same difficulties as man. But with her limited knowledge of life and her timidity in taking initiatives, how much more painful is the struggle for her! Since they are both companions in the struggle, would it not be simple justice and even an advantage to supply them with the same ammunition to defend themselves?

It is unquestionable that the essential condition for freedom is economic independence. The person who has to rely on another for his subsistence is in slavery. But earning a living or having a private income does not mean that one is free; it implies that one has the means to become so. And if proof is necessary, does it not lie in the fact that the women who command their own material destiny, be it by their dowry or their income, are abdicating their autonomy without revolt just like the others? It is not a painful step for them to *disindividualize* themselves or rather, they do not make any serious effort to acquire an individuality.

Hence, one reaches the conclusion that if economic independence is indispensable for emancipation, it does not really serve this object except in consciences that are already awakened.

We must therefore not only demand economic emancipation but also preach moral emancipation at the same time, and with the same ardor. The first without the second would be three-quarters sterile. The decisive revolution is the inner revolution; the freest of persons is, in the real sense of the word, the one who belongs the most to herself, and true freedom is ultimately measured by the degree of autonomy of the "ego." The worst tyrants are those we maintain, or allow to live within ourselves: our bad instincts, our mindless passions, our unreasonable temptations, and all our atavistic vices.

At present, when excellent projects are being proposed to strengthen the character, which will undoubtedly lead to a reform of the educational system, would it not be the time to let women profit from this new moral hygiene? [. . .]

In our request for equal pedagogical treatment for men and women, our adversaries would certainly see the proof that we are ambitious to wear "a bearded soul," according to the expression invented by one of them. In their animosity they confuse the legitimate claim to be classified as a human person with a ridiculous desire to *become masculine*. And this being only childishly absurd, they also accuse us of harboring the more serious intention of wanting to copy men, the better to declare war on them. Because we voice the wish not to be vassals any more, but companions, we are now considered enemies. That there should be but one law for all the individuals of the human species seems to them to be an exorbitant idea.

Could the intolerance of a slightly fanatical feminism have contributed to the spread of such ambiguity? Such zeal is excusable and even necessary, since one needs an excessive drive in order to tip ideas in the opposite direction from the one that custom has imposed on them.

But the great, initial spurt having been made, reasonable beings bring the effort into proper perspective.

In our doctrine there is only a wish for justice: not to exclude any human being from the right to live a complete life, from the right to develop all faculties fully and to exert them. Thus, far from *wanting to be masculine,* we want our womanly personality not to be dulled by pretexts of morality or social necessity. If we want everyone to be educated in a freedom that implies the exercise of responsibility, it is because we see that as the only means of ridding ourselves of the degrading uniformity that discipline imposes on souls.

How will the respect of the "ego" make the diversities of nature between man and woman disappear? Far, far from alleviating the original differences, it tends rather to accentuate what distinguishes each individual. It is necessary to repeat: when we talk about *equality,* we do not make any mistake concerning the meaning of the word; we do not confuse it with *identity*. We do not say that a woman resembles a man; we claim that she is of equivalent value.

We advocate the same educational system for women and for men. However, if one wants to suppress the distance that separates them on the mental plane, special attention must be given to the former.

The initial task is to give a woman confidence in herself. One remains forever without any will if one does not have some belief in one's power from the beginning. One desires strongly and risks success only when one has the first elements of success in oneself.

Women have been told so many times that it is by nature's decree that they are without power that they have become disastrously used to resignation. Resignation, so convenient for lazy souls, was misnamed a virtue by the strong so as to paralyze the weak. This is the reason why all religions that dominate souls preach resignation. Nevertheless, the human being who had never tired of hoping for happiness and of fighting to obtain it would not have listened to the counsel of renunciation if he had not been encouraged by the promise of eternal happiness after death. But now Paradise has spread, and humankind wants to know felicity on this earth. The gods do not live in a restricted, chimerical heaven any more, and the all-powerful god of willpower has come down to us, into us . . .

Resignation is a perpetual confession of impotence. From the moment that one recognizes defeat and seems to accept it, any possibility of victory recedes, whereas the very process of striving with all our strength increases it, and it becomes sufficient for reaching even a difficult goal. The goal must indeed be difficult. It is by looking up, very high, that one succeeds in raising oneself a little.

Thus, the first act of will would be to know exactly the point on which one should fix one's sights. This should be done not by chance, in a dream, but after having discerned and weighed all the motives of one's preference. Then, knowing that one must want, that one can want, and what one wants, all that remains is to orient each action in the direction of the ideal: not to dream it any longer but to live it.

Thus, the choice of what one wants implies a certain knowledge of things. A child who has been sheltered from life, even though he may feel the desire to make an effort when he grows up, will waste his energies stupidly; they will be of no use to him. He will not even have the negative goodness of the weak, since acts of will that have no conscious direction quickly become harmful.

The principle that one should shelter adolescents from the difficulties of life because they will suffer them in time is therefore false and dangerous. And indeed, they will suffer from them instead of being equipped to overcome them. This principle is maintained by the unconsidered love of parents and also because juvenile ignorance is found attractive—especially, of course, the inexperience and perfect candor of the young girl, candor, moreover, that risks being spoiled even faster because nothing warns her that she should avoid contact with experiences that will leave blemishes.

Instead of blinding young people, one should open their eyes wide to reality. Not everything is painful or abominable. Only souls disenchanted by a sudden fall from the heights of their illusions are incapable of seeing life's many beauties, whereas those accustomed to the rough but healthy contact with truth find a sufficient reason to live in the incessant desire to know it better.

By wanting to turn away from errors one becomes attentive to the spectacle of life. And this habit of examining everything must start early; because, if young intelligences are not offered occasions for comparison, they will be uncertain in their judgments later on—that is, if they are not totally deprived of critical sense.

It is said that this critical sense is particularly absent in women. They are held in contempt without anyone thinking that this faculty is not acquired between the candid walls of a girls' boarding school, or in the family home that is too cushioned to let in the educational turbulence of the outside world.

It is claimed that critical sense would shrivel feminine sentimentality. Could this be a confession that men, who are so proud of their reason, are defective in heart? They would be very angry if one assumed that they had insensitive souls. But it is their idea that a woman is fatally condemned to be incomplete. Do they allow her the exercise of one faculty? Then they want it immediately to be to the detriment of another. For them her soul does not exist without deficiencies; and to fill them would be useless, since an adjacent gap would immediately be created.

We believe, on the contrary, that for woman as well as man any feeling is more profound and solid if it can be subjected to the most minute examination of reason.

But this is a parenthesis. Returning to the relationship between critical sense and character formation, we must observe others not only in order to compare them among themselves, and be amused by their actions, but also and above all to let their actions teach us a lesson that results in a reliable equilibrium for ourselves.

No force is negligible in ensuring this equilibrium. The art of organizing our inner life consists especially in the use and harmonious development of our faculties. To sacrifice some of them is to renounce living a little; to dry up sources of energy.

When one perseveres in self-observation and has learned to recognize one's good and bad aspirations, it is vain to want to destroy the bad. The violence that one would use against them would imbue them with a dangerous importance. They can become useful sources of power if one exerts oneself, not to repress them, but to direct them well.

Anyhow, one does not create will in fiery and intermittent bursts. To will is to accept submitting to sensible and permanent commands that one gives quietly to oneself. This implies obedience both in thought and in action to an intimate and superior idea.

Moreover—is it necessary to say it?—this superior idea will never be an idea of pride against others. To adore oneself is not to belong to oneself anymore. It is, on the contrary, in an apparent exaltation of the will, to subordinate it to triumphant egoism, to manufacture from one's hereditary instincts, from one's passions, whatever they may be, even from one's weaknesses a shimmering and bad idol. It means substituting for ancient mysticisms, which are still somewhat important, not an ideal of self-liberation, but a doctrine of self-servitude that idolizes itself. It is to confuse the exhilaration of personality with the tranquil aspiration toward moral Betterment. It is also to withdraw from humanity in order to regard it from a standpoint of contemptuous pity, or to promise oneself not to get mixed up with it except to dominate it.

Far from teaching contempt or inspiring a taste for domination, putting into practice the cultivation of the "ego" is fertile in lessons of modesty and in suggestions of goodness.

During the rough struggles of internal progress one learns indulgence; one feels the generous desire to help others.

Thus the true doctrine of emancipation of the will leads to an enlightened and ardent altruism.

And this is true for all of humanity.

As there is only one truth, which does not depend on sex; as there is only one justice; there is only one principle of moral dignity, which must not be for the woman resignation, patience, submission and for the man free development. To all human beings without exception the same axiom applies: be yourselves, completely, through your mind, your heart, and your character.

Notes

1. The editors have found no biography of Harlor, although many biographical materials exist in the collection of the Bibliothèque Marguerite Durand. Pauline

Newman-Gordan of Stanford University is currently preparing an essay on Harlor and her novels.

2. Although Marguerite Durand (1864–1936) is not represented by a translation in this anthology, she was one of the most influential feminists of the belle époque because of her newspaper, *La Fronde,* which provided unity and leadership at a critical moment in the development of the women's movement. Most of the authors represented in this volume contributed to it at one time or another. There is a helpful biographical introduction to Durand in Goliber, "The Life and Times of Marguerite Durand." See also Klejman and Rochefort, *L'Egalité en marche,* 127–37.

3. Harlor is referring to the distinguished historian Jules Michelet (1798–1874), a leading figure of French romanticism, an eloquent nationalist, the author of a major history of the French Revolution, and a longtime professor at the Collège de France. The antifeminist opinions that Harlor mentions here are clearest in his *La Femme* (Paris, 1860); see also his *Le Prêtre, la femme, et la famille* (Paris, 1845), *L'Amour* (Paris, 1858), and *Les Femmes de la révolution* (Paris, 1854). For a discussion of Michelet's attitudes see Moses, *French Feminism,* esp. 158–61. For a fuller study, see Thérèse Moreau, *Le Sang de l'histoire.*

GABRIELLE REVAL

Gabrielle Reval was the literary pseudonym of Gabrielle Logerot, later Gabrielle Fleuret (1870–1938).[1] Logerot was one of the first graduates (class of 1890) of the *Ecole normale supérieure* for women founded at Sèvres in 1882, the training ground for women of the intellectual elite during the belle époque.[2] Logerot passed her *agrégation* in 1893 and taught at the *lycée* (secular high school) for girls at Niort until 1899. She wrote for several newspapers (notably *L'Oeuvre* and *Le Journal*), lectured all over Europe, and married the poet Fernand Fleuret. It is as the novelist Gabrielle Reval, however, that she became famous. Her novels earned her a variety of honors, including the Legion of Honor, the Prix du Président de la République (1934), and the Portugese Order of Santiago de l'Epée (1935). She also shaped women's writing as a member of the jury for the Fémina Prize.

As one of the first generation of Sévriennes, Reval concerned herself in her early novels with what must have been her own experience–that of young women struggling to pass competitive examinations and then going out to teach in the Third Republic's new secular schools for girls. She depicts the conflict between love and career, and she writes about the tremendous pressures that weighed on the pioneer women teachers in provincial France. These pressures chiefly came from the townspeople, who often refused to lodge teachers, watched them like hawks, and expected them to live as secular nuns; other pressures came from the injustices of operating within a school system created by, identified with, and led by men.[3] Reval's teachers were seen as subverters of tradition and the status quo, both of which the convent school protected–which is precisely what republican politicans had intended them to be.

The extract translated here is taken from *Un Lycée de jeunes filles* (A High School for Girls [1901]). This novel tells the story of a year in a provincial *lycée*. Berthe Passy (a character in Reval's previous novel about education, *Les Sévriennes*) welcomes and helps Marie Fleuret, a newly qualified Sévrienne who is innocent and idealistic in both her professional and her private lives. Berthe has other problems. A warm, outgoing, intelligent, and resourceful woman, she is more down-to-earth and outspoken than her colleagues. These traits derive from Berthe's peculiar history: she grew up in Montmartre, the daughter of a poet with whom she still lives. Her situation is unusual in that she has love and support at home and yet is free of the tasks and demands made of her colleagues. Also, although she is one of the new generation of teachers with a vision of what education might be, she views teaching as a job rather than a mission or a means to salvation. Such independence and lack of idealism bring her into conflict with a colleague who reports her to the school board. The scene that follows shows Berthe in a heated discussion with the government's inspector of schools.

The Perils of Teaching

"Word has reached me that people in town are calling you the *anarchist* and *companion!*"

"People around here are far too generous! And what, may I ask, brings me the honor of being called 'companion'?" said Berthe, with some acerbity.

"Your opinions and your language, Mademoiselle!"

Berthe raised her eyebrows, to show that she did not understand this reasoning.

In what way did her opinions resemble those of Sebastien Faure?[4] Just how was her language like that of *The Libertarian*? It would have been difficult for the Inspector to say, so he referred to the information in her dossier.

"These are the facts, as reported, Mademoiselle, and if your answers do not satisfy me, they may become the object of a serious inquiry."

This time Berthe was certain; she had been denounced according to the rules. Fidgeting on her chair and not the least bit alarmed, the young

Source: Gabrielle Reval (pseud.), *Un Lycée de jeunes filles* (Paris, 1901), 282–89. Trans. Jette Kjaer and Jennifer Waelti-Walters.

woman smoothed out her dress from neck to knee in the gesture of a cat enjoying stretching its legs and extending its claws.

The Inspector pulled out her dossier from a capacious briefcase, sorted the papers, and started reading out loud the following notes, dry and mean as a police report:

1. *Her private life*–She and her father ignore conventions of speech and behavior, both are lacking in dignity. Mademoiselle Passy calls her father, "My old Jules," a term never used by people who respect each other. And they occasionally clap each other on the back in a vulgar fashion–And who is this Rosalie who stays in the house, while the schoolmistress's father, in a sloppy state of undress, makes a show of peeling vegetables in the sight of passersby?

A teacher who truly respects herself and her profession would not discredit herself thus in other families' eyes!

2. *Her language*–Who would believe that this person had been to the best women's college?[5] One would think she had been born in a greasy spoon in Montmartre; her vulgarity is fit to delight Courteline's recruits.[6] Is it by speaking of *peepers* and *hoofs* and *mitts,* and using thousands of crude slang expressions, that one teaches literary language to young girls?–These families have good reason to wonder at finding such slang in the mouths of their children; several people have expressed a desire to take their little girls away from Mademoiselle Passy.

3. Finally, and most serious of all, in her teaching, Mademoiselle Passy shows no respect for the very *spirit* of our school.

Instead of conforming to the program and teaching her pupils our official doctrines, she starts philosophical discussions, and even political and religious ones, painting enticing pictures of utopias. The children's brains are too weak to retain anything from Mademoiselle Passy's very *advanced* doctrines except the seed of *revolt*.

Mademoiselle Passy insults the present and tries to detach children from their families. She is constantly advising them to free themselves of prejudice and question everything they learn. Nothing finds favor in her eyes; not family, society, or government. She and Mademoiselle Fleuret, who are full of these revolutionary doctrines, are actively spreading propaganda in the school. Since they have a real influence over their pupils, it would be wise for the Authorities to intervene; otherwise, our school will be brought down by these teachers.

Berthe, lost in thought, did not take her eyes off the *Magister* executing his duties. She reflected that her future lay at the mercy of somebody's hatred or jealousy, and yet nothing existed in this man's mind but the need to substantiate this "fable" and please the all-powerful Kriska.

Who else but she could have written this report? Narrow minded and domineering, this woman was the sworn enemy of the new spirit that Berthe and Marie represented in all its vigor and imprudent nobility, soaring high above the tacit Code, the harsh Code of honest people's opinion.

Berthe wanted to laugh and cry all at once. Laugh, because it was so ridiculous to watch the drama quietly being cooked up by this pen pusher!

And cry, because it was so distressing to be giving her soul and her blood to a task she would be prevented from accomplishing in the future.

She remained silent.

The irritated Inspector rose and, his hands behind his back, started pacing up and down the office; then, stopping by the fireplace, the tails of his frock coat lifted, he conveniently warmed himself.

Still Berthe did not say anything.

"Well, Mademoiselle! Do you acknowledge your wrongdoings?"

"Me?" said the young teacher, stunned. "But Inspector, there was nothing but praise in that report!"

"That's too much! Listen, Mademoiselle, don't forget you are talking to an Inspector of the Academy."

"God forbid, Sir. My father taught me to fear no one but a policeman . . . (and as the other knit his brows) . . . do you see one coming?"

"Get to the point, Mademoiselle. Vindicate yourself."

"I have very little to say to Mademoiselle Kriska's *precise* report; not for a moment would I affront Mademoiselle Gripou by supposing that she, our *Natural Guardian,* would make herself public prosecutor in front of you. I upset Mademoiselle Kriska and she wants to get rid of me. I am not leaving, that is my right!"

"You are forgetting your most fundamental duty, Mademoiselle," cried the Inspector furiously.

"Which is?"

"To obey your masters."

"My masters? My masters?" Berthe exclaimed, leaping to her feet. "Who on earth do you take me for, Sir? Am I your servant? Am I here in someone's pay? Neither you nor Mademoiselle Gripou is my master! Show me the merits, talents, or perfection by which you are my masters! No, I am your equal, we are all your equals here. You are demanding an obedience that is not your due. You want," she continued, caught up in her argument, "to make us schoolteachers and workers whom you enlist, passive, gullible, and submissive women in fear of punishment! You have us by the throat because you give us our daily bread! No matter that we slave and slog away and collapse on the job; as long as we obey, you are satisfied. It takes guts to go on when you have seen what I see: miserable women who have nothing left but their breath, and who are prepared to take on any drudgery; women crushed by labor that is worse than poverty. And you don't even send them the poor people's doctor! Oh, yes," she continued, transfigured, and bursting into harsh laughter, "you truly are their master, just as on a building site the man who gives out the pay is master of the beast that collapses under its burden and of the man, beaten unconscious, who falls down beside it! . . . "

The furious Inspector made a threatening gesture. Berthe's look stopped him; he could not sustain her angry gaze.

"Let me speak, Sir. Since you treat me as a culprit, I have the right to defend myself. It is not just my own cause I am pleading, but that of my sisters who remain defenseless before you, at the mercy of your orders. You will not get the mercenary obedience you are expecting from me. You can go ahead and condemn me. But there is one obedience in which I have not failed. Come into my classroom, observe, question, and dare tell me whether, in obeying my own conscience rigorously, I have sown the seeds of fanaticism or cultivated wisdom! Yes, I have dreamed of instructing my pupils and not cramming them with useless information. Yes, I wanted to make women who think, and not copies of Mnemosyne. What is the use of teaching pupils everything we teach if it doesn't open their eyes, if they remain paralyzed along the way, unable to reap the fruits of life? I want those who come by me to make an effort; I want the new world to be built in fraternity. We, too, are building our cathedral. Come and see the stones we are carrying. What does it matter if I use trivial language to raise souls toward what is noble! It expresses my thought in all its energy—thought rises above words—and the language of Rabelais still outdoes the long, philosophic-humanitarian tirades of your anteroom rhetoricians!"

"Nonsense! There is a wisdom older than yours, Mademoiselle, which must be respected: the one that says you must obey custom and not do anything that might offend public opinion."

"What a wretched shame!" cried Berthe, indignant at such cowardice. "What, then, is the use of so many secondary schools for girls, *imposed* at the price of gold, the cost of sweat and hunger, if we have nothing new to contribute, not even the hope of something better?"

"Just teach them to love the Republic, Mademoiselle, that is all we ask of you."

"All they ask!" murmured Berthe. "Poor women . . . "

For a moment she was silent, a knot of inexpressible emotion in her throat; she felt a decisive moment in her teaching career had come. Either she would defy the petty authority of the *administrators,* to defend her freedom of thought, or she would bow down like the rest and suffer shamefully for her silence.

She did not hesitate for a moment. Even before the Inspector, who was slightly stunned by her unpolished language, could have thought of giving any orders, Berthe continued very gravely:

"I have always believed a time would come when the large, dreamy eyes of Io would turn away from Jupiter. At that moment, the nymph, helped and loved, would be born again from the entrails of the Beast. She would finally be equal to God, and through her, happiness would enter the Mount Olympus of our dreams. But I see that the time has not yet come and that such dreams are the dreams of women, since you do not hear the protests that threaten, and the calls that implore you!"

"Ah," said the other, "What a clever little fellow he was who said:

> All my household reasons
> And reasoning banishes reason!

What you really want is to use our schools to emancipate women. Fine project, this feminist scheme! We have enough problems on our hands without your putting future incendiaries in our way."[7]

"Incendiaries! You are mistaken, Sir! These women are born of common stock . . . companions at the very most!"

"More rubbish!" And, feeling that he was going to have to make an effort to impose his authority, the man with the ermine decoration added:[8]

"Enough said. Besides, you are one of those women who cannot be converted. In the interest of your career, let go of these utopias, feminism and the rest! Follow the path we have shown you and, above all, respect mothers' prejudices; they are still the best guarantee of a girl's virtue."

"And if I disobey?"

"You will be dismissed," the other said dryly.

"I shall starve?"

"Humph, women like you don't die of hunger! . . . When good for nothing else, you can still make an excellent general maid," he added, between his teeth.

Berthe, having read the boor's lips, jumped up, ready to slap his face. A sudden thought stopped her.

"Sir, you have just spoken words that you will hear again one day; they will be at the head of the list of insults that must be atoned for. That day justice will be done, for all those women who submit to you—because they know that the only way to escape hunger is to beg for what you give them—those women will rise up without pity."

"Well done, you offer yourself as another Vallès!"[9]

"Were he still alive, I should call him my master!"

"More threats!"

"No," said Berthe, throwing him a look of contempt, "a commitment to myself."

When the door had closed, the Inspector of the Academy was stupefied by such a scene and the pathetic role he had played in front of *his inferior*.

Notes

1. There is no biography of Reval. For her writing, see Waelti-Walters, *Feminist Novelists,* 100–107. For interesting glimpses of her education and career as a teacher, see Margadant, *Madame le Professeur.*

2. Margadant's *Madame le Professeur* offers a collective biography of 213 members of the first generation of Sévriennes. She points out that Reval's perspective was somewhat more critical than that of other graduates (65, n.16).

3. For a glimpse of this clash of cultures in provincial France (without the issue of gender), see Barnett Singer, *Village Notables in 19th Century France: Priests, Mayors, and Schoolmasters* (Albany, 1983), esp. 108–46. For more evidence of the problems facing Logerot, see Danielle Delhome, Nicole Gault, and Josiane Gonthier, eds., *Les Premières institutrices laïques: documents* (Paris, 1980), pp.81–203.

4. Sébastien Faure (1858–1942) was a militant anarchist who publicized many of the anticlerical, antimilitarist, and neo-Malthusian ideas of the movement. In 1895 he and Louise Michel founded the anarchist weekly newspaper *Le Libertaire,* which he published until 1914. For Faure, the principle of authority was the source of the world's woes, and the schools were a branch of authority. He briefly led an experimental school for orphans, seeking to provide an emancipated education in the com-

munal life; see Roland Lewin, *Sébastien Faure et "La Ruche," ou l'Education libertaire* (Vauchrétien, 1989). For examples of Faure's ideas, see the collection of his articles entitled *Propos subversifs* (Paris, n.d.), which includes essays on women, children, and the family.

5. Reval refers to her own school, the *Ecole de Sèvres,* subsequently the *Ecole normale superieure de jeunes filles.*

6. Georges Courteline, the pseudonym of Georges Moineaux (1860–1929), was a writer known for his light novels often set in barracks.

7. Reval uses the French terms *"pétroleuses"* (incendiaries) and *"compagnonnes"* (companions), both of which were passionate political vocabulary. The *pétroleuses* were women who had participated in the Paris Commune of 1871; during the last days of bitter fighting, they set fire to parts of the city. See Gullickson, "The *Pétroleuse,"* and Edith Thomas, *The Women Incendiaries* (London, 1966). *Compagnonnes* were women members of the *compagnonnages,* secret societies of workers that aimed to provide mutual aid to their members; see Jean-Pierre Bayard, *Le Compagnonnage en France* (Paris, 1982).

8. Reval refers to his *"épitoge."* This is the decoration on the shoulder of an academic gown that (like a hood) indicates the subject of study and the level of degree.

9. Jules Vallès (1832–85) was a revolutionary journalist and novelist. He participated in the Commune and spent the next decade in exile. During the 1880s he collaborated on his newspaper, *Le Cri du peuple,* with a future feminist leader, Séverine (pseudonym of Caroline Guebhard, 1855–1929). He also published a succesful trilogy of autobiographical novels, known as the Jacques Vingtras trilogy (*L'Enfant, Le Bachelier,* and *L'Insurgé*). See Roger Bellet, *Jules Vallès, journalisme et révolution, 1857–1885* (Tusson, 1987), and Max Gallo, *Jules Vallès, ou la révolte d'une vie* (Paris, 1988). For Séverine, see Le Garrec, *Séverine,* and Lacache, *Séverine.* An anthology of her articles has been reprinted by Le Garrec, entitled *Séverine: Choix de papiers.* For her role in the women's suffrage campaign, see Hause with Kenney, *Women's Suffrage,* esp. 182–87.

LOUISE-MARIE COMPAIN

Louise-Marie Compain became a prominent feminist quite suddenly in 1903 with the publication of her first novel, *L'Un vers l'autre* (One Toward the Other).[1] The novel explores love and equality in marriage by focusing on a young, newly married girl (Laure Prevel) who expects to live a full and happy life as her husband's (Henri Deborda) equal and companion (see the excerpt on marriage in part 5).

The excerpt given here comes from the end of *L'Un vers l'autre*. Laure has refused to live in a marriage of servitude and has therefore set out to obtain economic independence. She obtains her teaching diploma and goes to work in a normal (teacher-training) school. There she finds a friend in the principal, Germaine Lachaud. Germaine approves of Laure's decision and supports her in her new career. In this excerpt, Germaine describes her own development as a teacher and as a woman–her ideals and the difficulties she has undergone. Her discussion of "preparing a new race of women" clearly shows why the novel was a feminist sensation.

A New Race of Women

"We are preparing a new race of women that is more reasonable, better able to deserve the respect they demand from men but often don't deserve by their frivolousness and unreasonableness. This possession, reason, purchased so dearly, since to win it we have usually had to give our deepest desires as a ransom, we bequeath to future generations. We are acting on today's generation by our example, by the education we are giving to the minds of our girls. We must make them not only good schoolteachers, but especially, women with the ability to govern themselves, tender and wise mothers who can offer good advice. Women of the future will be happier than we, they will blossom in the richness of their feminine nature. Men will love them deeply and respectfully, for although different from them, women will be their equals. Oppression shall end the day it is clear that there is no reason for it to exist. It is pleasant for me to think that I, for example, who have never known love, will be doing something for the happiness of my future sisters. For by my efforts I shall have contributed to making them worthier of love. We are a sacrificed generation. Incomplete human beings, unable to survive, it is we who are preparing the hatching of happier, more perfect human beings!"

For a moment she was silent. Then, no longer speaking seriously, she added playfully:

"Let me make a comparison. You have heard of the archaeopteryx, haven't you? This strange and ugly creature with feathers, teeth, and a tail like a snake? The breed died out, fortunately, but from this ridiculous creature birds were born. It existed only for a short while, yet it was necessary. Well, we too are archaeopteryxes, beings in transition, not lovable in themselves, perhaps, but beautiful by what they foretell."

Source: Louise-Marie Compain, *L'Un vers l'autre* (Paris, 1903), 249–50. Trans. Jette Kjaer.

Note

1. There is no biography of Compain. A brief sketch of her life appeared in *La Française* on December 24, 1911. For her writing, see Waelti-Walters, *Feminist Novelists,* esp. 126–37.

CHARLES THIÉBAUX

Charles Thiébaux was a turn-of-the-century lawyer who wrote a doctoral thesis on feminism. His thesis was well received, but Thiébaux did not go on to take an active role in the women's movement. He prepared *Le Féminisme et les socialistes depuis Saint-Simon à nos jours* (Feminism and the Socialists from Saint-Simon to the Present Day) under the direction of the distinguished economist Charles Gide, a champion of cooperationist socialism, an advocate of women's rights, and the father of the novelist André Gide.[1] Thiébaux successfully defended his thesis in 1906 and published it that same year. It examines nineteenth-century socialists (part 1) before turning to the author's contemporaries (part 2). Thiébaux surveys contemporary feminism in three categories: the civil and political emancipation of women, emancipation within marriage, and economic emancipation. The following excerpt is taken from the first of those topics, where Thiébaux examines the socialist ideal of holistic education. His remarks provide a helpful context for locating other feminists translated in this anthology, such as Harlor (part 1) and Marie Bonnevial (part 3).

The Pedagogical
Emancipation of Women

The development of a woman's feeling and ideas, and the final orientation of her life, is nearly always a function of the education received in her youth. Feminism has understood the full significance of educational issues in the problem of bettering the condition of women. Socialists have also been careful not to lose interest in these serious issues and in turn propose their formula for education and instruction. This is quite interesting to examine, for nowhere do the socialist tendencies toward regulation, tyranny, and sectarianism appear more evident than here.

In a brochure honored with a preface by M. Jules Guesde, M. Anatole Baju proposes the following: "If we want an egalitarian society, we must prepare for it.[2] And to do that, we must take all the youngest children before they have acquired any bad habits. We then give them the same care and attention, the same nourishment, and the same education." In an actual town of children, "boys and girls, mixed, receive a holistic education that is independent of the work they are destined to do one day." We find all the precepts of the socialists, who want to take charge of young souls, formulated in these few lines. For a slightly more detailed commentary on the regulation of education, we can look to a declaration made by Mlle de Bonnevial, a staunch feminist and ardent socialist, in her report of the Congress of the Feminist Left [*Congrès de la gauche féministe*] in 1900.[3]

Let us therefore examine what "holistic education" means in terms of socialism, according to those who propose it. We are forced to cite word for word the magnificent program that follows, for it would be impossible to summarize it without losing anything: "We want education to be holistic in its aims, all men and women having the same right to their full development. We want it to be holistic in its cultural methods and cultural means; that is, education must create an environment that allows human beings to come into contact with all areas of learning, so that they will wake up to their own personal initiative. Furthermore, education must protect children from being marked by slavery, while teaching them to observe, experiment, make deductions, and synthesize material. Thus, they will be able to define their

Source: Charles Thiébaux, *Le Féminisme et les socialistes depuis Saint-Simon à nos jours* (Paris, 1906), pt. 1, ch. 1, sect. 2. Trans. Jette Kjaer and Jennifer Waelti-Walters.

own set of morals instead of receiving them ready-made. Finally, education must cultivate and universalize children's aptitudes, their muscular development, and their sensual awareness by means of contact with essential material and tools. Hence, children will acquire general working skills, and thus be assured economic independence."[4] That, and nothing less, is what is required to "suppress ignorance and misery."

Moreover, it is hardly the personal opinion of Mlle de Bonnevial that we must consider, but that of the feminist or socialist groups. Now, we see that in 1900 the Congress on the Condition and the Rights of Women [*Congrès de la condition et des droits de des femmes*] passed the following motion: "This Congress declares itself in favor of holistic education; that is, education that cultivates the manifestation of human activity in everyone."[5] The wording is brief, but explanations and a development of the theme are abundant. Most of them are found in Mlle Harlor's report, presented at the same congress.[6] The program for holistic education involves "the totality of human knowledge." Its base must necessarily be encyclopaedic in nature, which means that young girls will learn something about everything at the risk of not knowing anything. Indeed, it is evident that a little learning is often more dangerous than complete ignorance.

This education must be obligatory and free for everyone; this comes from Mlle de Bonnevial's declaration at the congress: "It is quite obvious that for education to be holistic for everyone . . . it must be *imposed,* and for it to be imposed, it must be free."[7] It must also be secular, free of all denominational influences, and even beyond that, it must be anticlerical, for we must liberate all consciences so that women are no longer, as the socialists say so well, "toys of gross superstition, slaves of blind devotion, docile instruments of espionage in the hands of a few priests."[8]

Holistic, secular, free, and compulsory instruction will be an education and also will develop the mind and feelings of morality of the girls at the same time. By what miracle this will happen we do not know, but possibly by that of words alone.

It is true that socialists count greatly on the practice of "coeducation," which is originally American, to develop morality in children. [. . .]

The Congress of the Feminist Left also enthusiastically accepted the principle of coeducation, and in her closing speech, Mme Pognon announced:[9] "You have voted unanimously for coeducation, and this is an immense step forward. This is the first time a feminist congress has voted for coeducation in Paris, and that without contest. Look how far we have come in four years."[10]

Socialists maintain that this progress, on which advanced feminists congratulate themselves, is a step to the left, and they congratulate themselves in turn for having contributed to this. Under the pretext of holistic instruction and coeducation, they are making a great effort to attempt to regulate teaching methods. This would first of all mean the destruction of education in the home and, under their patronage and with their support, would form children of both sexes together, thus eliminating the separation that often exists between the emancipated male of ancient religious and conservative beliefs, and the woman who is still a slave of old-fashioned duties, to which, until this time, we have taught her from childhood that she should cling.

Notes

1. For cooperative socialism, see Ellen Furlough, *Consumer Cooperation in France: the Politics of Consumption, 1834–1930* (Ithaca, 1991), and Henri Desroche, *Solidarités ouvrières: sociétaires et compagnons dans les associations coopératives, 1831–1900* (Paris, 1981). For Gide, see Henri Desroche, *Charles Gide, 1847–1932: Trois étapes d'une créativité–Coopérative, sociale, universitaire* (Paris, 1982).

2. [Author's note in the original text: *Principe du socialisme* (Paris, 1895), 32.] Anatole Baju was a minor figure in belle époque socialism; Jules Guesde (1845–1922) was one of the most important figures in establishing Marxian socialism in France. He edited a Marxist weekly newspaper (*L'Egalité*), led in the formation of a Marxist workers' party (the Parti ouvrier), and represented Roubaix in the Chamber of Deputies; see Claude Willard, *Jules Guesde, l'apôtre et la loi* (Paris, 1991).

3. For Bonnevial, see part 3. The "Congress of the Feminist Left" refers to the *Congrès international de la condition et des droits des femmes* held in Paris in 1900. For more on this congress, see note 19 to the Roussel excerpt in part 1. Bonnevial's reports to this congress were published in *Le Mouvement socialiste* October 15 and November 1, 1900.

4. [Author's note in the original text: *Revue encyclopédique* November 28, 1896: 339.]

5. [Author's note in the original text: *La Fronde* September 8, 1900.]

6. *Congrès international de la condition et des droits des femmes. Paris 1900 (5, 6, 7, et 8 septembre) à l'Exposition universelle au Palais de l'économie sociale et des congrès* (Paris, 1901), 114–92. The education section met on Thursday the sixth and Friday the seventh. Bonnevial presided and Harlor made the opening statement.

7. Ibid, 134.

8. [Author's note in the original text: (Jules) Destrée, *Le Socialisme et les femmes*, 17.]

9. Maria Pognon (1844–1925) was one of the most important militants at the 1900 congress. She had succeeded Richer as the president of the LFDF in 1894 and served in that office until 1904, when she was succeeded by Bonnevial. Pognon was a frequent contributor to *La Fronde*, especially on political subjects; she wrote the first column to call for women's suffrage in that paper. Pognon was also a pacifist and served simultaneously as an officer of the *Ligue pour l'arbitrage international* (the League for International Arbitration). She left the feminist movement in 1904 to follow her husband overseas.

10. [Author's note in the original text: *Compte rendu du Congrès de la condition et des droits de la femme* [sic] (Paris, 1900), 225.] Cf. N.7.

MADELEINE PELLETIER

Madeleine Pelletier (1874–1939) was an unloved child of a poor family.[1] Her mother was a greengrocer; her father, who was paralyzed when she was four, died when she was sixteen. Pelletier left school at age twelve but continued to read. As a teenager, she discovered politics through the doctrine of nihilism, and she was soon attending anarchist meetings. Pelletier then decided that she wanted to be a doctor in order to be socially useful. Studying alone, she learned enough to pass the *baccalauréat* and enter medical school. After her mother's death, Pelletier was left destitute, but she obtained a grant from the city of Paris to continue her studies.

The medical profession had slowly opened to women in the years after 1875, when Madeleine Brès became the first French woman admitted to medical school. By 1900 there were 82 women physicians in France (69 of them in Paris) and 154 women enrolled in medical school. The legal profession, by contrast, had only one woman graduate (Jeanne Chauvin), only four women enrolled in law at Paris, and had not yet admitted women to the bar.[2] Pelletier thus graduated as a member of the trailblazing generation. She became the first woman physician to work for the welfare office (*Bureau de bienfaisance*). She was refused admission to the entrance examination for an internship in the psychiatric hospitals until Marguerite Durand took up her cause in *La Fronde*. Pelletier then succeeded in becoming the first woman physician to work in a French mental hospital.

In the early twentieth century, Madeleine Pelletier became active in a wide range of political organizations. She became one of the first women to join the Freemasons, one of the highest ranking women in the socialist party, and one of the most outspoken militant feminists. Her chief feminist positions were the presidency of a small radical feminist group named *Solidarité des femmes* (Women's Solidarity) and the editorship of a women's suffrage monthly that she founded, *La Suffragiste*.

In her own review and in a vast range of other periodicals, Pelletier wrote on almost all feminist issues.[3] The following excerpts on education are taken from her 1914 pamphlet entitled *L'Education féministe des filles* (A Feminist Education for Girls). This work, calling for egalitarian education, remains strikingly timely today. In it, Pelletier treats the values of education, the development of body and character, the education of the mind, and the still-controversial issue of sex education.

A Feminist
Education for Girls

The Formation of Body and Character

First of all, how should one dress a little girl? At first sight this question seems of minimal importance. On the contrary, however, it is very important. Clothing and the physiognomy are the most visible aspects of each of us; others judge us by them, and the impression thus created in others affects how we see ourselves. There is a reason why soldiers wear uniforms and monks and nuns wear habits. An army without uniforms would be worthless, and monks and nuns without habits would hardly differ from the laity. Elegant attire encourages pride and daring; it stimulates energy. Rags instill humility, indifference, and dread.

If from her earliest years you dress your little girl in dresses loaded with ribbons and trimmings, if you cover her with jewelry, you will make of her a coquette who thinks only of dolling herself up. All your efforts thereafter to make her into a serious and dignified person will be in vain. She will listen to you with apparent deference, but her real educators will be her little friends whose finery she will compare to her own. Once her childhood is over, if you are well off, you will have a society doll; if you are poor, you will

Source: Madeleine Pelletier, *L'Education féministe des filles* (Paris, 1914), reprinted in Claude Maignein, ed., *L'Education des filles et autres textes* (Paris, 1978), 69–76, 78–79, 82–83, 97–101, 109–10, 111–15. Trans. Lydia Willis and Jennifer Waelti-Walters.

be even worse off, for your child will be ready to do anything to obtain the trinkets she covets.

Therefore, a feminist mother should dress her little girl as a boy.[4] Masculine clothing will have a most beneficial influence on the child's character. First, its shape allows any kind of movement without indecency. Mothers will not be obliged to keep saying: "Pull your dress down. Don't lift your legs that way. It is unladylike." A child always wants to move, and constantly telling her not to do so shackles the little girl from her earliest years. It is obvious that one should not tell the child, as so many mothers and even feminist mothers do, "Little girls do not turn somersaults," or "Keep still, tomboy."

A mother who acts like this must not be surprised if her daughter becomes like other women in spite of secondary school and even the baccalaureate.

When observing little children's games, it is obvious that at the beginning of life the mentality is the same in both sexes. It is the mother who begins to create the psychological sex, and the feminine psychological sex is inferior. [...]

If dressing the little girl as a boy proves impossible, it is still advisable to keep her clothes simple, like a boy's. Dresses should be plain, correctly cut and without trimmings.

One should be careful that the child does not suffer too much from the way she is dressed, because if she were to suffer, all the good effects of the masculinization of the clothing would be destroyed. The little girl would want to free herself from her mother's authority so as to be able to dress *like everybody else*. Compensations should be made: for example, one could use more beautiful cloth or a better cut so that the little girl, although plainly dressed, will be better dressed than other children of her own social class. Mothers should train their daughters' eyes to recognize the superiority of their clothes.

One should attempt to correct the imperfections of feminine clothing. The child should have snugly fitting bloomers of dark material under her dress. Thus, she will be able to move freely and securely.

It will be best to cut her hair short. Long, curly hair suits the faces of children who are not yet marked by life and in whom one looks for no other beauty than prettiness. Avoiding all feminine coquetry must be the principal aim. Most little girls have their minds constantly on their braids. They compare their length and thickness with those of their friends; they undo and redo their hair ribbons from morning till night. If one has a boy as well as a girl, it might be well to let the hair of both grow to shoulder length and curl it. It is not coquetry that is dangerous in itself; it is the attitude the little girl acquires to her femininity. This danger is partly removed when the brother has a hairstyle like his sister's.

Toys will be considered carefully by the feminist educator, because they influence to a large extent the development of the mind and character. Toys such as dolls, toy furniture, and kitchen stoves, which teach the little girl from the cradle onward that she will be a housewife, should be banned. Games requiring patience or building toys that train children to concentrate, even military toys, can be given.

The name of the little girl should be chosen from among those that are common to both sexes, differing only by their spelling: Andrée, Renée, and Paule are to be preferred to Marie, Louise, or Georgette. Once the equality of the sexes is a *fait accompli* in law and custom, it will be unnecessary to masculinize the names of little girls, but as things are, this masculinization cannot be emphasized enough. Society will do as much as it can and even more than necessary to undo whatever we have accomplished in this direction.

To accomplish the best possible results, the feminist educator will be compelled to isolate her daughter from other children of the same sex, for otherwise anything she does will be undone. However great the mother's influence, the influence of friends is greater, especially if the mother has ideas that are in opposition to the whole of her social class, as is the case here. If the mother is well educated, she can act as her daughter's teacher. If she is wealthy, she can have a teacher come to the house, and it should be a man, not a woman. The teacher will always give a little of himself in his teaching. It is true that the man will have contempt for his little pupil, who is going to be only a woman, which to him means an inferior being, but neither contempt nor admiration are stable attitudes. Most of the time the teacher will forget the sex of the child seated in front of him. He will see just a pupil, and whether he wants it or not, his teaching will have a virile character.[5] A female teacher would make of the little girl a slave like herself. Without even being conscious of it she would constantly project ideas of servitude.

When the female teacher realizes the mother's ideas, she will consciously thwart them, being horrified by their peculiarity, and this feeling would be even stronger than her material interest in keeping her position.

A mother who is poor or insufficiently educated will be obliged to send her daughter to a secondary or other type of school. She will then have to resign herself to a problematic result, but she can alleviate as much as possible the bad effects of a public education by prohibiting her daughter from going with other classmates after school hours.

Such a prohibition should not be imposed in an authoritarian manner. The mother should explain to the child that she is afraid of bad examples for her, and she will compensate for this deprivation by giving her more beautiful toys, walks, and travel if the necessary means are available. Besides, the little girl can be encouraged to get together with little boys, and this will be even easier if she has a brother.

Observing children's games, one can notice on many occasions that boys, even brothers, will humiliate little girls by repeating remarks they have picked up everywhere about the inferiority of the female: "women are useless," "women do not know how to earn money," "women are not soldiers," "you do not know how to somersault; one can see that you are only a girl." Occasionally, the *stronger* sex would like to apologize, but the effect will be just as bad. "Obviously, your somersault was poor, but for a girl it's quite good."

The mother must never cease to intervene under such circumstances. If the guilty party is her son, she must explain to him why the common opinion is wrong. If he wanted to vex his sister, she should shame him for his lack of heart and the abuse of his strength, which he did not earn by any merit of his own but which was granted by society because of his sex. Then she should punish him severely. If the boy does not belong to the family, the mother should still give the same explanations, and then she should forbid him to visit for a certain time.

The mother should not stop at defending her daughter but, better still, should teach her to defend herself. She should tell her daughter what replies to give, and if she needs to uphold, together with her own honor, the honor of her sex by hitting the young antifeminists-to-be, the mother, far from blaming her, should congratulate her.

Generally, a mother should avoid protecting her daughter against other children. The girl must get used to defending herself and to returning blow for blow. Educators are imbued with a "code" of passivity, especially when little girls are concerned. If there is an exchange of slaps they punish the defender as much as the attacker.

Because of this stupid type of upbringing, women, already weak by nature, are deprived of that instinct to defend themselves, which should move them to retaliate without thinking when attacked. The feminist educator should once again take the stance opposite to tradition. She should accustom her daughter to defend herself, and if she is beaten, far from pitying her, she should pretend to despise her.

The mother should also make certain that the brother does not attempt to pose as his sister's protector, in imitation of what he has seen elsewhere, and reciprocally, if the need arises, she should thwart her daughter's tendency to put herself under her brother's protection. If the boy is guilty, the mother should analyze for him the feeling that motivates him to offer his protection, and she should demonstrate that the basis of his action is not altruism but egoistic pride. If the girl solicits protection, she should be made to feel ashamed for her weakness, and the mother should pretend to have great contempt for her; the girl should be given coarse food and clothing, as though she were an inferior being.

The mother should initiate her daughter, and her son if she has one, into household duties, as one must foresee that one could be poor and obliged to do such work oneself. Therefore, the child should learn to sweep, to scrub, to cook simple meals, and to mend clothes and underwear as well as possible. But she should not try to make them *like* these duties. She should explain to them the error of those who laud this work as an honorable duty for women. She should show household work for what it really is: an inferior and boring activity but unavoidable for those who are not favored by riches. However, one should avoid teaching knitting, crochet, lace making, and embroidery. If one has money one can buy ready-made all these things that women spend thousands of hours of their lives making, dulling their wits in the process. If one is too poor to buy such things, one can do without them perfectly well. There is nothing more dull than women who, instead of taking up a book, a magazine, or a newspaper, spend days embroidering a handkerchief. [. . .]

Mothers should teach their daughters energetic habits.[6] If the girl is in good health, she should be made to wash in cold water each morning and at all times of the year. She should not be dressed too warmly. While letting her eat to satisfy her hunger, greediness should not be tolerated. She should be encouraged to be proud of doing without sweets.

Mothers should, however, avoid the error of some educators who would confuse children with a multiplicity of regulations, as they only dull their lives without any positive results. [. . .]

Generally speaking, one should not needlessly restrain children. There are some mothers especially who seem to spend their time forbidding their daughters to do things: don't go so far; close that door; have you finished jumping about; stand up straight and don't run like that. Mothers often give such orders without any reason other than to keep busy. To a large extent, children are entitled to be free, and if they do nothing harmful then they should be allowed to act as they please. [. . .]

Books should be chosen with care. I do not refer here to schoolbooks, which will be dealt with in our chapter on intellectual education. During the early years one is obliged to give little stories; one should choose those taken from masterpieces of French and foreign literature such as *Don Quixote* and *William Tell;* one should forbid touching stories of little girls devoted to their sick mothers. One should also avoid *Cinderella,* which exalts coquetry and teaches that there is no greater pleasure in the world for a young girl than to go to a ball in a magnificent gown.[7]

Bluebeard should not be read, since the man is a fearsome master of the woman. Certainly Bluebeard is not the sympathetic character in the story—our sympathy goes out to his unfortunate spouse—but still, it would not be advisable to make a little girl, a future feminist, read stories in which the wife trembles before her husband. One would be wrong to imagine that such tales have no educational importance, serving only to amuse little children. Everything that penetrates through the senses to the mind affects one's education; reading for amusement influences just as much as schoolbooks or lessons. In reading *Bluebeard* the little girl imagines the man as a wicked but very strong person whom the woman must obey for fear of her life. I know that it might be said that it is only a tale without any semblance of reality, but the impression will still be made. It is better not to produce a bad impression than to have to correct it later. [. . .]

The Education of the Mind

No more for women than for men should education be merely a diversion or a last resort. Whatever their sex may be, persons are entitled to intellectual enlightenment and the full blossoming of the spirit. No one ever has enough instruction; it is not up to the teacher to set for the pupil a limit that may not be exceeded. The pupil will determine her own limit when her intelligence encounters problems that are beyond it. A feminist should push the education of her daughter as far as possible.

If the child goes to a secondary or other school, the mother must supplement the teaching. Primary schools and especially secondary schools for girls are quite inferior to those for boys. The secondary school for girls represents progress over the convent school, but not much. In place of philosophy, young girls are taught drawing-room psychology and a moral code whose assumptions are never analyzed. The teaching of mathematics and sciences is much less advanced. The mother herself must make up for these deficiencies if she is capable of it or should seek help from teachers or courses. If the child goes to a secondary school, she should be encouraged to obtain the baccalaureate, which opens the doors of universities, instead of the school-leaving certificate, which leads only to teaching.

The teaching should be watched very closely. The sciences are straightforward. Because they are concerned only with facts and natural laws, they do not provide room for comment; therefore, it is advisable to follow the program imposed by the secondary school. In girls' secondary schools, however, the study of general scientific laws is quickly set aside in favor of their application within the household. For example, the domestic uses of chloride and acetic acid will be emphasized in chemistry classes. This is not bad in itself. It is not detrimental to know about the household uses of chemicals, but the spirit behind this teaching is obviously pernicious. The young girl will draw the conclusion, and this is precisely what society wants, that she needs to know little about general scientific laws but much about their household application, for, since she is a woman, her destiny will be to direct a household. When the girl is old enough to understand, the mother should explain to her the deficiencies of this kind of instruction.

The secondary school is especially poor in the teaching of literature. Here the unchangeable laws of nature no longer apply; one is dealing with relationships among humans, and in novels and in dramatic compositions a woman occupies a primary role. From this source the young girl will absorb her ideas on what a woman is, what she has to be, and what her role is with respect to man and society. The heroines imagined by authors, all of whom consider women as inferior beings, do not inspire the pupils who study them to become feminists. For a young girl, the heroine of a novel is either an Agnès, as insignificant as she is pretty, a weak person without any willpower or personality who as a victim of evil inspires mainly pity, or an equally weak person, but one who, armed with cunning, succeeds only through duplicity. Spouse or mother, the heroine in literature is a dull individual whose sexual or maternal love is her whole life. "I have not kissed him yet today!" (Racine)[8]

Such heroines do not grasp superior ideas. Horace would have wasted his time if he had tried to explain to his sister Camille that the murder of Curiace was essential to the salvation of Rome. Camille does not care about the salvation of Rome, and she says so in a fiery tirade. She understands only one thing: her fiancé has been killed, and for those who committed this crime she can feel only hatred. Thus, since Horace cannot make her understand, he kills her, and in my view he does well.[9]

In all justice one must say that such female characters represent reality. A woman who has always been a slave cannot have the mentality of a free being. The feminist educator is compelled to have her pupils study such heroines. She cannot prohibit the whole of literature, but at the same time this study need not be enslaving, because she could comment on the works as appropriate. For example, with respect to Camille, she could point out how such a woman is worthy of contempt because she wants the whole world to revolve around her nuptials.

Feminist propaganda has been successful among female teachers.[10] Nowadays, there are a certain number who interject a few ideas of emancipation into the curriculum. But one should not trust the teaching profession, since, as they are both women and civil servants, the teachers of secondary schools for girls have two reasons to be fearful. Through natural timidity and fear of their superiors, female teachers show feminism only hesitatingly to their pupils. In order to correct a statement that seems extreme, they might actually make an antifeminist speech. Obviously, women have rights to this, but they should not believe that they are permitted to do that; soon the pupil no longer knows what to believe. Such teaching has also the defect, especially contemptible, of imprinting her character with fear and hesitation. The young feminist must know what to believe and should not be afraid to speak out.

On what subjects should one insist? Pedagogues have written many books about this. Some have advised the study of mathematics because this, as they say, teaches reasoning. Others have advised the study of science, which teaches precision. Still others have advised the study of literature and the humanities, which provide a more brilliant culture.

To think thus is to ignore the psychological reality. Mathematics on its own does not promote reasoning, any more than science promotes precision and literature a culture. Most of the time these subjects are ingested by the pupil who does not make the effort to digest them. A pupil who will excel in solving a geometrical problem may, nevertheless, demonstrate illogicality in other subjects. Scientists who may excel in their own specialities may be very ordinary thinkers in other fields. Finally, the humanities can produce prigs or insignificant minds who will quickly forget. A program of studies is only a group of subjects. It shapes the mind only on condition that the teacher takes care in elaborating on these subjects. *To stimulate reflection* is the objective of all teaching, and such reflection should be applied just as much in chemistry as it should be in geometry or literature.

One should make sure that children *have understood* what they have learned. Most children learn like parrots. To appreciate this, it may be sufficient to interrogate them on a lesson they have just recited without a mistake.

The paragraph they knew so well they no longer know once a few words have been changed. The children of the lower classes, who have difficulty in forming ideas even to the level of their primary lessons, sometimes most comically transpose into more familiar expressions the words that they do not understand. [. . .]

In more enlightened circles parrot-type learning is less common but is far from disappearing. It has even invaded higher education.

A feminist mother should fight against this parroting with all her power, and she should not rest until her children prove that they have understood their lessons. She should make them discover on their own, without any assistance, the applications or consequences of the knowledge they have acquired.

A very young girl whom I am bringing up recently learned in her geography lesson that a pond is a small lake. During a trip we passed a pond and I asked her:

"What does one call such a body of water?"

"I do not know."

"Why is it that you don't know? Yesterday you recited perfectly the meaning of a lake and of a pond."

"Oh yes!" And then, with a vague expression in her eyes, forgetting completely the pond in front of her, she recited again the paragraphs of her geography lesson. Obviously, for her and for children in general, books are one thing and the world another. [. . .]

The foremost idea of the feminist and of everybody in general, since this applies to boys as well as to girls, should be to give as much intellectual culture as possible, whatever happens. The prospect of obstacles raised by society before educated young women who are poor should not stop them. First of all, a young woman can succeed in a liberal profession, and even though it may not be a brilliant profession, it is still better than the enslaving and badly paid labor of a female worker. Even if she does not succeed and is obliged to seek employment in commerce or industry, she will bring with her qualities of intelligence that should put her in a better position. In her leisure time she can enjoy books and music, visit museums with great interest, and enjoy the beauties of nature. It is true that this could keep her from marrying a working man, but we do not see a great disadvantage in this. On the contrary, we think that a woman must raise herself for her own sake and not for a man.

The partisans of ignorance for the poor say, in support of their theories, that a good education leads to an unhappy life for the poor because it gives them desires they cannot fulfill. This point of view is false and criminal, because if a child born to poor parents cannot fulfill his desire for a happy life, whose fault is it? It is still better to desire in vain than to live the beastly life of the ignorant worker.

The desire to raise oneself incites to effort, and sometimes such effort is rewarded by a degree of success.

If poor people were educated, one would rapidly see the end of social inequality. It is precisely because they are ignorant that inequality persists. Their vague desires to better themselves make them the dupes of unscrupulous politicians.

I am well aware that a poor mother will have great difficulty in giving her daughter a high intellectual culture. Secondary schools or courses are too expensive, and since the mother may be unable to pay for them, she will be compelled to put her daughter into an elementary school. She should supplement the teaching by buying books that she should study herself and then have her daughter study. The baccalaureate can be prepared at home with the help of manuals. Obviously, oral teaching would be better, but with perseverance one can succeed. To make the studies less dry and more intelligent, one should add to the manuals some literary and philosophical works. The mother should make her daughter read historical memoirs, which give a good idea of the times. Generally speaking, they have also the advantage of making pleasant reading. For a change, the mother should give historical novels in preference to others. Her child will see the development of the leading personalities of their times. These novels will give the child ideas of social development in contrast to other novels that deal only with the loves and misfortunes of ordinary people.

Up to what age should a child be left in school? In principle she should be left as long as possible. A primary school teacher, a postal employee, or a typist earns a living at age eighteen, but younger than this a girl earns very little in any occupation. It would be better for a parent to do without a garment, a piece of furniture, or a few pleasures than to sacrifice the life of a girl by sending her at thirteen years of age to earn ten cents a day in a workshop. There are some cases of extreme poverty where ten cents represents a precious resource and it is impossible to do otherwise, but such cases are rare. Most of today's working-class households could leave their children at school up to the age of fifteen without feeling any deprivation. If they do not do so, it is because they do not understand the usefulness of the culture of the mind, and the time spent in school seems wasteful.

Every young girl, rich or poor, must have a career. Rich men have one because they generally believe that a completely idle life would not be worth living. The wealthy feminist should reach the same conclusion. What pleasure is it to spend all one's life dressing and undressing, receiving and making tedious visits to women who are generally of little intelligence and enjoy only gossiping about frivolities? Obviously, a wealthy young girl will not become a teacher in a secondary school or a typist in a ministry. Besides taking away the bread from a poor girl whose position she would occupy, she would endure this drudgery uselessly. She can obtain higher diplomas in science or in literature and then work as a lawyer or seek voluntary work in a laboratory or an institute.

If she prefers, she can learn to fly, drive a car, or fence. Women look on sport only as a source of amusement; why should they not make a disinterested career out of it like men? Most sports require great natural vigor. Women are inferior to men in this respect, but what is to prevent them from forming groups of female pilots, drivers, cyclists, or boxers, etc.?

A poor mother will obviously be compelled to limit her choice to remunerative careers, since the objective is to enable her daughter to earn a living by herself without the assistance of a man.

She should prefer the civil service to private industry. Perhaps doors will open to women, because the men who used to want to become civil servants do not care for such positions any longer. The advantage of the civil service lies in its security for the future and the quasi certainty of not losing one's job except for serious offences. Furthermore, the working environment of the civil service, even though it is not ideal, is still better than the industrial or commercial environment.

The entry to a career must certainly not mean the end of education. Only coarse people think this should be so. For them, the acquisition of knowledge is simply a means of financial gain. Education has its own ends, and it must continue throughout life.

Sex Education

Sex education is now topical.[11] More and more, old ideas that stipulated that it was moral to ignore sexuality and keep silent about its worst turpitudes are now being rejected. How many girls got married believing that marriage consisted in dressing in white and going by the side of a gentleman to the town hall and then to church? The revelation of reality was a surprise, always unpleasant and sometimes horrifying. If it so happened that the bride complained indignantly to her mother, the mother then preached resignation: "Women," she said, "are made to submit and to suffer; nature wants it this way—and the good Lord!" Many men did not recognize a woman as a human being, but only as an instrument of pleasure that they had the right to use and abuse. Many didn't and many don't (one can speak of it in the present because sexual education of women is still far from teaching them to be on their guard), many men don't have any scruples about getting married even when they are suffering from gonorrhea. After a few weeks of marriage the woman falls ill; she takes to her bed and has no idea of the cause of her illness. Hypocrisy and ignorance are accomplices in deceiving her. Relatives and friends will then say how fragile the female sex is; this young woman has been married for only two months and here she is in bed. The surgeon talks about an operation.

One day one of my professors in medicine interrogated the patients on a hospital ward. He stopped at the bedside of a young person: "And you, what is wrong with you?" "My belly hurts." He made an evasive gesture: "My belly hurts, my belly hurts. Oh, women's bellies!" He was forgetting, although he knew, because the masculine viewpoint dominates men's minds so completely that this doctor was forgetting his pathology; he did not remember that when women's abdomens are affected, it's men's fault most of the time. [. . .]

A feminist worthy of the name wants nobody's pity. It is up to her and to her alone to direct her life. She will be on guard against the dangers of sexuality, just as she is on guard against disease and dangers of all kinds that surround us all. But the educator, resolutely disregarding the prejudices that even the most liberal people face only timidly, must give her daughter a sex education so that she is capable of that self-protection.

Certain people with advanced opinions advocate that children should be told about sexuality from their tenderest age, because, as it is said, one should never lie. This is a simplistic viewpoint. Obviously, one should not lie without cause, but I see no need to attract the attention of children to organs they are not thinking about yet. The naïve explanations that one gives to little children about the conception of babies are not without charm. Roses that open to give birth to beautiful babies embellish the imaginations of small children. There will be plenty of time to reveal the ugly reality. Along these lines I would go so far as to keep the fairies, the genii, and the angels, a puerile supernatural world that represents no danger for the future. One should start to give a glimpse of the truth about reproduction at about six or seven because such truth should not be discovered by children on their own. It is essential to expose the mystery with which sexuality is usually shrouded in order to remove its perverse character. Toward their seventh year one should therefore start to tell little girls that children are born not from cabbages or roses but from their mother's belly.

As for intersexual relations for procreation, this should not be revealed before the age of twelve. In healthy surroundings, it is quite rare that a childish mind becomes preoccupied with them before the twelfth year. Sexuality should be treated simply as a matter of natural history. There will be nothing shameful attached to it. One should draw for the little girl a chart of reproduction in plants, inferior animals, then birds and mammals. Then one should explain that since man belongs to the mammals, he is reproduced according to the laws that apply to them.

From the age of twelve, especially if the girl goes out on her own, which is the case of our young feminist, she must be put on guard against men. It would be useless at such a tender age to show the ugliness of sexuality in too strong a light. One should simply explain that it is dangerous for children, boys or girls, to go with unknown persons even if they are well dressed. To support this one should quote from newspapers that tell of offences committed by sexual perverts. The child will be content with summary explanations such as, for example, that men who appear quite normal are really afflicted by a morbid urge to kill children. This will be sufficient to inspire the girl with a healthy terror of male advances.

It is toward the age of fifteen that one should reveal the whole truth. After this no more caution is indicated; physical, sentimental, normal, and pathological love should be presented as they are. It is obvious that one should explain love in great detail from a social point of view: the seduction and the artifices of men in persuading young girls to yield to them, motherhood within marriage and out of marriage, neo-Malthusian practices,[12] venereal diseases, the condition of kept women, and the lives of courtesans and common prostitutes. As far as possible, one should show examples. One should take the girl to the doors of department stores at a time when the employees are leaving. One should then show her the young or old lovers waiting for their mistresses. Frequent walks to the poor districts of Paris will allow the girl to witness fights between husbands and wives. Nocturnal walks will give her a glimpse of street prostitution. One should try to be in front of a police station when prostitutes climb out of the "Black Maria." Finally, one should go to the races to see the courtesans.

How should one deal with sexuality from a moral point of view? Because I consider that women are as entitled to love as men, I obviously cannot advise feminist mothers to follow tradition. It is not bad to accept a lover. What is bad is to be kept by him, since one then becomes a seller of love, worthy only of the greatest contempt. Before thinking of sexuality, the young feminist must be in a position to earn a living if she is poor, and, if she is rich, she must make sure of her intellectual life. One should explain that if she indulges in sexuality too early, it may disturb her preparation for a career and make her a reprobate for the rest of her life.

It may be said that the abyss that separates justice and logic from present reality is very deep. Society does not grant women the immutable right to love that they ought to possess. Nevertheless, since we live in society, it is good to take some of its prejudices into consideration. It would not do, for example, that because a girl is convinced of her right to love she should become the dupe of men and thus expose herself to rejection by society and be classed as a disreputable woman. Nowadays, society hardly distinguishes between young women living in a free union and kept women.

In view of this antagonism between true justice and social reality, it will be good to keep a casual eye on a daughter up to the age of twenty, while allowing her a great amount of freedom. She should be restrained not more but to the same extent as bourgeois families restrain their sons. The reasoning capacity of a girl of fifteen or sixteen is still quite weak in spite of advice and even examples. She might yield to the natural attraction that youth exerts on youth and lose, little by little, all her good habits of study and regular work.

At the age of twenty a girl has all her reasoning capacity, and she should be left completely free at her own risk and peril.

If the girl prefers to eliminate sexuality from her life, she should be encouraged to do so. Laws and customs enslave the woman, and she can find freedom only by doing without love. Even in a free union the woman is under guardianship. The man considers himself the master, and to obtain independence the young feminist must keep fighting at all times, which makes her life intolerable. Doctors who have written about the dangers of chastity have thought only of men, since women do not have such a strong sex drive. Many nuns in convents live to a great age and in better health than married women. The nervousness of old maids is due to their idleness and not to their continence. If they are often sad, it is because celibacy has been imposed on them by circumstances in spite of their great desire for marriage.

Our young feminist will have her occupation to fill her life, and she will add one or several voluntary activities to give it more meaning. She will learn a science or an art, or she will be active in politics or social work. If she has friends, she may prefer life in common with several young women. She will thus avoid the solitude that is the great sadness of the unmarried state.

But if the young woman wants to include sexuality in her life, what advice should one give her? This will depend on her social class. If the family is wealthy, the young woman should get married. A free union would put her outside her social class, and marriage among the leading classes is still less enslaving for the woman than in the lower middle class or especially in the working class.

Notes

1. Pelletier has attracted more scholarly interest than any other feminist of the belle époque. She is a central figure in Charles Sowerwine's works on feminism and socialism, *Les Femmes et le socialisme* and the revised translation, *Sisters or Citizens?* Sowerwine has produced two short pieces focusing on Pelletier: "Madeleine Pelletier (1874–1939)," and "Socialism, Feminism, and Violence." His biography of Pelletier is forthcoming in a French edition. The first full biography of Pelletier is Felicia Gordon's *The Integral Feminist*. See also the works of Marilyn Boxer, including her 1975 dissertation at the University of California–Riverside, "Socialism Faces Feminism," and her summary of it in *Socialist Women*. Boxer also focused on Pelletier in another essay, "When Radical and Socialist Women Were Joined," in Slaughter and Kern, eds., *European Women on the Left*. Finally, see Claudine Mitchell, "Madeleine Pelletier (1874–1939)."

2. Data from Maurice Bardèche, *Histoire des femmes*. 2:341–42. By 1906, France

had 73 women in law school and 264 women in medical school, although in both cases the majority of the students were foreign women. See the discussion of this in *Le Petit Almanach féministe illustré: 1907* (Paris, 1907), 22–23.

3. Even the lengthy bibliography listed at the back of this book is not a complete list of Pelletier's writings. For a fuller list, see "Published Works of Madeleine (Anne) Pelletier" in Gordon, *The Integral Feminist* 278–81.

4. Pelletier practised this principle in her own life and dressed as a man. She intended this to be a political statement rather than a sexual statement. Joan Scott has explored this subject in a lecture and essay entitled "Madeleine Pelletier: la femme en homme," which will be a chapter in her forthcoming book on feminist claims for political rights in France, 1789–1945.

5. [Author's note in original text: "The men who are feminists are a lot more feminist than the women. Raised in freedom, they immediately see all the shackles which laws and customs impose on women, and they rise up against them. On the other hand, women, raised in these shackles, do not notice them. Thus, most often, far from wanting to break free of them, they rise up against those rare women who do, because they see more clearly than the others. Like birds in cages, freedom frightens them."]

6. Pelletier's close associate in feminist and socialist activities, Caroline Kauffmann (d. 1926), was a strong advocate of physical fitness and physical education for girls, and she stressed this point to Pelletier. See Kauffmann's *L'Importance de l'éducation physique scientifique combinée avec l'éducation intellectuelle morale* (Paris, 1989).

7. For an examination of the books used in the education of girls, see Linda Clark, *Schooling the Daughters of Marianne.*

8. Racine, *Andromaque,* Act I, Scene iv. Andromaque is here speaking of her son.

9. Pelletier is referring here to Pierre Corneille's tragedy, *Horace* (1640), based on Livy's history of early Rome. Horace and his two brothers represent Rome in a battle with Curiace and his two brothers, representing the town of Alba. Camille, Horace's sister, is engaged to marry Curiace and curses Horace and Rome for the murder of Curiace. Horace then kills Camille. After their father pleads on Horace's behalf, and a sister of Horace and Camille (Sabine) offers to take Horace's punishment, he is forgiven for killing Camille.

10. For this subject see Hunt, "Revolutionary Syndicalism"; Clark, "The Battle of the Sexes"; Moch, "Government Policy"; Quartararo, "The Ecoles normales primaires"; and Hause with Kenney, *Women's Suffrage,* 124–28.

11. This was a controversial subject during the belle époque. For conflicting views of French feminists (especially Jane Misme and Marguerite Witt-Schlumberger), see *Les Ecrits pour et contre: l'éducation sexuelle* (Paris, 1924).

12. Birth control practices. See Nelly Roussel on this subject in part 6.

3

WORK

CLOTILDE DISSARD

The 1890s were a transitional period for French feminism.[1] The dominant figures from the founding of the women's movement in the 1870s and 1880s–Léon Richer (1824–1911), Maria Deraismes (1828–94), and Hubertine Auclert (1848–1914)–were no longer active. Richer retired in 1891 and turned his *Ligue française pour les droits des femmes* over to a younger generation of feminists such as Marie Bonnevial, who is represented in the next chapter. Auclert (see parts 6 and 7) married in 1888 and followed her husband to Algeria. Deraismes died in 1894, leaving her well-financed organization, *Amélioration*, in the hands of her more moderate sister, Anna Feresse-Deraismes.

Clotilde Dissard was one of the most prominent new leaders of French feminism during the 1890s.[2] Dissard considered herself a pioneering sociologist, but she is best remembered for her feminist writings. In 1895 she founded a monthly journal, *La Revue féministe* (The Feminist Review), which she edited for nearly three years. This effort led Dissard to participate in the LFDF congress of 1896 and to publish a book based on that experience, *Opinions féministes à propos du congrès féministe de 1896*.[3] She closed her review in the following year, but the appearance of *La Fronde* gave her a continuing feminist forum that she used for several years. Dissard had multiple interests, however, and later devoted her energy to the Russian immigrant community in France.

Clotilde Dissard recognized that there were many competing forms of feminism in belle époque France. She opposed most militant feminism as hopelessly quixotic and advocated, in its place, a period of reflection on feminist goals, which she called *"féminisme d'étude"* (feminist study), and a new understanding of women's roles in the home, which she called "familial feminism." She opposed forms of feminism (such as Roussel's and Pelletier's) that she considered to be linked with extreme left-wing political doctrines. Instead of advocating socialist-inspired "egalitarian feminism," she called for an "individualist feminism" that would be compatible with most of the tenets of classical liberalism. Dissard thus concentrated on rights such as the equal educational opportunities for women and the equal treatment of working women. The following translation is of an article she wrote in 1900 criticizing the paternalistic labor laws that treated women and men differently.

The Protection of Female Labor

The new law concerning the work of women and children has yet to be voted on by the Senate, and already protests can be heard from all over the working class and the feminist milieu.[4]

What do feminists have against this law? That it does not put the male and female worker on a perfectly equal footing but wants to protect the woman, whereas the man is already considered pure work muscle, totally insignificant and quite unworthy of care from the State. This hypocritical concern of our legislators for female workers is normally liked and greatly appreciated by the trade unions, who are so preoccupied with the competition between the sexes, so very disposed to eliminating women from the lucrative jobs, and stupidly hostile to female labor, under the pretext that female labor lowers the rate of the salaries. These gentlemen deliberately condemn young and unattached women, widows, and unmarried mothers: all those women who suffer and are prepared to work for a starvation wage and who, consequently, are the cause of the meager salaries that the men themselves earn.

In certain trades, typesetting for example, competition is so fierce that the unions refuse membership to female workers and forbid their members to work in printshops that employ women. Whereas the law of November 2, 1892, which was voted on at the instigation of the unions, authorizes women to fold newspapers at night—for this work is very poorly paid—it refuses to let women print these same newspapers, since the good wages must be reserved for the men.

Source: Clotilde Dissard, "La Protection du travail féminin," *La Fronde* January 29, 1900. Trans. Jette Kjaer.

Perhaps you imagine that our legislators will make these strange abnormalities disappear in the new law? Think again. If a more equitable clause is written into the code, it will not be applied, because in our society women cannot provoke just treatment, have their rights validated, or obtain the benefit of laws which are in their favor.

The law of November 2, 1892, was never enforced in the tulle industry. This was revealed in the interesting discussion that took place in the general assembly of the French Union for Male and Female Tulle Workers of Calais.

This trade union declares that the law of November 2, 1892, has never been enforced in the tulle industry and that the length of the workday for children and women has never been reduced to ten hours. Furthermore, that in Calais, where men work twelve hours, women and children have likewise always worked twelve hours and in many cases *thirteen and fourteen hours. Finally, that children below the age of sixteen working as assemblers in the workshops have always continued to work during the night, in violation of the law.*

Despite the many good reasons that are brought forward concerning the necessity of protecting female labor, and the possibility of protecting the mother and pregnant woman against the demands of her employer, the law is enforced only in cases where men demand it, believing that it will protect their salaries. As for children, adolescents, girls, and minors, nobody worries about them, because they share with women the privilege of not placing a vote in the ballot box.

Notes

1. See Hause, *Hubertine Auclert,* 152–56; Klejman and Rochefort, *L'Egalité en marche,* 87–113.

2. No biography of Dissard has been published. See the discussion of her in Klejman and Rochefort, *L'Egalité en marche,* 105–06.

3. For the congress of 1896, see Wilkins, "The Paris International Feminist Congress of 1896."

4. Dissard is referring to a law on the conditions of work for women and children, adopted on March 30, 1900 (two months after she wrote this article). This law modified a law of November 2, 1892. It temporarily restored the eleven hour working day for girls between thirteen and sixteen years of age, which had been reduced to ten hours. The law of 1900 added provisions for security and hygiene in the factories. See the detailed discussion of both protective laws in Stewart, *Women, Work, and the French State.* Stewart's appendix provides translations of key Articles of the labor laws of 1892 and 1900 (203–04).

MARIE BONNEVIAL

Marie Bonnevial (1841–1918) was one of the first generation of French women to profit from expanded educational opportunities.[1] Raised in a small village outside Lyons by a blacksmith uncle and a laundress aunt, Bonnevial continued her education until she obtained her credentials as a primary school teacher. She became involved in radical politics (the republican movement of the 1860s and the Commune of 1871), however, and the conservative government of the 1870s prohibited her from teaching either in the public schools or even privately as a tutor. Bonnevial thus spent several years in voluntary exile, joining her brother in Constantinople and teaching there. When the republican reformers of the 1880s created a freer environment in France, Bonnevial returned to open a school in Paris.

Marie Bonnevial subsequently participated in a variety of radical political organizations. She was one of the first women to be active in freemasonry, the socialist party, and the League of the Rights of Man. The feminist congress of 1896 and the foundation of *La Fronde* in 1897 added the women's movement to her interests. She joined Durand's staff at *La Fronde* and contributed many columns on working women; she also joined the LFDF, quickly becoming one of its officers. Bonnevial's greatest feminist interests were the educational and economic rights of women, and she was well placed to work for both causes: she was the first woman named to sit on the government's *Conseil supérieur du travail* (the High Labor Council) and to the post of administrator of school funds. The following translation is of Bonnevial's study of women in the trade union movement at the turn of the century, which appeared in 1901.

The Women's Trade-Union Movement in France

The methodical organization of the proletariat into economic groups whose aim is to study and defend the interests of the worker is relatively recent. It is arranged by profession, grouped by industry, and united in a vast workers' confederation. This trade-union organization can be distinguished from the old associations for working women, whose single aim was either assistance or resistance, by the spreading of manifold action.

In 1871, under the energetic impulse of the communalistic movement, the first trade unions were founded.[2] The proletarian brain was becoming organized. The liberality of the communalistic principle would inspire a broader, more altruistic concept of the roles of corporative groups than the one from which were born those different kinds of professional associations that followed the *trade guilds* of the Middle Ages.

But the movement was at first essentially masculine. Few women were able to penetrate even timidly into the male unions of their occupations.

In Paris, one of the first mixed trade unions to be established was the *Membres de l'enseignement* [the Members of the Teaching Profession], founded in 1872. Here men and women were on an equal footing, participating in equal numbers in the administrative functions of the trade union. Lyons imitated Paris the following year, and within ten or twelve years, in all the branches of the work force, there developed cells of the great female workers' hive that makes up the totality of the organized corporations.

The Waldeck-Rousseau law, promulgated in March 1884, helped the development of these groupings considerably by making their existence legal. As we have already said, it was the working men who first understood the valuable advantages of the unions, while the women remained outside the movement.

Indeed, the official statistics from the Board of Trade reveal that in 1884 there were:

Employers' federations	101
Workers' unions	66
Mixed workers' unions	1
Agricultural unions	5
Total	173

Source: Marie Bonnevial, "Le Mouvement syndical féminin en France," *Revue de morale sociale,* no.11 (1901): 251–67. Trans. Jette Kjaer and Jennifer Waelti-Walters.

Thus there were only sixty-seven workingmen's unions—only one of them mixed—in France at that time. Moreover, they did not declare how many members they had.

Still, it is worth adding that the official figure does not represent all of the existing unions.

In the beginning, many refused to declare their coming into being, protesting against Article 4, which obliges the names of the directors to be declared. At one point the unknown unions, especially in Paris, were almost as numerous as those acknowledged by law.

This explains why, in 1888, the Labor Exchange in Paris alone numbers 135 unions, including the mixed Teachers' Union and the Union of Cooks, Lady's Maids, etc. In 1892, we arrive at a total of 213!

A new female union figures in this number, that of the sewing maids.

How slowly women leave their isolation.

Why such inertia?

Because women have always been kept outside real life; because religious dogma, education, custom, and habit have made them believe in their inferiority and have instilled in them a spirit of resignation and sacrifice.

And, forced to leave the home, or to bring home work from the workshop or store to do on top of the household duties, they have accepted a derisory wage without thinking of complaining; even when the work done by both sexes is exactly the same in nature and quantity, this pay is always inferior to that given to men, which is already unfair! [. . .]

Fortunately, people are becoming more aware of the situation. Many militants have understood the necessity of giving their oppressed sisters a hand in helping them become organized; that is how the mixed unions, which become more prosperous every year, are being founded, at the same time as a number of female unions are coming into being.

From the year 1884 on, the only precise data we have about the union movement begin with the year 1894. The Labor Bureau, founded in 1891, published as early as 1894 a bulletin with various information concerning work; it relates month by month the unions that were created and those that disappeared.

Here is a summary of the mixed and female unions that sprang up from 1894 to the middle of 1901:

Year	Mixed unions	Female unions
1894	3	1
1895	5	5
1896	10	6
1897	7	1
1898	4	3
1899	10	5
1900	18	3
1901 1st semester	18	12

Thus, a total of 75 mixed unions and 36 female unions; that is, 111 known unions in which we find the female worker. Let us in our minds add all those that, having neglected legal formalities, do not figure on the *Official Bulletin*. There is without doubt a notable quantity among the mixed unions; but female unions that shy away from declaring themselves are probably less numerous, because unionized women are generally anxious to assure themselves of protection under the law.

Furthermore, certain titles do not reveal the nature of the workers who constitute the group: teachers, journalists, and socialists, for example. One must be familiar with the trade-union environment to know that these groups include female members.

But while lacking the precise number of existing unions and the number of members in each, we can draw attention to the progression of the movement, mentioning the rapid expansion that the union concept underwent as early as 1896, and especially from 1899 onward, when the socialist Millerand entered parliament.[3]

It would be interesting to determine at least what proportion of women enter the union movement.

But even a proportional average is difficult to establish, for it does not depend just on the proportion of people in a trade or profession.

For example, aside from the male and female workers in the tobacco trade [*Tabacs*], where women in Paris account for nine-elevenths in manufacturing and find themselves in the same proportions in the union, if we look at store employees, we see a proportion of only one-twentieth women becoming unionized, whereas they are about equal in number with men in the corporation.

Yet this powerful organization, which amounts to 5,000 members in Paris, fully supports ideas of economic equality between the sexes and is fervently campaigning to awaken a spirit of solidarity in female employees.

The same observation can be made about the dressmakers' and ladies' tailors' union, which has greatly developed since last winter's strike, and where women make up hardly a quarter. It is nevertheless encouraging to note their progress, since before the strike they were represented by only a few units.

In general, we can say that a sense of solidarity develops where there is a large agglomeration of workers, whereas it degenerates in isolation.

That is why the Congress of Zurich for the Protection of Female Workers, dealing with the question of female labor, having heard the speeches of Bebel, Liebknecht, and Vandervelde, came down in favor of work in workshops, and against work in the home, which isolates the worker and cannot be controlled.[4]

Which are the occupations where we have seen the most abundant flourishing of groups within the past few years?

The figures will tell us:

Textile industry	19
Central department stores	12
Dry cleaners and laundering	7
Military outfits and equipment	6
Stockings	6
Hat shops	4

So groups flourish in the industries where men and women work together and have a chance to exchange reflections about their situation every day. Through speech and example, working men are winning their companions over to the idea of trade unions.

Strikes are also frequent opportunities for creating, or at least developing, mixed or separate groupings. Women and men take part in conferences where the militants examine present work conditions and ways to improve them. And the good socialist word advocating unity usually falls on fertile ground.

From the last brocade weavers' strike, the female brocade weavers' union was created; it has its own existence, yet its founding is due in large part to the male union.

In Tenay, in the Ain region, it was also a strike that created the mixed spinning and rope-making unions. *All the women employed at the factory,* that is, about 600, belong to the union.

Were I to treat the union question in its entirety, I would indicate the admirable movement of harbor strikes that are spreading so methodically one would think that a well-defined plan was controlling their organization. In fact, the power of example and the spread of success are the true causes for the generalization. It would be easy to demonstrate that all unrest created by the demand of a right is the cause or result of union organization. Moreover, a large movement within any corporation is sure to have repercussions: considerable moral influence over the other professional and trade groups.

Finally, one would have to be blind or prejudiced not to recognize the beneficial action of the female workers' laws, which are the result of the initiative of Minister Millerand. The Labor Councils and Superior Labor Council have to recruit their members from the unionized workers; the principle of arbitration in workshop conflicts, where the union intervening as a powerful representative of work opposite capital is recognized legally; obligatory relations between the work inspectors on the one hand and the unions and trade-union centers on the other. All of these creations, let us say, are indeed made to favor the development of the union groups.

Indeed, in 1898, there were only seven mixed or female unions, while in 1899, fifteen more were created; in 1900, twenty-one; and in the first half of this year, thirty!!

To be completely accurate, let us mention still other influences that have strongly affected women's minds, such as the study groups like the League for Women's Rights [*Ligue pour le droit des femmes*], so masterfully directed by its president, Maria Pognon.[5] The feminist congresses, of 1896 and 1900 in particular, although frequented only by a small female proletarian élite, have also done some excellent campaigning.

This advertising is increased a hundredfold, given shape, and made permanent by the newspaper *La Fronde,* which every day sends out to all parts of the country news of the workers' movement, including claim attempts, testing of groups, and results of strikes. Its valiant founder, Marguerite Durand, has moreover taken on the job of morally and materially helping working women to become unionized. The following unions are among those born at *La Fronde,* because of the enlightened dedication of its director: the union of female typesetters, female shorthand typists, cashiers-accountants, the student association.

And nothing less than these numerous efforts, this daily instruction in fraternal duty to one's occupation, was needed to convince and bring along female workers from offices or stores. These women are much more rebellious than those from workshops when it comes to the idea of unions.

The momentum now exists, and the movement can do nothing but broaden and gather speed. It is reaching all trades and professions. Here are a few of the occupations that have one to three unions, mixed or female: diamonds, gunpowder, pewter sheets, paper bags, umbrellas, hosiery, feathers, glass jewelry, chocolate, suspenders, brushes, refinery, cardboard, gloves, brooms.

Soon it will be not only exclusively female occupations forming female unions. The future definitely lies in mixed unions, for the more members, the more authority the representatives have to speak before the employers in the name of the corporations. Further, it is in the interest of workingmen to raise women's salaries, so that they come closer to their own. For the lower women's wages are, the lower men's wages tend to fall.

However, in some cases separation is essential. In certain occupations the men declare that they are ready to accept women into their union, but on condition that they be given equal pay. Now, insisting that women claim equal pay from one day to the next means the suppression of female labor. And that is what certain workingmen, who sing the sentimental ballad of the housewife, are clearly asking for. These men brutally shut the union door on female workers.

I shall not spend time demonstrating, as so many others have done, that the extra salary from a woman's workday is often essential in sustaining the home.

I shall go further and say that even if economic necessities did not impose work on a woman outside the home, it is her full right to direct her efforts where she chooses.

It is for her to know how to reconcile her duties.

It is for her to demand shorter days that leave her enough spare time to be at once wife, mother, housewife, and producer of goods, if she so wishes.

At the present time, a woman has no choice. This miserable extra income is essential for putting a bit of wood on the fire and a little bread in the bin.

There is only one way for working conditions to improve: by forming groups and uniting. And when workingmen refuse women entry into a union, women must organize themselves in similar fashion. That is what happened to female typesetters, whose union, founded in 1899, is thriving prosperously and has about 300 members.

Besides, there is a certain advantage to having separate groups; it forces those concerned to become aware of their aptitudes and begin putting them into practice.

Organizing and managing are tasks that suit women very well. Are not women the ones who manage the household and organize the budget, which is usually difficult enough to balance?

And yet when it comes to using similar skills outside the home, the timidity one has taken pains to cultivate in her prevails over her desire to do the requested service. This explains why in the mixed unions, where the men are more willing to apply the principle of equality, it is hard to get one or two women onto the councils.

However, left to their own strength and having no one to count on but themselves, the unionized women administer themselves very well.

Therefore, I believe it would not be a bad idea if working women first learned to act for themselves and then joined the male unions after having demonstrated their moral and social worth. They would bring the following as a dowry to their community: number, order, good feeling, and a sense of collective interest.

But there are no absolute rules. Thus, male and female workers in the tobacco union [*Tabacs*] sometimes act together and sometimes in parallel.

In Marseille, Bordeaux, and Nantes, the two unions, which work well together and come to an agreement whenever a common claim must be presented, have completely separate existences otherwise.

But in Paris the union is mixed, and it suits the workers. Nevertheless, there is a particular organization, a type of sanction. The men and women have their own special executives, which can discuss separately when there is a particular issue concerning one or the other but reunite to deliberate together over the general interests of the corporation and name a delegation, with members from both executives, when there is a claim to bring before the authorities.

In one form or another, working women must unite. It matters little if the majority of women initially see nothing but their own immediate interests; by grouping together alone, they act in solidarity. Soon their horizons will be expanded; women's expansive qualities will develop; their minds open to wider concepts and they will go to the *Union des syndicats* [Federation of Unions] to discuss general work interests with groups from all other occupations.

To use only the larger cities as an example, we draw your attention to the following mixed unions that belong to the Federation of Unions of Lyons and southeastern France:

Power Weaving—where women are in the majority, the Weavers' Union, the Employers' Federation of Weavers, Dressers of Tulle, Chenille Workers, Esparto Workers, Clothes Makers, Pedlars, Paperboys, Trimmers and Braid Makers, Cardboard Manufacturers, Makers of Tulle (on an assembly line), Costermongers, etc.

And the female unions: Laundry Women (800 members), Funeral Wreath Makers, Ladies Reunited (employees or in service), Embroideresses, and Seamstresses.

In the Seine Federation of Unions figure: the Seamstresses—a female union that is outside the mixed Tailors' and Seamstresses' Union, the Flower and Feather Workers, Laundresses, Female Collar and Tie Workers, Female Stenographers, Cashiers-Accountants, and soon, Female Typesetters.

The list is too long to name all the mixed unions, but I cannot resist mentioning the Teachers' Union. For not only is it one of the oldest unions, but its members consider it an honor to claim their title of *worker* and, by their presence in the large family of workers, show the close solidarity that must unite the school with the workshop.

From this assessment of the female union movement, it follows that women are now aware of their economic rights and have opened their eyes to the social iniquities of which they are the most sacrificial victims; they see clearly the path that must be taken in order to find a cure.

Let those who have understood bring along the others! Let them make the rest appreciate the economic and educational role of the union.

Let all women be persuaded that only by grouping willpower and force into a single, powerful unit shall we obtain increased salaries and reduced work hours, the double condition necessary for domestic happiness.

Let them join the union and get used to discussion; become part of the organization and administration; become familiar with the statistics that will show them the ever-increasing profits that work makes for capital and from which so little returns; that will show them the state of production and consumption both nationally and internationally. In a word, let them mentally rise above miserable egotism, be it personal, familial, or national, up to the great human fraternity, that altruism that opens the heart and increases moral pleasures a hundredfold.

Perhaps more than man, woman, as mother and educator, has the duty of learning all about collective living; for the workers in the city of the future must come from her hands, her artist's hands, like long-awaited masterpieces, pure of line and vibrant with life—that full, harmonious, complete life that makes one capable of "feeling the heart of humanity beat in one's heart" as said Fan-ta-gen in his beautiful thesis on *Happiness* (*Cité française,* Eug. Simon).[6]

Perhaps it will not take many more generations working actively like ours to bring this glorious dream into being.

Happy the ones who will see it!

Notes

1. Marie Bonnevial was a leader of the LFDF for nearly thirty years, so the league published several biographical sketches of her. See her obituary by Maria Vérone, *Le Droit des femmes* February 1919: 21–26, and the discussion of her in the league's pamphlet (*Cinquante ans* 78–81). For her feminism, see Hause with Kenney, *Women's Suffrage,* esp. 52. For her socialism, see Sowerwine, *Sisters or Citizens?,* 72–76. For her syndicalism and a bibliography of her articles in *La Fronde,* see Guibert, *Les Femmes.*

2. Trade unions were illegal in France following the Chapelier Law of June 1791, which abolished trade and craft associations, such as the guilds. Napoleon III modified this situation during the last years of his reign: strikes were permitted by a law of May 1864, and trade unionism, although technically illegal, was encouraged by a labor law of March 1868. The Trade Union Act of 1884, also known as the Waldeck-Rousseau Act (for its author), legalized unions. For the role of women in the labor movement, see the work of Marie-Hélène Zylberberg-Hocquard, especially her *Féminisme et syndicalisme en France,* and of Madeleine Guibert, especially *Les Femmes et l'ogranisation syndicale.*

By "the communalistic movement" Bonnevial means the Commune of 1871; she personally participated in the Commune of Lyons. There is an enormous historical literature on the Commune. For recent general accounts, see Stewart Edwards, *The Paris Commune, 1871* (London, 1971), or William Serment, *La Commune de Paris (1871)* (Paris, 1986). For the perspective of a militant woman participant, see Louise Michel, *La Commune* (Paris, 1878). For a study of the role of women in the Commune, see Edith Thomas, *The Women Incendiaries* (London, 1966). For the Commune in Lyons, see Maurice Moissonier, *La Première internationale et la commune à Lyon* (Paris, 1972) and Louis M. Greenberg, *Sisters of Liberty: Marseille, Lyon, Paris, and the Reaction to a Centralized State, 1868–1871* (Cambridge, MA, 1971).

3. Alexandre Millerand (1859–1943) was a moderate socialist lawyer who won recognition for defending workers in notorious cases of the 1880s and 1890s. He was elected to the Chamber of Deputies in 1885 (not 1889) and joined the socialists

in 1891. He became a controversial figure in French socialism in 1899, when he became the first socialist to serve in the cabinet; revolutionary socialists denounced him for collaborating with the bourgeois enemy. In later years, Millerand became increasingly conservative, and he was elected president of France in 1920. See Leslie Derfler, *Alexandre Millerand: The Socialist Years* (The Hague, 1977), and Marjorie Farrar, *Principled Pragmatist: The Political Career of Alexandre Millerand* (New York, 1991).

4. August Bebel (1840–1913), Wilhelm Liebknecht (1826–1900), and Emile Vandervelde (1866–1938) were leaders of the international socialist movement. Bebel was a leader of the German Social Democratic Party (SPD), a deputy in the German Reichstag, the editor of the socialist newspaper *Vorwärts,* and the author of a noted feminist work, *Die Frau und der Sozialismus* (Women and Socialism, [1883]). Liebknecht was an ally of Karl Marx, the founder of the German socialist party in 1869, and a longtime socialist deputy. Vandervelde was a leader of the Belgian socialist party who held several cabinet posts.

5. Maria Pognon (1844–1925) and Bonnevial were close associates in the LFDF. While Pognon was president of the league, Bonnevial held the post of secretary-general, which meant that she did most of the work.

6. Eugène G. Simon, *La Cité française, par le lettré Fan-ta-gen* (Paris, 1890).

LOUISE-MARIE COMPAIN

Louise-Marie Compain's career as a feminist novelist led her naturally into the women's rights movement (see her introduction in part 2). After publishing her second novel, *L'Opprobre* (Disgrace), she devoted much of her time and energy to two issues: women's suffrage and women's work.

Compain was a member of the founding committee of the society that organized mass suffragism in France, the *Union française pour le suffrage des femmes* (French Union for Women's Suffrage, or UFSF).[1] She served as a member of the UFSF executive committee throughout the prewar period; for several years (a period of rapid expansion), she served as publicist for the union. As an officer of the UFSF, Compain participated in the 1911 convention of the International Women's Suffrage Alliance (IWSA) in Stockholm and numerous meetings in France. She valued the international network she encountered and consequently became an officer of Marya Chéliga's Permanent Congress of International Feminism. Her job as publicist for the UFSF required Compain to place articles about these activities in the French press, and she succeeded in placing feminist news in such unsympathetic papers as *Le Matin*.[2] This work led, in turn, to Compain becoming a columnist for *La Petite République* in 1912, greatly expanding the reach of feminist journalism.

At the same time that she served the suffrage movement so energetically, Compain also devoted herself to women's work and labor law, lecturing and writing on the conditions of working-class women. Although she generally argued the socialist position on such questions, her role in the labor movement provoked controversy and criticism from the leaders of the French trade union movement.[3] One of Compain's controversial essays, "The Consequences of Woman's Work," is translated here.

The Consequences of Woman's Work

Woman's work, woman's participation in the life of society, is a reality that each person may judge deplorable or fortunate according to his own tendencies. To research all its causes would be very lengthy. In fact, they are almost all known, and it is essential to put at the top of the list the economic necessities of the present time that have forced girls without dowries to find means to support themselves and the progress of technology that has driven female workers into workshops. However, in our opinion, the pressure of economic circumstance is not sufficient to explain the entry of women into the work force and into the public domain. "An impulse stronger than her own nature, a breath of the incomprehensible, underlying all things," pushes her, said Selma Lagerlöf at the Congress for Women's Suffrage, which was held at Stockholm in June 1911.[4] We may be able to translate this with even more precision: the modern woman obeys an irresistible urge created by forces as yet inadequately understood that transform human beings and are responsible for the evolution of life.

We should not linger in trying to discover the explicable and the mysterious in feminine evolution, though, once more, we cannot not state it.

But what will be the consequences of this social problem that demands our attention? That is the interesting and even fascinating question that this fact arouses in those who think, who find one of their dearest and most disinterested satisfactions in foreseeing the future based on present information. It is for those who take the facts into account that we should like to try to lay out where we are already and what we see the individual domestic and social consequences of woman's work to be.

We shall pay particular attention to the transformations that occur in the middle classes, because it is mainly in this milieu that feminine evolution is taking place at present. The woman of the lower classes has been working for her bread for a long time. As for the women of the upper classes, they play but an insignificant role in social evolution, in view of their small num-

Source: Louise-Marie Compain, "Les Conséquences du travail de la femme," *La Grande Revue,* no.10 (1913): 364–76. Trans. Lydia Willis and Jennifer Waelti-Walters.

bers; besides, we see some of their most interesting representatives following the present movement.

Individual Consequences

It is true that one feels a certain embarrassment in describing the psychological transformations that may occur among women engaged in very different occupations. Particular characteristics will certainly distinguish the
secondary or elementary school teacher, the lawyer, the government employee, the typist, the physician, the writer, and the artist. However, for the
observer who has been in touch with the world of intellectual workers, and
who has seen the life of that disconcerting new being, the modern young
woman, common character traits emerge, like a family resemblance, that we
shall try to describe here.

The possession of a working skill assures the young girl of material independence and brings her at the same time a new moral independence with
respect to marriage. This certainly does not mean that the modern young
girl does not want love and does not desire marriage; but she no longer perceives marriage, or perceives it less and less, as a state one has to acquire at
any price. She wants to love the man she marries, and she is not ready to
marry the first comer who finds her pretty, because she has less time to lose
in debilitating dreams and because she is more aware of reality. In a word,
she has almost always conquered what we would call freedom of choice, and
one can say that this freedom is the most considerable gain the conquest
of an occupation has brought her, and its value by far exceeds the material
benefits.

Engaging in an occupation ensures the moral dignity of the young
woman and at the same time puts her in more direct contact with life. The
lawyer who has received the painful confessions of the guilty and the oppressed, the woman doctor who has spent the most beautiful hours of her
youth with the sick and the dead, the employee who is in contact with the
public, the secretary who is in charge of the mail of a large business or a
member of parliament, a teacher, or a nurse will know life better than the
young girl of old who only went out accompanied by her mother or her
maid to take courses in literature or music.

Certainly, contact with reality does not happen without bruises, and it is
possible that the young girl arrives at marriage with so few illusions that her

mother is astounded and afflicted by this precocious experience. One young woman told us the other day: "I have watched men too closely; I know that the best of them are unfaithful to their wives; I know what to expect and I suffer ahead of time." This lucidity is perhaps exaggerated, but it is certainly a lesser evil than the evil of ignorance that gripped the inactive girl of twenty years ago and aroused in a brain deprived of stimuli a love of the romantic that deformed her judgment and later on kept it from tasting the bitter but invigorating flavors of reality.

Better informed, today's young girl is, however, always very gay. She is gay, because, for a start, she has very little time to be bored, and undoubtedly for a deeper reason as well; because action, although rich in deceptions, is nevertheless the main element of life; and what is gaiety but an abundance of vitality?

The growth of a sense of her dignity as a woman, a loftier ideal of love, a deeper knowledge of life and more zest for it, these seem to us to summarize the moral gains for the female mentality that come from the material independence won by working.

Could one place on the other side of the scale the loss of those special qualities that seem more particularly feminine (sweetness, goodness, grace) or the acquisition of faults that seemed until now to be reserved for men?

This question is not easy to answer. It is said that the struggle is crueler for women than for men. The struggle is hard for both, and to face it, qualities of flexibility are just as useful as qualities of aggression. Nevertheless, we shall hardly contest the idea that the woman who has entered public life suffers more there than she who has remained sheltered by a happy home; but it does not seem to us that this suffering, being inseparable from action, should diminish the qualities of her heart (and this statement does not contradict what we said before). Is not a woman teacher more devoted to her pupils than a male teacher? [. . .] No, the soul's tenderness can remain intact in the working woman; but she has to accept a greater amount of suffering.

It seems to us that one could be more afraid that the exercise of a profession might imprint on women's brains that regrettable defect so common in men: specialization. Everybody knows physicians who ignore everything in life but medicine, professors who are always handing out grades, lawyers who never cease pleading their case. We would not dare deny that one can also recognize a woman teacher by a certain pedantry of speech, or a woman lawyer by her mania for quibbling. This is a stumbling block a woman does not always avoid. However, if she is careful, is there not reason to hope that the innate flexibility of a woman's spirit will enable her to escape the professional barriers and remain in contact with life around her?

Domestic and Social Consequences

Now let us discuss the domestic and social consequences of feminine evolution.

There are two choices: upon marriage, the woman will leave the occupation that she had pursued (and this will not always depend on the husband's income, but also on the love that the woman had for her work), or she will continue to exercise her profession.

In the first case the moral gain the young girl acquired remains intact and adds to the family's happiness. There is no doubt that the woman whose spirit has developed in contact with life is, as a wife, more comprehending of her husband's work and of the struggles he will have to face. It is also certain that as a mother she will be better suited to direct the education of her children, perhaps more aware of the differences in their natures, more apt to become their friend.

If the moral gain remains intact, the material gain also persists in part as a precious insurance in case of sickness, financial misfortunes, or the husband's death. If one of those misfortunes should strike the developing family, the woman would not only find indispensable resources in the profession she exercises, but the previous apprenticeship would find her better equipped for the brutal assault of adverse circumstances.

However, will this woman, who has left paid employment to devote herself completely to her family, have no other ideal but to live in her home sheltered from the outside world? It would mean that she had failed to experience to any degree the profound joy of work, that she had worked only to earn her bread. We believe that this could happen, but that it will become more and more rare. The appeal of life outside the home is felt even in the hearts of happy women who have not studied for any practical purpose. Thus, one sees more and more young women who, after the initial tasks of motherhood are over, feel the need for activity outside the home. She returns to or enters the world outside her home by way of social activity. She becomes involved with charity, education, or propaganda. She does not abandon her home, but she can no longer live there as a recluse. But has it not always been like this? Are there many women who do not give a large part of their time to what is called the world, after having fulfilled their domestic tasks with a more or less enlightened or demanding conscience? The modern young woman who has experienced work devotes less time to visiting and shopping; she devotes more time to living; she replaces visiting with committee meetings, mornings spent helping at neonatal clinics and dispensaries, in charitable or instructive inquiries, antialcoholic propaganda, even propaganda for women's suffrage. Such a young woman, between thirty and forty, who sometimes leaves home and children to take part in social action, surprises her mother.

"How can you find time to busy yourself outside the house?" the mother asks. "You have only one maid; I used to have two, and I only ever looked after my home; you must be neglecting your duties."

And the young woman replies:

"I am sure I fulfill all of them; my children are surrounded by as much love as I received myself; I must divide the time I devote to them better. I have only one maid, but my apartment is heated and lit; I have simplified many tasks that occupied your time to no purpose. I do not make jam any more; I do not waste precious time going to sales; in my home there are no heavy drapes that require extensive cleaning; my simplified material life leaves me with some leisure time to devote to useful work. As for my children, I do not believe it necessary that they should never leave me. I am a mother, but I am also a woman who sometimes gets impatient and nervous; I do not want my little ones to suffer from the irritation that their noisy games and constant demands sometimes cause me; unjust punishment horrifies me. It is good that I return to them with a will refreshed by the distraction of another occupation. Besides, I do not entrust them to hands any the less tender or intelligent than mine. I do not send them to the maid but to a kindergarten, where women who are superior educators teach them how to use their eyes and their hands and develop their tastes and their attention by charming exercises that I could not offer them at home. They find their little friends; they learn how to play and to act together; they take their first steps in social life. When they are older they will go to schools that, perhaps one day, will also be converted to educational centers."

Thus, the modern woman who has no paid occupation, but who has retained from her work the taste for outside activities, uses the simplifications of her material existence and the tendency for collective social life to maintain her participation in everyday life. One question remains. What is the husband going to say? Will he willingly accept not only that his wife leave the home (she has always done that) but that she possess in her life another interest besides the interest in her family; another love besides his love? As we have said in a previous article, a brutal and short statement sums up the opinion that man has of his role and that of woman:[5] "man is made for life and woman is made for man."

It is possible a man feels that the interest a woman takes in her outside activities diminishes her love for him. This is a revolt of the masculine instinct of property toward his woman. But is this instinct justifiable? Is it sensible? Should it not be sufficient for the husband to be first in his wife's heart? And if we look at the question more closely, could not the love that we assume exists between the spouses be justified by their common effort? Most often the social activity of the woman, if the marriage has really been a marriage of free choice, will be in the direction of the ideas and tendencies of the husband; he will approve of his wife's activities; he will love her; and she herself could not act joyfully if she were going against the will or the wishes of her husband. Thus the hours and the thoughts that the woman seems to take from the hours and thoughts reserved for the husband can, on the contrary, be moments when their hearts and wills move closer. Thus their love is purified and deepened. And this result will depend very much on the way in which the woman is able to make the man who loves her accept her leaving him for a moment, to return joined to him by new bonds. This is all a matter of tact, measure, and love. And true love will gain from it.

We now arrive at the case where a married woman must, for financial reasons or because of an irresistible vocation, spend several hours of the day outside the home, absorbed by an occupation of her choice.

Even more pressingly than the woman whose desire to work outside the home is a moral need, will she not feel the need both for material simplification of her life and for a society organized more collectively?

It is very likely that this will be so.

To start with let us talk about household tasks. We are certainly of the opinion that the households of intellectual women are better organized than those of women who have no other interests. A novel that presented a thesis to the contrary and raised some clamor a few years ago appeared so weak on this point that the following year the author denied it herself by making a model housewife of the woman lawyer, her heroine.[6] It still remains that in an apartment where good taste has eliminated dust catchers, knickknacks without any artistic value, it is still necessary, for example, to cook every day.

It is the lot of every housewife to awaken to the worry of preparing her menu; it must be economical, good, varied, and take into account the age and temperament of the members of the family. Whether the mistress of the house does it herself or leaves it to her cook, an oven will be lit every morning and every evening in the tiny apartment, and this for the needs of only a few people. The same thing occurs from the top to the bottom of the building; ten, fifteen, twenty, or fifty kitchen ovens are lit at the same time in all the city's buildings. If one stops to imagine it, this sight is very funny and shows egoistic customs that encourage a tremendous waste. What an outlay of fuel, of foodstuffs, and of work that could so easily be reduced! Twenty or thirty women are occupied, where a good cook and two or three assistants would be sufficient! Where only one large oven would be necessary, thirty little ones are being lit!

"What?" people will cry, "You want to destroy the family table!" Such is not my intention! On the contrary, I wish that all the happy people who like to get together for two hours every day around this symbolic table should continue to do so; but is it really necessary that the cooking should be done in their own apartments? Besides, it is so complicated in the families where everybody follows a different diet, and this is more and more the rule (because the same food does not suit all ages or temperaments). The baby needs soup, the husband red meat, the wife white meat; one likes fried potatoes, the other digests only purées; finally, a third is vegetarian! So much work for the cook and impossible to carry out even in a modest household! Would it not be simpler if a large kitchen were installed on the ground floor of the building, its operating expenses divided among the tenants pro rata according to their rents, where housewives could order suitable meals?

"Utopian dream!" But no! Those kitchens are starting to appear. "And where, in which circles?" Precisely in the circles where the woman has for a long time worked outside the home, in workers' cooperatives. The Egalitarian [*L'Egalitaire*], the large socialist cooperative of Sambre-et-Meuse Street, operates not only a restaurant but also a cooperative kitchen where women returning from the factory, who have not prepared their meals at home, may purchase ready-cooked food.

This kitchen renders such great services to housewives that in their Charonne district branch, the Egalitarian has also installed a kitchen. The Claim [*Revendication*] in Puteaux operates a cooperative restaurant and also, like Potin's grocery store, prepares many dishes that can be taken home. Finally, in Germany, bourgeois houses have recently been erected with a central kitchen in their basements. In the heart of Paris, the "Electric House"

[*"Maison Electrique"*] offers some examples of simplification of services provided by electrical current. There is not only a vacuum cleaner but a scrubbing brush-broom, an electrical washing machine, and table service accomplished without the help of domestic staff.

Nowadays these simplifications are very expensive; but one can easily foresee the lowering of their prices following their coming into general use. A telephone subscription costs only ninety francs for a Swedish citizen; it is four hundred francs for a French person.

We recognize that neither the cooperative restaurants of the Egalitarian and the Claim nor their cooking offers all the comfort and elegance that one might desire, but it is possible to imagine a pleasant and comfortable cooperative restaurant in every street for those people who like to take their meals in company, and a well-provided kitchen in each building, with elevators and dumbwaiters allowing easy communication, for those who enjoy domestic intimacy.

Let us note that the simplification of life will have the inestimable advantage of gradually resolving the problem of domestic service, which every day becomes more onerous and more odious for both masters and servants. The chef who cooks for twenty or thirty families, the waiter who takes the meals up to the various floors while awaiting the advent of facilities that will replace him, and the waiter who serves in restaurants are not domestic servants but employees; they do their work, but they are not in the service of the people whose needs they meet. Like the cobbler, the launderer, the baker, and the teacher, they are not domestic servants.

Let us deal now with the question of children's education, which is by far the most important problem resulting from the woman's *compulsory work* outside the home. It is complex. Such work can be reconciled with the tasks of motherhood: for example, that of the teacher whose days are far from being completely absorbed by her professional work. The primary school teacher, at least in small communities, has her apartment located in the school where she teaches and can therefore have her children in her classroom. We know of principals who have fulfilled their double task, domestic and professional, admirably. However, their prematurely white hair bears witness to their efforts.

But all feminine occupations do not have so many regular holidays, so few and such regular working hours as teachers. A woman doctor or a woman office worker can find herself facing more painful choices between her motherly and her professional duty. Will the woman doctor leave her own sick child and care for another woman's?

It seems, in spite of all the facilities that a widening of collective education will be able to offer to a woman in the future, that it will be difficult for her to earn a living like a man and to look after their children like a mother. A woman will be able to do so in certain situations, but not in all. And while it is desirable that when calamity strikes she should be able to assume this double task, one would wish that she could either work a few hours each day at home (as a writer or a consulting lawyer, for example) or live on her husband's earnings. Then, later, as the work and the worries of maternity no longer absorb her time, she should take her place again in social or public life with her broader experience.

Spinsterhood and Work

We have looked at the consequences of work only for the young girl and the married woman.

This sketch would not be complete if we did not talk about the woman who, caught between work she loves that keeps her and a marriage that does not satisfy her highest aims, opts for celibacy.

Would she have chosen it? In the majority of cases certainly not. But one sees too many of today's men dreading the risks of a moneyless marriage. The young girl has to accept independent solitude or a marriage of reason. There is also a third option that we shall now discuss. Should one pity the woman who, deliberately, out of pride, has chosen solitude? Yes, because in a sense she will not know the fullness of life and the joys of love. Nevertheless, her isolated life can be rich in sublime satisfactions and fruitful in blessings. Has one not observed that the unmarried teacher gives herself more fully to her students than the married teacher? And what devotion is offered by a woman doctor who gives not only her care but the best of her thoughts to her patients! Another kind of love grows in those hearts that do not dry up: a love of their work, a love of life in the deepest sense of the word. Perhaps it is necessary that life should be deprived of personal motives of happiness for its infinite riches to be revealed to the human heart. Those women who have given all their love to their work exist, and they are an inestimable blessing for society. Have they not always existed, in fact? But long ago (still today for those who, although born yesterday, belong nevertheless to past centuries), they remained in cloisters and dressed in the austere and rough garments that showed their vocation. Nowadays they circulate freely, and their clothing does not distinguish them from the masses. They no longer live in communities, and maybe this is regrettable. Many dream of homes that are pleasant and comfortable, not cold and bare, where each, while conserving her liberty, can enjoy in her leisure hours the company of those who love life more than they love individuals. [. . .]

However, many reading these lines will shake their heads and evoke the growing number of spinsters who lead an independent life full of regret. We know some of them, although there are fewer of them than the others. The woman on her own who has not been able to find a source of life in her work, or has not known how, is to be pitied. I do not know whether she is more an object of pity than the unmarried daughter who grew old within her family, a constant burden on her father or brother. In the life of the woman who supports herself by her work, there is a pride that the other woman is lacking; but pride cannot make for happiness, and the woman who does not feel in her heart an ardent love for her work will be better off in a marriage of reason than as a spinster.

This is why the question of choice of work is so important for a woman. She must like her work even more than a man must.

A very serious problem now arises: does the fact of women working turn men away from marriage? It is possible. It is possible that the first generations of women who have envisioned work as the only means of ensuring the dignity of their life and their love must pay a ransom for the progress of their sex: the sacrifice of their most feminine faculties. That is hard. But what progress in the material or moral order has ever been accomplished without there being some dead and wounded before the victory? The Latin man has difficulty in following the woman in this evolution where forces superior to any individual will are pushing them. He is perhaps still afraid that, in the brutal contact with life, woman will lose the qualities of tenderness and charm that captivated him. He is still in love with mastery. Is he, perhaps, moving away from it somewhat? If so, it is perhaps the best men who are moving away; those who want to keep their protective instinct, which gives them nobility of their hearts.

It is the challenging task of women to persuade men that their desire to participate in the whole of life makes them no less loving women than before.

However, progress cannot come from them only. And women's evolution requires a corresponding masculine evolution, perhaps an evolution of love or, at least, of the feeling of property that is so strong in men.

While many women have in fact ceased to ask themselves whether they are inferior or superior to men; while they are already beyond the stage of revolt, and feel only the sweetness of putting a more intelligent and wiser personality at the service of the one they love, the man still wants to exercise his mastery. He thinks that the protective instinct, which is his best virtue, corresponds to the right of domination. He still wants to be not only the first but the only object of his woman's care. In this he is undoubtedly in error, because a being that exists only for another is always on the verge of the greatest unhappiness. Men and women belong to the whole of life; their greatest happiness will be realized only when they love each other within such a life, united by a common objective. Love that absorbs all the forces of an individual is a frightening feeling; it is called passion, and a man should no more wish its perpetual presence in his wife than in himself.

As for the instinct of protection, we think it is deviant when it is coupled with a sense of mastery. To protect and to seize are not synonymous; to protect and to oppress even less so. Would not protection mean the lending of strength that is returned in tenderness and in gratitude? And when wills are united, who wants to know who leads and who commands? The service is reciprocal, and quarrels caused by vanity are unknown.

It is possible that this necessary evolution of love is still to come. But already we see unions where the woman's activity does not offend the man's love; where woman and man love each other not only through the senses but in a harmony of wills. There is no doubt that such unions are the happiest that have ever existed. However, they have not waited for the twentieth century to be born; but we feel especially strongly nowadays that instead of fortunate exceptions they must become the general rule.

We wish to repeat that it is possible after all that the happiness of the evolving woman is held back today because man is not advancing; this halt in progress is very understandable, because it is caused by surprise. Woman, in her present state of evolution, pushed by circumstances and deep feelings, is an object of surprise to herself. How then could it be otherwise for men?

Since we have tried in the preceding pages to draw out some of the consequences from the wealth of reflections and ideas arising from the spectacle of the feminine evolution, we shall try, to conclude our essay with clarity, to sum them up.

We have noted first:

A growth in women's personality, in the strength of women's intelligence and reason, and a more active and comprehensive love of life;

a deeper moral union between mother, children, and husband, resulting precisely from the growth of intelligence in woman;

probable material changes in the life of the family and of society that will become simpler and more collective (collective kitchens, household facilities, etc.);

changes in children's education that will also be more social and start earlier (kindergartens, more motherly schools, etc.);

changes in feminine social life (abandonment of futile and worldly occupations, creation of clubs);

new types of single women who live in their own buildings but remain in contact with the whole of life outside, seen as an invigorating experience;

finally, an ennoblement of love.

In conclusion, we ask all those who have kindly followed us thus far to open their eyes on the world surrounding them, to look at it carefully, and to see whether they do not discover signs of the changes that we believe we have noticed ourselves.

Notes

1. The UFSF was created in 1909 as a result of the efforts of Jeanne Schmahl, the woman who had been instrumental in winning the Married Women's Property Law of 1907. Other founders included Jane Misme, the editor of *La Française,* which had succeeded *La Fronde* as the major feminist newspaper, and Amélie Hammer (Harlor's mother; see part 2). By 1914, under the direction of Cécile Brunschwicg (1877–1946), the UFSF had 12,000 members and chapters in seventy-five departments of France. See Hause with Kenney, *Women's Suffrage,* 109–14 and 132–45.

2. Several of Compain's articles survive in the Dossier Congrès national de l'UFSF at the Bibliothèque Marguerite Durand.

3. For Compain's syndicalist activities, see Guibert, *Les Femmes,* esp. 371.

4. Selma Lagerlöf (1858–1940) was a feminist novelist from Sweden. She was the second woman to win the Nobel Prize, which she received in 1909 for her work *The Legend of Gösta Berling.*

5. [Author's note in the original text: "L'Action sociale des femmes," *La Grande Revue* February 25, 1912.]

6. The author is probably thinking of Collette Yver's *Les Dames du Palais* (Ladies of the Lawcourts; see part 5).

HÉLÈNE BRION

Hélène Brion (1882–1962) was a socialist feminist who, like Pelletier and Bonnevial, studied hard to escape an impoverished background.[1] Orphaned at an early age, she was raised by her grandmother and studied to be an elementary school teacher. She soon became an activist, both as a militant feminist and within the teachers' union. Her energy in these activities led her friend, Madeleine Vernet, who directed the workers' orphanage at Epone, to describe her thus: "And who is this Hélène Brion? Comrade, it will take a while to reply. Officially Hélène Brion is an elementary school teacher, secretary of the Federation of Unions of the Schoolteachers of France and the Colonies; secretary of the workers' orphanage in Epone; member of the confederal committee of the *Confédération générale du travail* (the CGT, General Confederation of Labor); archivist of the socialist division of Pantin; member of the action committee and of the special commission of the Committee for the Resumption of International Relations and of a number of feminist associations. . . . Ouf!"[2]

During World War I, Brion caused a major controversy by speaking against the war in defiance of legislation against "defeatist propaganda." In late 1917 (a period marked by the Bolshevik Revolution in Russia and mutinies in the French army), Brion was brought to trial. According to *Le Matin* (Nov. 18, 1917), Brion was accused of "malthusianism, defeatism, antimilitarism, and anarchy" as "a member of several revolutionary groups, treasurer of a feminist association, and if that is not enough, a schoolteacher!" Despite the support of many noted feminists and socialists, Brion was convicted and sentenced to three years in prison and suspension from teaching until 1925.[3] After her release from prison she played a major role in the postwar debate on women's suffrage. In her later years, Brion compiled a handwritten feminist encyclopedia of nearly 5,000 entries, which survives at the Bibliothèque Marguerite Durand.

The following excerpt is from one of Brion's speeches, which she subsequently published as a brochure. It was originally published in 1916, but we have included it here because it shows some of the problems in the relations between feminists and socialists during the belle époque.[4]

The Feminist Way:
Prewar Political Parties and Feminism

Woman, dare to exist!
Félix Pécaut[5]

The progressive parties willingly tell us feminists that when we fight on their side we are led by the force of circumstance to fill out their demands with our demands as women.[6] Easily vexed and not understanding the situation, the progressive parties often ask us:

"What is your feminism exactly? What does it want that we are not offering?"

They are divided into two groups, both equally convinced and singing almost the same refrain: socialism is all-sufficient! True feminism is to be socialist! You do not have to be feminists; you should be satisfied just to be fully and completely socialist—the whole social question rests there!

The other gang declares: the union movement is all-sufficient! True feminism is to be a unionist. If you are a true unionist, this should satisfy you, because complete unionism is the true answer to the social question, and you do not have to deal with the humbug of parliamentary action!

There are getting to be quite a few feminist militants who have heard these refrains!

In the name of all of them I should like to try to explain why this is false, why even militant men themselves hardly believe in it and feel troubled and worried when faced with a feminism that is asserting itself and that they

Source: Hélène Brion, *La Voie féministe* (Paris, 1916). Trans. Lydia Willis and Jennifer Waelti-Walters. Reproduced by permission of the Bibliothèque Historique de la Ville de Paris.

do not understand. This is why militant women must continue to display more than ever the label of a doctrine that alone resolves a great many social questions, the very existence of which seems to be ignored by the socialist and union movements.

Socialism and unionism attempt above all to improve the lot of the workers and the poorer classes.

However, women are even more exploited as women by the male community than they are as producers by the capitalists.

While on the subject of the working classes, it is easy to prove that the greatest injustice perpetrated on the female worker–factory worker, employee, or civil servant–is unequal pay for equal work, which is visible to us all. Now, this injustice affects her as a woman and not as a producer. It is the woman whose value as a worker is depreciated by such an odious and absurd procedure, established by secular practice.[7] [. . .]

In the workshop the woman has fixed wages, however small. She has regular working hours, even though they may be long, and she has free time, too. At the workshop she feels a certain dignity in working and producing. She says proudly, "my money," in talking of her wages, however small. However miserable her position at the workshop, she will not be beaten by the manager or the foreman without public opinion rallying to her aid to obtain justice.

Within the family . . . there is no limit to her working hours. Every hour of the day or night she is at the disposal of everyone: elderly parents, husband, children, sick or in health; she never feels that her task is finished. For this crushing labor, for this permanent slavery, she does not earn a *centime* and she is not entitled to the title of worker. She is not a producer. You will often hear men of the lower classes and even of the lower middle class say with pride:

"Oh, my wife does nothing. I do not want her to work. She only does 'housework.' "

The man who talks like this truly feels that he feeds his wife so that she can do nothing; he will gladly tell her so and make her feel that he is the master.

And the law, the expression of the wishes and thoughts *of men only,* judges in this way and reinforces such feelings. This is especially true of the law governing workers' pensions, which classifies household work as an occupation only if it is done for wages.

It is clear that it is in the family that the woman is most oppressed. In the workshop or the factory she achieves an appearance of independence that, together with the powerful attraction of a more varied life elsewhere, is an important factor in the social movement that increasingly draws women out of the home.

It is precisely where the woman is most oppressed, in the family, in *her* home, that the union movement cannot help her; already it can do very little to stop the exploitation of the female worker who is doing piecework at home; to defend the woman who suffers the oppression of domestic exploitation, it has no power at all.

The household as it presently exists is a hell that weighs on the whole of a woman's life and prevents any show of independence and thought. We feminists well remember the typical example of the Lebaudy strike a few years before the war, an example that should still cause some of our male comrades to reflect, if only they had the time.

In the middle of a strike, picketing women and a number of men are at the door of the factory observing dismissals and preventing the entry of women workers too timid to strike unless forced. Hence they "force" them. They say a few words to the few women who try to come to work and make gestures as though defending the entrance to the factory. This is enough; the workers go away or remain to watch. Suddenly, what do they all see? A woman arrives crying, cringing with shame, followed by a man who forces her onward by *hitting her with a stick and kicking her*. She is one of the strikers of the previous two days whom her tsar forces back to work because he is displeased that his wife is striking.

The knights of the strike remain motionless, powerless before this man who, under their very eyes, pushes the door open and, still hitting his wife, shoves her inside the "prison."

If a foreman had hit a female worker the whole of the union would have been up in arms; but it was the husband. Hence, it was a private matter, a domestic matter! Unions deal only with questions touching work. We do not reproach them about this, but they should not reproach us for dealing with questions that are just as important to us as labor disputes!

Our comrades should understand that for a woman the center of her life is not the workshop, that being a worker is but a moment in her life. It is family life that occupies her the most, even if the family is only elderly parents who are dependent on her. She takes her worries to the workshop more often than she brings back worries from the workshop. Her work at the workshop or factory is most often the work of a laborer, which does not demand any intelligent effort and so leaves her mind and heart empty. She does not need any creative or inventive spirit in her work. Her professional training and the prospects open to her in manual work, sewing excepted, are customarily very limited.

A man can have a passion for his occupation; he can endeavor to better himself and improve the machines and tools he uses. Conditions urge and invite him to do so, while at present everything pushes a woman toward the only permissible center of her activities: the family.

The union movement alone is not sufficient to ensure women's emancipation, because it deals only with the female worker. We feminists do not limit our efforts to that—and occasionally we have the very real fear that we shall have to fight the unions some day if they do not make clear their intentions toward us.

Many unionists still hold the old image of women that was dear to Proudhon: housewife or harlot.[8] As a harlot a woman has a definite use. As a housewife she has that use and many others. She is a cook, dishwasher, laundress, ironer, mender, linen maid, mother, wet-nurse, children's maid, nurse, etc.

Such a full life does not satisfy her any more than the other. She wants the right to have a third choice, a life of freedom with elements that she herself chooses.

While feminists have always demanded the right to work and the right to a free life for women, many unionists reject this.

The notorious and fairly recent Couriau case proves my statement. To review the facts:[9] Mme Couriau, a woman typographer who, along with her husband, had been a union member for years working at the union rate, arrived at Lyons, and they found work there together. The unionized comrades in Lyons did not allow women typographers to work among them. They urged the husband to forbid his wife to work. Couriau emphatically refused, daring to maintain that his wife was free and so was he, and they were not doing any harm to anyone since they both worked at the union rate.

Our good unionized comrades went to see the employer and threatened a general strike if Mme Couriau continued to work. The employer was compelled to give in: Mme Couriau was dismissed, and both she and her husband were thrown out of the union.

The whole feminist world rose in protest against this odious, arbitrary action, but not a single voice from the *official* union movement was heard in condemnation. [. . .]

What pushes our unionized comrades to act in this way is simply the masculine instinct, accustomed for centuries to subjugating the female and now upset over her potential liberation. It is the brutal instinct for domination of the Roman Caesar or the slavemaster exasperated at the idea that his slaves may escape.

You can see this plainly in the following newspaper item copied from the old *Lanterne* dated March 1907.[10]

Two coachmen, in a manner scarcely gallant, have shown the frustration caused by the competition of female coach drivers, minor though it be.

At the corner of Rue de Sèvres and Rue Vanneau a coachman endeavored to run down a coach driven by a woman. He succeeded in damaging the back of the fiacre and then fled, satisfied.

Another person was less fortunate. Mme Decourcelles, a coach driver in the service of the Valentine Coach Company, was driving two ladies at about five o'clock in the afternoon when in front of No. 144, Rue de Rivoli, she was suddenly cut off by a coach belonging to the Urbaine Company, driven by coachman D***.

To avoid a collision she skillfully managed to turn her horse aside but unfortunately hit a passing car. Both of the coach's springs were broken, the windows shattered, and the jumpseat smashed!

Mme Decourcelles, who is not only a skillful coach driver but also an energetic woman, jumped off her seat and went in hot pursuit of D***, who, whipping his horse, tried to get away at top speed. Grabbing him bravely by the collar, she brought him back and called the police, who interrogated witnesses.

D*** was charged by M. Bureau, Commissioner of Police for the Halles District, with interfering with the freedom to work and violent behavior.

You will find the same instinct at the other end of the social scale in the sons of the upper classes who, at the end of the nineteenth century, invaded a feminist congress singing obscene songs and throwing garbage into the assembly hall. You will find it among students who, in the streets of Paris one year, pursued with insults two of the first female doctors.[11]

It is the same instinct that caused chic young men from the boulevards, only a few years ago, to assault the models of the Rue de la Paix who were trying to promote the fashion of culottes. The same instinct stirred up the Yankees of the free United States of America against the Bloomerites who had been so audacious as to wear a "biped" costume.[12]

From the female doctor to the female coach driver, from the Misses Garrett and Blackwell to Mmes Dufaut and Decourcelles, all those who reached for or tried to reach for a few fragments of freedom have had to fight.[13] This has happened not only in France and Europe but in Turkey, in Persia, in China, and in India, wherever the enslaved sex, finally touched by the holy spirit of rebellion, tried to react against a miserable destiny.

Both unionism and socialism are mainly interested in the poor and in material conditions.

People generally and especially women, even rich women, can suffer a thousand moral miseries as painful as poverty, perhaps even more so.

I shall not insult the large majority of our comrades by thinking that they do not believe my statement. If there is a small number of brutes who seem to believe that money is a remedy for all evils, that one should not be pitied when all one's material needs are met, I know they are the exception and that the large majority has a more equitable appreciation of life's complexities and of the human soul.

The latter will understand, and all women will understand, if we state that there are rich women, even great ladies, who have suffered and continue to suffer as much and perhaps even more than factory workers in our social system. Capacity for suffering depends on the development and the degree of culture of the individual.

A "great lady," whose life is spent in charitable and social work fighting against poverty and vice, has perhaps suffered more deeply through social injustice than the poor woman rescued by her, but who is too stupefied by her own poverty to think about it.

In fact, women like Josephine Buttler [sic] and Pauline de Grandpré, who wore themselves out all their lives in the fight against prostitution, have suffered from the social system.[14] Miss Garrett and the two Misses Blackwell have suffered through male injustice, using their fortune and energies for many years in pleading against the universities of London, Edinburgh, and fourteen American universities, which refused them the right to study medicine because they were women! Elizabeth Cady Stanton, the ardent antislavery fighter and feminist, suffered when, after having covered 5,000 kilometers to attend an antislavery congress in England in 1840, she was ejected, although a delegate, because she was a woman.[15]

Let us not make a list of the innumerable emotional sufferings of woman, or mother, whatever her social rank, nationality, or race! Rather, let us speak about them! Everybody, male or female, will find a vast number of martyrs created by the world's phallocratic traditions, from the Indian widow burned alive on her master's grave and the Chinese woman with her broken feet to Mme Lafarge and Mme Doeckes, without forgetting the female pharmacist and her little padlock.[16]

Unionist comrades, your ideal is not good enough. Few of you could answer immediately in one or two clear sentences if we turn back on you the question you keep asking in order to "embarrass" us: What is your feminism?; if we asked you point-blank: What is your unionism? If I added a second question to the first, such as: What position is there for me as a woman in your union movement? I am quite certain that there would be no reply, only a great surprise, embarrassment lasting a second, annoyance, and a vague worry that a thousand unexpected problems might suddenly arise from the shadows.

Then the usual self-sufficiency would take over; we would have either the contemptuous shrug of the shoulders or the series of clichés on the role of woman and her "natural place" in the home, in the shadow and wake of a man. Banal and hollow sentences, sickening to hear for anyone who thinks at all and that shock you even more on the lips of those fierce revolutionaries because you have already heard and read similar ones, identical in their platitudinousness and conventionalities, coming from the "bourgeois" opposition and the "upright" people of all shades of opinion and all parties.

I cannot hear them without being reminded of the grotesque and bombastic speech made by Chaumette as he chased from the Convention of the 29 Brumaire the female revolutionary republicans who had come once again to claim their rights.[17]

"The premises where the magistrates of the people deliberate," cried out this fierce friend of freedom—for himself—"must be forbidden to all beings who *are an outrage to nature!* Since when is it allowed to disclaim one's sex? Since when is it decent to see women abandon the pious care of their homes and come into the public arena, into the tribunes to harangue us, or onto the Assembly's platform? Impudent women, who want to become men, etc."

This brings us to the issue of political rights and to the examination of the party's action on behalf of women, a party that represents the interests of the oppressed in the political arena.

Without going back to the Deluge or to the first Republic, without interrogating Saint-Simon, Fourier,[18] or even the aforementioned Proudhon about their conception of our social role and the position reserved for us in a future society, let us just consider the Third Republic. Now let us see what has been done for us by this party, which without any shame whatsoever wants to prevent us from any social action that lies outside its scope.

Here, listed in chronological order, are some of the reforms of interest to us.[19]

1884–86: Reestablishment of divorce: author Naquet.[20]

1904: M. Vallé: Constitution of a commission for the revision of the Civil Code, revision "*pro feminae*."[21]

1905: Bill Charles Beauquier against the legal incapacity of married women to manage their own affairs.[22]

1906: M. Chéron, formation of a Parliamentary Group for the Rights of Women. Henri Coulon, Extra-Parliamentary Commission for marriage reform.[23]

1907: Goirand Law concerning the salaries of married women.[24]

1907–08: Women's eligibility for membership in the Trade Disputes Arbitrators Council.

1913: Paul Strauss, a daily allocation to mothers of newborn babies: 0.50 francs a day.[25]

A bill granting women guardianship, which naturally lay dormant in the Chamber's files for many years before being passed a few months ago, reminds us of the names of Castelnau, Marc Réville, and Maurice Violette.

There is a mass of bills pending: Bill Dussaussoy-Buisson for the municipal vote; the bill of President Magnaud, "the Good Judge," that the separation of property become the legal basis for marriage without contract; Bill Martin and Maurice Violette, for divorce by mutual consent; Bill E. Giraud, that legal guardianship be granted to a woman rather than an interned husband; Bill Chautemps-Borel, that adulteries and divorces be examined *in camera;* Bill Beauquier, for the abolition of the legal incapacity of the married woman and proposing to make insanity a cause of divorce . . . , etc.

Among all those names, socialist comrades, not one is yours.

Among all those reforms or fragments of reforms hauled through by the constant work and effort of feminism, not one was initiated by you!

The famous bill on determination of paternity, which was discussed for thirty years, owes nothing to socialist endeavors either.[26]

However, the brave gentlemen who worked on it have not succeeded too well. This was to be expected. In a matter so delicate, touching women so closely, only they could have found a satisfactory solution. The determination of paternity is a false principle that we, the avant-garde feminists, fight against because it perpetuates the thousand-year-old error of the family based on the man, while its natural and logical base is the woman and the woman only. In starting from a false principle, in spite of all their zeal and their legal science, our good legislators could come up with only an imperfect law. This is what happened. We feminists are nevertheless grateful to them for having worked so hard to endeavor to remedy an obvious evil even though its deep causes escaped them.

Once more we are compelled to note that there were no socialists in their ranks.

Not so long ago our feminist delegations, when coming to the Chamber for a feminist claim, had to approach the Radicals or Radical Socialists if they wanted to be certain of being received.[27] This occurred in spite of the fact that almost all members of such a delegation were members of the Socialist party.

We know that you have included women's suffrage in the party's political program. We even know that just before the beginning of the war, at the last municipal and legislative elections, the party made the effort to *support* (?) female and feminist candidates. Elisabeth Renaud, in Isère, and Madeleine Pelletier and Caroline Kauffmann, in Paris, ran in the elections under the colors of the PSU (United Socialist Party) in hopeless districts with no possible chance of winning, but playing simply what is called in racing terms, "the stable game."[28]

We remember well the complex feelings that disturbed us when we were passionately taking part in the election campaign; the gleam of hope and happiness in fighting our own battle, in serving justice in the highest cause, closest to our hearts. Then deep and painful shame, bitterness, and humiliation.

To see an intelligence like that of Madeleine Pelletier, for example, fighting against the popular cretinism of the most reactionary districts of Paris; to see that intellectual power and competence, which could have served our party in parliament, condemned to wasteful display in that vulgar schoolyard before such a badly informed public; to see this when we knew that in more favorable districts candidates who were hardly her equal in value and with much less knowledge were winning hands down!

I know that it was a great honor for feminism that the Socialist party extended its endorsement to female candidates. But it would have done an even greater honor to itself, and would have acquired without contest indefeasible rights to our gratitude, if only it had arranged for one candidate, one woman, to be elected.

I can hear the cries now. It would have been necessary to sacrifice a good district, disturb some petty dealings and upset a few mediocrities . . . What a flurry in the Republic of Comrades!

But what moral victory for the party and what enthusiasm for it in the feminist world! A moral victory of inestimable importance on the eve of the tragic conflict in which the world is now engaged! A gesture of enormous importance that would have introduced into the political world a new force with unknown powers, unlimited enthusiasm and faith, perhaps capable of changing it single-handedly and of making a healthier, purified, and renewed world by sparing it the horrors and crimes of the present hour!

Therefore, neither unionism nor socialism are sufficient for us. In the greater interest of justice and in our own interest, we must continue the feminist struggle alongside and on the margins of all others.

We shall not fail. We have taken a clear position toward our comrades of the extreme avant-garde in the following declaration addressed to them almost a year ago:

Feminist Declaration

to

The Committee for the Resumption of International Relations[29]

We who have been unable to prevent war because we have no civil or political rights are with you with all our hearts in wanting its end.

We are with you in wanting to endeavor to install in Europe, after the end of the war or on the occasion of its end, a more just and equitable social system, which, on the one hand, will make wars less frequent by a sort of federation of nations and, on the other, will ensure a better and less precarious life for the immense masses of workers within each nation.

We women are with the mass of the workers because they are oppressed everywhere and because we women are also oppressed everywhere, even more so than any class of worker.

Like you workers, and even more than you, we suffer from war, and that is why we should like to try to prevent further conflict.

Before entering into a more decisive phase of action at your side, we should like to show clearly the motives behind our actions and comment on your attitude as indicated by the facts.

You workers have never been just to the women who have helped you in your struggles.

At the dawn of '89 [1789], when a new era seemed about to commence for the world, the women approached you with confidence because you talked of freedom and they thought they would obtain theirs. You rejected them.

Proud of your freshly acquired rights as "citizens," instead of stretching out a fraternal hand to those who had for centuries pulled the plough beside you and, like you, had eaten the grass of the field in the years of great famine, you mocked and despised them. You, who would not accept further despots, took fright at the possible emancipation of your perpetual slaves. You have closed women's clubs, confiscated women's newspapers, withdrawn from women the right of petition, and forbidden women all thought and all action. You have pushed women brutally back into the ignorance they wanted to leave behind, into the arms of the Church from which they wanted to escape. More than half the women who were the soul of the Vendean revolt for fourteen years confidently joined the '89 Revolution. When they were rejected, they rebelled, as the black populations of the colonies, rejected before them, had rebelled. Legouvé was later able to write that the Revolution failed because women were left out of it.[30]

However, in spite of your harshness toward women, many who still hoped remained by your side on the barricades. You all know Mme Roland, Charlotte Corday, Théroigne de Méricourt, Rose Lacombe, Olympe de Gouges, Sophie Lapierre, Babeuf's female followers, and many others who sealed their revolutionary faith with their blood.[31]

During the whole of the nineteenth century, through all the periods of crisis, women accompanied or preceded you. In 1830, in 1848, in 1851, and in 1871 we find Flora Tristan, Jeanne Deroin, Pauline Roland, Eugénie Niboyet, Adèle Esquiros, André Léo, Olympe Audouard, Louise Julien, Louise Michel, Hubertine Auclert, Eliska Vincent, Nathalie Lemel, and so many others, whose names you scarcely know or do not know at all. They are as dear to us feminists as the names of national heroes are to oppressed peoples.[32]

In every period, the women joined with those who fought for more freedom and well-being and for a more intelligent and human life. Feminist pioneers have devoted themselves to your cause while trying to link the women's cause to it and to make you understand the close relationship between the two. They acted not from egoism and for personal profit but out of love of justice, in the interest of all sisters who suffer and also in your interest, you workers who do not understand.

You have always accepted their collaboration, sometimes with a little shame and blushing to think of the debt you owed them, as happened in the trial of Jeanne Deroin's 107 working women's associations.[33]

While you accept their efforts you have failed to consider sharing with women at the opportune moment the all-too-slight advantages they had helped you wrench from the authorities. You have not understood or did not want to understand that your cause will be truly just and sacred the day you do not allow slaves among you. As long as it seems natural to you to withhold privileges from more than half a nation, you are hardly entitled to protest against privileges that others still deny you. If you want justice for yourselves, practice it toward your inferiors, women.

Workers, a social crisis is looming that is even more serious than all those of the nineteenth century. Women, as always, flock to you instinctively, ready to give their devotion unstintingly the day you act.

The feminists come to you too, with the same devotion and the same will. But they are determined to tell you: "If this time you again accept the participation of women—and you cannot not accept it—without thinking of granting them social redress, if you keep them slaves instead of making them your economic, civic, and political equals, all your efforts will fail!"

They come to remind you, or to teach you, that as early as 1843, a woman, Flora Tristan, was the first to think of an International Association of Workers, and we quote this often-forgotten passage of the manifesto that preceded the statutes and epitomizes its spirit: "We proletarians declare that we see clearly and are convinced that the omission of and the contempt for women's rights are the only causes of the world's evils and we have resolved to include women's sacred and inalienable rights in a solemn declaration . . .

"We want women to be informed of our declaration so that they will refuse to be oppressed and debased by man's injustice and tyranny, and we want all men to extend to women, their mothers, the freedom and equality they themselves enjoy!"[34]

To workers who read this the feminists say: If you had been inspired by the statutes and the spirit of the very first International, which you do not even count in your history, the second International would not have met with the lamentable failure from which the world is now suffering.

Workers, avant-garde feminists are awaiting your reply and leave you to meditate on the saying of Considérant:[35]

"The day women are allowed to participate in social questions, revolutions will no longer be made with guns!"

> Transmitted to the Committee by Hélène Brion.
> Handed over to M. Merrheim on October 23, 1916.[36]

Notes

1. For Brion, see Huguette Bouchardeau's introduction to her reprint edition of Brion's *La Voie féministe* and the sketch by H. Dubief, "Hélène Brion."

2. Quoted in *Hélène Brion, une belle conscience et une sombre affaire* (Epone, 1917).

3. See Annie Kriegel, "Procès de guerre."

4. This subject has attracted a great deal of scholarly attention; see note 3 to Countess Lecointre in part 1.

5. Félix Pécaut (1828–98) was trained as a Protestant pastor but became a prominent educator. He joined Ferdinand Buisson's group of liberal Protestants, which shaped the French educational system in the 1880s. As director of the *École normale* founded at Fontenay-aux-Roses to train women teachers, he influenced the first generation of women teaching in the secular schools; these women widely quoted his motto, "Dare to exist!"

6. Brion is referring to parties of the socialist left. For a full discussion of this, see Bouchardeau's notes to *La Voie féministe*.

7. In the late nineteenth century, French women earned fifty percent (sometimes less) of men's wages for the same job. Brion gives the average figures of thirty francs per week for women and seventy-five francs for men.

8. The Lebaudy strike, from which Brion draws the following story, was a bitter strike of workers at a sugar refinery in the department of Seine-et-Oise (suburban Paris). The Lebaudy family, which owned the refinery, were prominent members of the industrial *patronat* and included two deputies during the belle époque.

9. For an analysis of the Couriau affair, see Charles Sowerwine's "Workers and Women in France."

10. *La Lanterne* was an old name in French radical journalism, chiefly as a republican paper opposed to the Second Empire and as an anticlerical voice of the early Third Republic. At the turn of the century, its editor was a future premier, Aristide Briand (1862–1932), who opened it to socialist politicians. This orientation did not survive, and the paper abandoned its historic support of women's rights. To trace its history (and other belle époque newspapers), see Claude Bellanger, et al., eds., *Histoire générale de la presse française*. (Paris, 1972), vol.3 (1871–1940).

11. See the discussion of women in medicine in the introduction to Madeleine Pelletier in part 2.

12. An American feminist, Amelia Bloomer, proposed in 1851 that women wear knickerbockers under a short skirt for active occupations. The popularity of the bicycle in the 1890s made "bloomers" fashionable without the skirt. In France, the wearing of trousers was technically a crime for a woman until 1909.

13. Elisabeth Garett, Elisabeth Blackwell, and Emily Blackwell were pioneers of women in medicine in Britain and the United States; Mmes Dufaut and Decourcelles fought their battles in France.

14. Josephine Butler (1828–1906) was an English feminist who led the campaign against the Contagious Diseases Acts of 1866–69, which regulated prostitution in Britain. Pauline de Grandpré (1828–1908) founded an organization that helped French prostitutes when they were released from jail.

15. Elizabeth Cady Stanton (1815–1902) was a leading activist in the abolitionist, prohibitionist, and women's rights movements in the United States.

16. Marie Lafarge (1816–52) was involved in a notorious murder trial in 1839, accused of poisoning her new husband because he had married her for her dowry. She was sentenced to life in prison, but doubts about her guilt persisted in French popular culture. See Rayner Heppenstall, *French Crime in the Romantic Age* (London, 1970), esp. 200–202.

17. Pierre Chaumette (1764–93) was a leader of the revolutionary reign of terror. He had a violent hatred of women, and he attempted to send large numbers of prostitutes to the guillotine. In the Convention he spoke against women's rights; his speech of November 1793 contributed to the rejection of political rights for women. For such issues during the Revolution, see the documents in Darline G. Levy, et al.,

eds., *Women in Revolutionary Paris, 1789–1795* (Urbana, 1979). For Chaumette, see Jean Tulard, et al., eds., *Histoire et dictionnaire de la révolution française, 1789–1799* (Paris, 1987), 644–45.

18. For Fourier and Saint-Simon, see note 9 to Lecointre in part 1.

19. Compare this list to that given by the Countess Lecointre, p. 43.

20. Alfred Naquet (1834–1916) was a chemistry professor who took up radical politics and served a long career in the Chamber of Deputies and the Senate. His divorce bill of 1884 was significantly influenced by Léon Richer, but it displeased many feminists because it kept strict limits on divorce; see Phillips, *Putting Asunder*, 422–38.

21. Ernest Vallé (1845–1920) was the Minister of Justice in the French government of 1902–05. When the 1904 centennial celebration of the Napoleonic Code led to feminist protests against the code, Vallé named a commission to consider revising it. The commission was notorious because it contained no women; see Hause with Kenney, *Women's Suffrage*, 75–77.

22. Charles Beauquier (1833–1916) was a radical deputy who supported feminist reforms and organized a women's rights group in the Chamber of Deputies. Feresse-Deraismes honored him with a vice presidency of *Amélioration*. In 1905 he introduced a bill that would have suppressed all articles in the legal code that denied or restricted the rights of married women.

23. Henry Cheron (1867–1936) expanded Beauquier's parliamentary group to include 200 deputies. Henri Coulon was a lawyer who organized a committee of prominent citizens to study the marriage laws in France and seek reforms. Coulon served as president of this committee and named Avril de Sainte-Croix (see part 4) as his vice-president. Other feminists, including Jeanne Oddo-Deflou, Héra Mirtel, Jeanne Schmahl, and Séverine, participated in the committee's meetings.

24. Léopold Goirand (1845–1926) introduced the married women's property bill in the Chamber of Deputies in 1894 and defended it there and in the Senate (which he entered in 1906).

25. Paul Strauss (1852–1943) devoted his career in the French Senate to social welfare. He served on the Council of Public Assistance and became one of the first ministers of public assistance (welfare). The law of 1913, known as the Law of Large Families, provided both assistance to encourage a high birth rate in France and family welfare.

26. Brion is referring to the law of 1912, based on a Viviani Bill of 1906, which permitted the first paternity suits in French history.

27. The Radicals and Radical Socialists (who were not socialists) had a mixed record on women's rights. They endorsed women's rights in principle and worked for

many of the reforms that Brion mentions; they dominated the French parliament, however, and could have achieved far more if they had been more sincerely feminist. See the discussion of this in Hause with Kenney, *Women's Suffrage,* passim, and James F. McMillan, *Housewife or Harlot,* 182–83.

28. Women did not have the right to be candidates, but French suffragists used the tactic of women's candidacies for publicity. They made several such efforts in the 1880s, a few scattered attempts, and then a wave of candidacies in 1910. For the 1880s, see Bidelman, *Pariahs Stand Up!,* 137–46, and Hause, *Hubertine Auclert,* 116–26. For 1908, see Steven C. Hause and Anne R. Kenney, "Women's Suffrage." For 1910, see Hause with Kenney, *Women's Suffrage,* 145–51.

29. The committee comprised socialists and unionists (especially metal workers and teachers). This group supported the Zimmerwald meeting in Switzerland during World War I; their declaration obtained no response.

30. Ernest Legouvé (1807–1903) was a professor at the Collège de France who included women in his history courses. He was an early member of the feminist league of Richer and Deraismes. See Karen Offen, "Ernest Legouvé."

31. These women were important participants in the French Revolution, but for quite different reasons. Madame Roland (1754–93), Charlotte Corday (1768–93), and Olympe de Gouges (1748–93) were all guillotined during the Reign of Terror. Roland was an influential Girondist who supported the Revolution but opposed Robespierre. Corday, the assassin of Jean-Paul Marat, was the daughter of destitute aristocrats. De Gouges became one of the leading feminist voices of the era with the publication of her Declaration of the Rights of Woman (1791), but she was executed for royalist politics. Rose (Claire) Lacombe (1765–96) and Théroigne de Méricourt (1762–1817) were prominent feminists during the Revolution; both were denounced and imprisoned. Sophie Lapierre was arrested in 1795 for singing revolutionary songs in a café, but she was soon released. Gracchus Babeuf (1760–97) was an egalitarian revolutionary who formed the Conspiracy of Equals and was executed for its plots; he was later hailed as a revolutionary precursor of communism. For further information on women during the French Revolution, see Jane Abray, "Feminism in the French Revolution," *American Historical Review* 80 (1975): 43–62; Paule-Marie Duhet, *Les Femmes et la révolution, 1789–1794* (Paris, 1971); Sara Melzer and Leslie Rabine, eds., *Rebel Daughters: Women and the French Revolution* (New York, 1991); and the documents in Levy, et al., *Women in Revolutionary Paris.*

32. All these women were active in the women's rights movement between 1815 and 1871. Flora Tristan (1803–44) was especially active in the workers' movement. Jeanne Deroin (1805–94), Pauline Roland (1805–52), and Eugénie Niboyet (1796–1883) were active in utopian socialism and the revolution of 1848. They also

founded a tradition of feminist journalism and edited a variety of newspapers, such as Deroin's *La Politique des femmes* or Niboyet's *La Voix des femmes*. Adèle Esquiros (1819–86) was a writer who defended women's rights and edited *La Soeur de charité* (The Sister of Charity). André Léo (the pseudonym of Léodile Champseix, 1824–1900), Eliska Vincent (1841–1914), and Olympe Audouard were among the founders of Richer's and Deraismes's feminist league of the 1860s. Léo published several novels about women and their dependence on their family. Vincent became a prominent militant feminist of the belle époque and led an organization named *Egalité* (Equality). Louise Julien was the woman at whose grave Victor Hugo made his famous feminist speech of 1853. Louise Michel (1830–1905) and Nathalie Lemel were participants in the Paris Commune of 1871.

For further information, see the work of Claire Moses, especially *French Feminism;* Albistur and Armogathe, *Histoire du féminisme français,* vol. 2; Laure Adler, *L'Aube du féminisme: les premières journalistes, 1830–1850* (Paris, 1979); and Bidelman, *Pariahs Stand Up!* See also the many writings of these women.

33. In 1849, Deroin founded the Union of Workers' Association, which attracted members with a program of cooperativist (mutualist) socialism, in which the workers agreed on cooperative production and distribution of goods. The union's plans included equality between the sexes. In May 1850, however, Deroin's union was raided by the police, and she was arrested. Her trial in June 1851 became a feminist issue of the era, foreshadowing Brion's own trial shortly after she wrote this passage. In 1852, Deroin fled to England and spent the rest of her life in exile.

34. Quoted from Flora Tristan, *L'Union ouvrière* (Reprint: Paris, 1986 [1844]).

35. Victor Considérant (1808–93) was a prominent utopian socialist who spoke for Fourierists after the death of Fourier in 1837. His idealistic socialism of the 1840s (which included women's rights) led to his election to the revolutionary parliament of 1848. During the conservative era that followed, Considérant fled to the United States and attempted to create utopian communities in Texas.

36. Alphonse Merrheim (1871–1925) was a copper worker who rose to become one of the leaders of French trade unionism (secretary of the CGT). He presided over the meeting at which Brion spoke.

4

PROSTITUTION AND THE DOUBLE STANDARD

GHÉNIA AVRIL
DE SAINTE-CROIX

One of the most noteworthy varieties of belle époque feminism was Protestant feminism. France had a Protestant population of approximately 620,000 at the beginning of the twentieth century. These 80,000 Lutherans and 540,000 Reformed Church Calvinists represented less than two percent of the population. Nonetheless throughout the late nineteenth century the Protestant minority had shaped many of the institutions and movements of France, including the women's rights movement.[1]

The largest (by a huge margin) of the women's rights organizations of the early twentieth century was the *Conseil national des femmes françaises* (the CNFF, National Council of French Women). It was a coalition of women's associations with a combined membership of 21,000 in 1901, when no other feminist league could claim 500 members; by 1914, the council had nearly 100,000 members, whereas all other feminist groups had a combined membership of 15,000. As a coalition, the CNFF represented French women from a wide variety of backgrounds, but the founders and leaders of the council, the women who shaped it and set its policies, came overwhelmingly from the elite of Protestant philanthropy. The coalition's first president, Sarah Monod (1901–12), and second president, Julie Siegfried (1912–22), were both daughters of Protestant pastors who devoted themselves to philanthropy.[2]

Ghénia Avril de Sainte-Croix (1855–1939) was one of the animating spirits of the CNFF.[3] She joined Monod and Siegfried in founding the council and served as its secretary-general throughout the belle époque. She too came to feminism from the philanthropic background of the "HSP" (*haute société protestante,* Protestant high society).[4] In the 1890s, she had begun to participate (under her birthname, Ghénia Glaisette) in the annual meeting of Protestant women's charities known as the Conference of Versailles.[5] A wide range of organizations reported to this meeting, especially social reform groups dedicated to the suppression of pornography, alcoholism, and legalized prostitution. This led Glaisette (in 1900, Madame Avril) into the "abolitionist" campaign against legalized, government-regulated prostitution. A variety of organizations relied on the zeal of Protestant abolitionists such as Emilie de Morsier (1843–96), the daughter of another prominent pastoral family.[6] Morsier was one of many Protestants active in the *Oeuvre des libérées de Saint-Lazare,* who focused their concern on women (chiefly prostitutes) being released from Saint-Lazare Prison.[7]

Madame Avril had already established a literary reputation using the pseudonym "Savioz," which was a slightly modified form of her mother's family name, Savuiz. For her feminist activities, she added the pseudonym "de Sainte-Croix" (of the Holy Cross) to her name and became publicly known as Mme Avril de Sainte-Croix. She quickly became one of the most energetic activists in this Protestant women's movement and was one of the leaders who converted a feminine movement to feminism.

While directing the CNFF, Avril de Sainte-Croix continued to devote her energies to abolitionism. In 1901 she founded another philanthrophic society, *L'Oeuvre libératrice,* to assist prostitutes released from prison. Simultaneously, she published *La Serve* (The Female Serf), from which the following translation is taken, to exhort the French public to save young girls on the streets. She continued to speak out on this subject for the remainder of her life.[8]

The Female Serf

It is no longer just a few rare, isolated people, considered utopians and mild maniacs by the masses, who are disturbed by the suffering of prostitutes. It is no longer just a few women, the very few there were ten years ago, who are protesting. No, those protesting are the people who are preoccupied with social issues, sickened by the injustice being done, and wanting to see humanity move by means of greater justice toward a more moral beauty. And beside them, in serried ranks, march the women who are at last aware of the scandal, who understand at last that regulating prostitution is the final, most solid link that still joins the new Eve to ancient slavery.[9] And that this regulation, together with its fortresses and prison-hospitals, places the poorest, most wretched women outside the law.

Women are protesting vehemently, while men, usurping the title of moralists, say that they want this institution maintained above all to safeguard honest women and the purity of the household.

According to one of the women fighting the most eloquently against those who would regulate prostitution, women reply: "If we really are the ones concerned, then it is only fair that our voices be heard; silence implies our agreement. We cannot accept protection exerted by such means."

For some years now the abolitionist movement has become so general among women that not one society has been founded without the abolition of regulated prostitution being written into its program, together with the necessity of seeing a single morality established for both sexes.

Some of these societies are represented here. Among them, *The Improvement of Women's Lot and the Claiming of Her Rights; Equality; The French League for the Rights of Women;* and *The Forerunner,* presided over by the dedicated and knowledgeable Mme Jeanne Schmahl.[10] Others have sent us letters expressing their regret at not being able to attend our meetings and also agendas voted on by their members on this subject.

The opinion held by all societies is unanimous. All reject regulated prostitution as being unjust and detrimental to the dignity of women.

Le Conseil national des femmes françaises, founded in Paris this past April, has not yet had time to declare itself officially. However, I believe I can affirm that all the representatives of its member societies are equally hostile to regulated prostitution. [. . .]

Source: Ghénia Avril de Sainte-Croix, *La Serve: iniquité sociale* (Paris, 1901), 4–12. Trans. Jette Kjaer and Jennifer Waelti-Walters.

The feminist newspapers and magazines have also declared themselves against regulated prostitution.

For two years, *La Fronde* has led an unwavering campaign. The *Féminisme chrétien* has always condemned the dealings of the *police des moeurs* [vice squad]. *Le Journal des femmes,* founded by Mme Maria Martin, has dedicated lengthy articles to it, and in *Le Pain,* a Catholic journal dealing with female social issues, Mme Paul Vigneron writes: "The very fact of being forced to support as if it were an advanced idea the fact that there is only one civil code proves in itself just how low our society has fallen . . . only by observing moral law, developing a sense of responsibility in individuals of both sexes, and reforming economic conditions will polygamy in Christian countries—which is here more shameful and barbaric than it is in the Orient—be diminished."[11]

Clearly, therefore, the same opinion is held from one pole of feminism to the other, and the names I have just listed prove it.

Now, if we approach this from another angle, we see that the male associations for social studies have generally declared themselves in our favor.

Conferences have been organized in the Workers' Universities [*Universités populaires*], the lay patronage institutions [*Patronages laïques*], and at the Paris Labor Exchange [*Bourse du travail de Paris*].[12] The League of the Rights of Man has, as you know, opened an inquiry that can only turn to our advantage, since several branches have already declared their support.[13]

We have won over to our cause all those who have spoken of justice. Some, influenced by their past, may still hesitate and stop the advance for a moment, but they too will come to us. Carried foward by the truth, they will perhaps be obliged to attack the edifice they used to defend, in order to remain consistent with themselves.

Working-class men too, those whom work bows down and poverty makes old before their time, have finally understood that it is their daughters, sisters, and wives we are defending. They recall Benoît Malon's eloquent speech:[14]

"Women and the Proletariat make up the two great downtrodden groups left over from the ancient order. They must necessarily be the two great collectivities that revolt in our time. From their common effort will spring social transformation and a renewal of morals; and, from being the driving aspiration of the present, this will become a harmonious and fraternal realization in the future."

And they tell themselves that the streetwalker shivering on the streets, the sad prostitute condemned by her registration never to leave prostitution, is also to be pitied, perhaps even more than the others. From all around supporters come to us, touching in their sincerity and pity.

How could it be otherwise? What honest man would dare to come here and, without sheltering behind dangerous sophisms and false hygienic reasons, claim that the vice squad is a justifiable system? What man, having once spoken of law and justice, would dare to claim that this odious system is a social necessity?

Even if regulated prostitution were useful from a moral standpoint and advantageous from a hygienic one, we would still reject it. Because from the viewpoint of individual freedom, it is, first and foremost, a violation of rights.

No one has the right, at any price or under any pretext, to place women outside the law or turn them into slaves and then find himself, to a degrading ext˅
anyone have the right to put them, without a single resort, at the mercy of pimps or white-slave traders licensed by the government.

Justice must be neither inconsistent nor behind the times; it must be complete and equal for all.

Moreover, the unfortunate fallen woman who is at the mercy of the police has a right not only to justice but also to immeasurable pity, for she is the expiatory victim in a society that takes its revenge on the weakest.

It is no longer possible for card-carrying prostitutes to rise again.

Registration links them to a chain of slavery, and forced, periodic medical visits have destroyed what modesty they might have had. Grossly unjust in principle, the practices of the vice squad have deplorable consequences, because, having abolished women's freedom, it also abolishes men's responsibility.

Furthermore, in an appalling lesson, they teach that by selling themselves women commit such a monstrous crime that they are not even treated with the consideration given to the worst criminal offenders, whereas men who pay these women perform a natural and legitimate act in which the authorities must intervene to guarantee the quality of the merchandise.

By regulating prostitution the State is thrice guilty. First, it aims a serious blow at a woman's freedom by registering her as a prostitute; second, it destroys the principle of equality by punishing her for what is considered a pardonable offence in her accomplice; and finally, it is harmful to morality and creates pimping because of the registration that authorizes a woman to do business with her body.

Besides, these odious regulations are not just the product of an ill-fated concept of a double morality different for both sexes, a morality that has its source in ancestral contempt and that has weighed down women through the ages. They are also applied differently, for while police track down and pursue the unfortunate, starving "streetwalker," the poor merchant of love on the streets looking for something to appease her hunger or pacify her landlord, these same police stop respectfully in front of the apartments of the great courtesans. Impassively, paternally even, they watch scandals taking place before their very eyes in brothels, where minors, virtual children, are brought in to satisfy a choice *clientèle*.

I repeat, it is only the most unfortunate, the very poorest, who are treated severely and for whom arbitrary measures are considered necessary. These women are shut up in St. Lazare, handed over to the keepers, and if by any chance they should try to escape from this hell, this inferno forgotten by Dante, everything rises up against them and unites to push them into the gutter. Furthermore, while international congresses and secret meetings work to prevent and repress the White-Slave Trade, those nations that have sent their delegates sell licences at home to the meanest white-slavers, licences that, without the shameful markets, could not exist.

Lastly, because of regulated prostitution, which by tolerating these brothels makes it possible for dealers in human flesh to take in a supply of women and to shut up minors, we have seen young French women sold like cattle to foreign countries, at prices varying from eighty to three hundred francs. To escape from their brothels, these women have had to steal the house key from the dead-drunk brothelkeeper in order to flee, half-naked, in the middle of the night.

And do not think that is a product of my imagination. We have seen these women; we know where their misfortunes lie.

We would like to convince those who are still in doubt by showing all the proof that we have in our hands. But that is impossible. Therefore, let us quote in their touching simplicity the letters of an unhappy woman who tried in vain to get away from prostitution and whom our present system sent mercilessly, not into prostitution, with which she refused to have any dealing, but to her death.

Mr. Mayor,

I am writing to ask for your protection with regards to prostitution. It is true that, when I was young, I had the misfortune of conducting myself badly. But it has now been five years since I have been crossed off the list, and today the superintendent called me in and declared that I must go for a medical checkup. I wanted to prove that I had been living honestly for five years, but he wouldn't listen. It is truly unfortunate, when I have been rehabilitated from my past conduct, to find myself blamed when I don't deserve it. Therefore I beg you, Mr. Mayor, to intervene on my behalf with the superintendent and ask the police whether they have seen me on the streets in the past five years. For, having been put among the prostitutes without being one, never will I go for the medical inspection.

> I remain your very humble and devoted servant.
>
> January 17, 18 . . .
>
> M. A. . . .

Evidently, the poor woman's request was not taken into consideration, because the following letter, found in the same file as the preceding one, proves that nothing was done on her behalf.

Mr. Mayor,

I beg you to please be so kind as to intervene and have me crossed off the list of registered prostitutes, for I do not deserve to be on it. Mr. X . . . , the town ex-superintendent, when he still occupied his position, told me to make a request to you, and on your recommendation he would cross me off. For he knows that I work and cause no trouble. This is very unfortunate for me; for six months now, I have passed in the eyes of others for what I am not.

> Your very sincere and humble servant,
>
> M. A. . . .
>
> July 19, same year.

In the margin of this last letter was written: "deceased."

Death had been more merciful than life; it finally released the poor woman.

I hope these letters will provide reflection for those who wish to fight against the white-slave trade while maintaining brothels.

Last year, following two feminist congresses that unanimously voted "the suppression of all exceptional measures concerning morality," the question of regulated prostitution was again brought up in the papers. I cannot resist citing some passages from articles that appeared at the time: "I once spoke on this serious issue (the regulation of prostitution)," wrote M. Jules Bois in *Le Figaro*, "and as a result of the notion of justice that it encompasses, united the votes of the parties the most opposed to each other. It is obvious that we are too biased; society, so indulgent toward masculine errors, is pitiless when it comes to the mistakes made by women. There are many articles for the legislators to take up again, and several ideas for the psychologists to spread."

"It is a legacy [regulated prostitution]," explains M. Georges Montorgueil in *L'Eclair,* "of that morality that was a strength, but whose time has passed. We are more and more the State, more and more the authorities, and we feel humiliated by this commerce of women under the aegis of the authorities and the State. For long enough we have asked civil servants to hold a cane in one hand and a candle in the other. Let us return to a healthier practice of justice. Common law is enough to keep the streets decent and respected."

"The disgrace of courtesans is what accentuates women's misery," says M. François de Nion quite accurately in *L'Echo de Paris.* "Why have rules, exceptional legislation against the debauchery of one sex, freedom and protection for the other?"

"Why harrass like a skunk the poor woman abandoned by her bourgeois lover, whom hunger has forced into giving her sad and weary body to the first passerby?" we read in *L'Epoque,* under the name of M. J. Torlet.

"Prostitution is an unavoidable necessity in our present-day society. Since women, who are our serfs, must occasionally arouse desire and search for venal embraces in order to live, let us not bear down on them but rather extend a helping and fraternal hand."

"There is no problem in discovering where man's infamy and society's hypocrisy spread themselves most crudely," Urbain Gohier cries in *L'Aurore,* "Prostitution, clericalism, and militarism are the three ulcers in this decaying world. When we have thrown down the Church, the brothel, and the barracks, then we will see the birth of a new order."

In *Le Paris,* M. R. de Verpré asks that we "Let her [the prostitute] exercise her sad profession while waiting for the day when she is free and has the franchise along with the proletariat. Meeting all her own needs, no longer depending on anything from men, in short, our equal, she can without a backward thought give herself to the man she has freely chosen, give and recover herself."

We see from these quotations that regulated prostitution is equally condemned by all . . .

Notes

1. For the argument that Protestantism was influential in shaping and supporting the development of French feminism, see Hause with Kenney, *Women's Suffrage*, esp. 255–59; McMillan, *Housewife or Harlot*, 88–89; Klejman and Rochefort, *L'Egalité en marche*, 151–52. For the development of this theme in an international comparison (with close attention to the subject of prostitution), see Anne-Marie Käppeli, *Sublime croisade*.

2. For Monod, see Gustave Monod, *La Famille Monod: portraits et souvenirs* (Paris, 1890); for Siegfried, see Elisa Sabatier, *Madame Jules Siegfried, 1848–1922* (Privas, 1922).

3. There is no full biography of Ghénia Avril de Sainte-Croix, but she figures prominently in two histories of belle époque feminism: Klejman and Rochefort, *L'Egalité en marche* (see esp. 155), and Hause with Kenney, *Women's Suffrage*. Avril left a large collection of her scrapbooks to the library of the Musée Social.

4. There is some scholarly disagreement on whether Avril de Sainte-Croix was a Protestant or merely a participant in predominantly Protestant women's circles. McMillan asserts that she was "another non-Protestant" (*Housewife or Harlot*, 89); Michelle Perrot puts Avril at the head of a list of "les philanthropes protestantes, affranchies du conservatisme catholique" (preface to Klejman and Rochefort, *L'Egalité en marche*, 17).

5. For disentangling Avril's names, see Klejman and Rochefort, *L'Egalité en marche*, 155, n.1. For the Conférence de Versailles, ibid., 150–52, and Hause with Kenney, *Women's Suffrage*, 37–39 and 47–48.

6. See Käppeli, *Sublime croisade*, 55–77, and the collection of Morsier's speeches, *La Mission de la femme*.

7. For the legalized prostitution of the belle époque, the abolitionist campaign against it, and Saint Lazare Prison for women, see Jill Harsin, *Policing Prostitution;* Alain Corbin, *Women for Hire;* and Elizabeth Weston, "Prostitution in Paris." For the work of *L'Oeuvre des libérées*, see Morsier's speech and the works of Isabelle Bogelot, especially *Mémoire sur l'oeuvre des libérées*.

8. For Avril's later thoughts, see her speech *L'Esclave blanche*.

9. "The new Eve" was a widely used term in nineteenth-century French feminist thought. See especially the writings of Maria Deraismes, such as *Eve dans l'humanité*, which has been reprinted with a preface by Laurence Klejman (Paris, 1990).

10. These three small societies, with a total of fewer than 500 members among them, were among the most ardent voices of French feminism when Avril wrote in 1900. Improvement of Women's Lot (*L'Amélioration du sort de la femme*) was the

society founded by Maria Deraismes in 1870; in 1900 it was led by her sister, Anna Feresse-Deraismes. Equality (*Egalité*) was a militant group led by long-time activist Eliska Vincent. The Forerunner (*L'Avant-Courrière*) was the society that Jeanne Schmahl created to work for the Married Women's Property Law.

11. Avril knew *La Fronde*'s policy on regulated prostitution very well indeed (just as she knew the CNFF's) because she wrote the paper's columns on that subject. *Le Journal des femmes* was a vigorous voice of militant feminism; it had appeared as the successor to Hubertine Auclert's *La Citoyenne* (see Hause, *Hubertine Auclert,* 143–48). *Le Féminisme chrétien* was the voice of Marie Maugeret's group of the same name, the most feminist segment of the Catholic women's movement (see Hause and Kenney, "The Development of the Catholic Women's Suffrage Movement"). *Le Pain* was a short-lived social Catholic newspaper.

12. The *universités populaires* were not part of the French educational system. They were self-help institutions founded in 1898 by a cooperativist socialist and autodidact, Georges Deherme (1870–1937). While they had an important pedagogical function, they were also dedicated to the creation of an alternative sociability among workers. See Lucien Mercier, *Les Universités populaires, 1899–1914: Education populaire et mouvement ouvrier au début du siècle* (Paris, 1986).

13. The League of the Rights of Man, which took its name from the title of the French bill of rights (The Declaration of the Rights of Man and the Citizen), was a vigorous human rights league founded at the peak of the Dreyfus affair. Wendy Ellen Perry of the University of North Carolina is currently completing a doctoral dissertation on the league.

14. Benoît Malon (1841–93) was a dye worker and labor leader who participated in the Paris Commune and spent the 1870s in exile. During the 1880s and 1890s he was one of the leading socialists who refused to join the French Marxist party; see K. Steven Vincent, *Between Marxism and Anarchism: Benoît Malon and French Reformist Socialism* (Berkeley, 1992).

CASE STUDIES OF
BELLE EPOQUE
PROSTITUTES

It is difficult to estimate the number of prostitutes in belle époque France, but the number was, without question, startlingly high. Police records in Paris for the year 1894, for example, show that 5,104 women were inscribed as legal prostitutes (only ten percent of them in brothels) and that, additionally, the police arrested 29,695 women as prostitutes.[1] The police estimated that 35,000 to 40,000 Parisian women earned part or all of their income through prostitution in 1900. Whatever the correct number, prostitutes were so ubiquitous that they became a basic feature in stereotypes of the belle époque. Prostitutes filled the paintings of Degas and Toulouse-Lautrec, the novels of Zola, and the imaginations of foreigners.[2]

Such cultural images of belle epoque prostitution often mislead observers into visualizing a glamorous world. The following contemporary documents provide a different perspective. They are the blunt case histories of a few Parisian prostitutes in the years 1906 to 1909. The first case appeared in a daily newspaper, *Le Matin;* the others are from anonymous interviews.

Prostitutes, 1906–09

A Heartrending Story

This story is a commonplace, everyday occurrence, and it is very sad:

Twenty years ago, Emilie B. . . . became an orphan. She was not taught any skills and so she fell into the low life. During her nocturnal wanderings on the boulevards, she fell in love with a commercial employee without a job. She helped him until he found a situation that paid enough. From that moment on, the young man, who belonged to a respectable family, wanted his benefactress to get back on the right track. Courageously, he married her. And immediately she was crossed off the register at the Paris police headquarters. Shortly thereafter, the young wife brought a little girl into the world, who never knew of her mother's past. Two years ago, Mme Emilie B.'s daughter became a mother in her turn. But the child was brought into the world at a sad time. M. B. died, and misery settled in their home once more. In order to raise the child they cherished, both mother and daughter worked day and night making clothing, for a paltry wage. Despite the women's labor, the child did not always get what it needed. Therefore the grandmother, now forty-five years of age, armed herself with incredible courage. Shamefacedly, with tears in her eyes, she went to claim her "card" at the police station.

"I have made up my mind that I will do anything," she declared, "for my granddaughter to have bread and milk every day . . . I shall arrange it so my daughter doesn't find out."

Given this information, M. Lépine comforted the poor grandmother and gave her assistance until he could find her a job that would permit her to live honorably.

Prostitution: Case Histories from Paris[3]

Louise D. . . . born in Lyons, twenty-eight years of age. Had a child she gave over to public assistance [*l'Assistance publique*], since she couldn't pay the wet nurse.

"How did you come to this, my poor child?"

Source: For "A Heartrending Story," *Le Matin,* Nov. 16, 1908 (trans. Jette Kjaer); for "Prostitution: Case Histories," anon. mss., in dossier "Prostitution 1906–1909" (DOS 351 PRO), Bibliothèque Marguerite Durand, Paris (trans. Jette Kjaer and Jennifer Waelti-Walters).

For a minute she hesitated, then burst into tears:

"When people discovered that I had had a child, they drove me away. Then one evening, a friend from the maternity ward who had also given up her child said to me:

" 'Go on, you're silly to let yourself die of hunger. Come with me, I'll help you make some money!' "

"I followed her; it was nine in the evening, I shall always remember it. I would rather have died, and my teeth were chattering, although it was July. Yes, nine o'clock, and at eleven I was caught in a raid, brought to Saint-Lazare, and when they let me go I had to be registered, because I had been singled out to be under police supervision!"[4]

"What did your mother do? When did you leave her?"

"My father and mother worked in a silk-spinning factory. They both died of consumption and so I was taken in by nuns, out of charity, and I stayed at the convent, where I sewed, until I was twenty-one."

"And after that?"

"Afterward I got a position as a lady's maid, but I did not sew very well, and I couldn't dress hair. So then I got a job as a general maid, and that's where I had my poor baby. Oh, it wasn't my fault, madam, I swear I didn't know! My mistress and the children were in the country, and Monsieur stayed behind to do business. One evening he came into my room, and he frightened me so much that I gave in . . . for fear of losing my job.

"And when I left the maternity ward and had to pay thirty-five francs a month for a wet nurse I couldn't manage, even by going without the clothes and shoes I needed for the different positions I had. My mistresses asked me what happened to the money I earned; they searched and found out and dismissed me. That's how it went in six successive places until the evening I told you about."

Marie R. . . . from Paris, twenty-eight years old, sewing maid, dying of tuberculosis (they haven't taken her card away from her).

Same question as before. Why?

"Because for three days I had lived on dry bread and I no longer had a place to live. I was turned out by my landlord, to whom I owed one quarter's rent and who kept my parents' furniture (except the bed and one chair) as payment. I accepted the hospitality of a friend for a few days, but I could see that it bothered her husband, so I went to the night shelter. But since they only keep you three days, I started wandering around like a lost dog, accepting the hospitality of those I met and paying by lying on my back.

"One fine day, a woman in a bar who made all sorts of promises, you can guess which ones, took me with her. I listened to her because I was tired of sewing eighteen hours a day without being able to make a living and earning nothing in the off-season. Then, less than six months after having been imprisoned in a country house where the lady had taken me, I began to cough, and I was sent away.

"By spring, my few savings (from being a prisoner of pleasure) were exhausted, and since I was feeling much better, I took the necessary steps to get my card back. But I soon had a relapse, and here I am, done for."

"Have you been an orphan for long?"

"Oh, yes. I lived with a sister from my father's first marriage, who is also dead. But before that I was taken in by nuns for four years, who taught me how to sew, and that's how I became a sewing maid."

Georgette V. . . . twenty-four years old, clandestine for a year. "Got nabbed after having been denounced." Left the Nuns of St. Vincent and, at the age of ten, during her mother's illness, was employed by a lady doing good works. She had had enough of all the kids and of sewing all the time, liked having fun. Was then employed as a maid at the *Grand Neptune* and at *Point du Jour,* where she learned how to sing in the evenings with an actor. Would no doubt have been able to have a singing career if she had not been taken ill (tuberculosis, 2d degree).

Marie L. . . . forty years old, registered prostitute, dishwasher in a pub. Caught in a brawl one night while returning home after work . . . Had her arm broken. Has never been clandestine, had a card since she began, at the age of twenty-eight. Has repented, but it is too late. Daughter of working-class people, she says, crying: "If my poor mother could see me." Was led to the job by poverty, mostly, but also by bad company.

Marie R. . . . Nothing special. When she was nineteen, she had a child at her employer's. Does not know if the father is monsieur or madame's younger brother, but clearly he is one of the two, since she had never been with other men at the time. She did herself up so tightly that she had an adhesion; the child was born deformed and lived only for six weeks. Was sick for almost six months after giving birth. When she left the hospital she was so weak and anemic that she was turned out from all her situations. Took the advice of a woman she knew in the maternity ward. Regrets this because she is "dying of starvation" anyway, seeing she is often ill from uterine hemorrhage. Has had a dilation and curetage.

Diagnosis from the doctor, inflammation of the womb.

The concierge said to me before I went up: "What are you visiting that piece of trash for? She's registered. Oh! what a mess, she is half-rotten. Sunday night she had a wild time with two men, and Monday she had a discharge. We should let drug addicts like that die in the gutter. I got to give her her f . . . notice!"

Marie T. . . . Student at the Good Pastor school of Ch. . . . Servant. Two children by her master, the manager of a bar and *tabac,* widower. Sent away after the second child. Wanted to raise the second (the father had forced her to give the first one over to public assistance). Gave it to a wet nurse and went into service as a maid for a wine dealer. Paid the wet nurse for half a year. The dealer didn't pay her, so she could not send anything to the wet nurse, who threatened to return the baby, so she gave it up. Her boss went bankrupt. She went into service with another wine dealer and got pregnant for the third time, by the dealer himself. Had a miscarriage . . . Had hemorrhages and was sent away because she could no longer do the work. Didn't want to leave, and to take revenge threw syphon bottles through the shop window and the mirrors. She was sent to prison. The boss and customers bore witness, the boss said she wanted to blackmail him, that he had never slept with such trash, etc. etc. . . . Coming out of Saint-Lazare, and following the advice of a woman she has met there, she enters into the business.

Notes

1. Harsin gives registration data from 1812 (1,293) to 1900 (6,222) and arrest data from 1857 (7,471) to 1894 (29,695) (*Policing Prostitution,* 361–67). See also the data in Benjamin F. Martin, *Crime and Criminal Justice Under the Third Republic: The Shame of Marianne* (Baton Rouge, 1990), e.g., 77. Martin also found police estimates that the average prostitute charged forty sous and that two percent of the registered prostitutes and forty percent of the nonregistered prostitutes had veneral diseases.

2. See Charles Bernheimer, *Figures of Ill Repute,* especially his chapters on Degas, Zola, and Huysmans.

3. These case histories are unpublished in French. They are found among eighty-one similar cases, recorded anonymously in manuscript form at the Bibliothèque Marguerite Durand.

4. Saint-Lazare was the Parisian women's prison. See note 7 to Avril de Sainte-Croix in part 4.

MADELEINE PELLETIER

Madeleine Pelletier has already been seen, in part 2, stating advanced ideas about the education of girls. "A feminist mother," she argued, "should dress her little girl as a boy." That idea, along with strong feelings about such diverse subjects as haircuts and toys, was intended to prepare girls (and society) for genuine equality, beginning with an equal education. "Whatever their sex may be," Pelletier argued, "persons are entitled to intellectual enlightenment and the full blossoming of the spirit."

Pelletier naturally carried the same ardent attachment to complete equality, and the same capacity for radical ideas, into her discussion of male-female relationships. Her most important work to deal with this subject was a book published in 1911 under the title of *L'Emancipation sexuelle de la femme* (The Sexual Emancipation of Women). The title may seem to imply a wider and more active sex life for women, but that was not Pelletier's goal. Indeed, she personally chose a life of virginity, as the title of her autobiographical novel of 1933 makes clear: *La Femme vierge* (The Virgin Woman).[1] This did not mean that Pelletier had chosen or advocated lesbianism (nor that she rejected it more than heterosexuality).[2] Pelletier sought a sexual equality that started with the abolition of the double standard. She made that point and many of its implications clear in the following excerpt from the first chapter of *L'Emancipation sexuelle de la femme*.

One Morality for Both Sexes

According to whether one is male or female, the word "honest" has a different meaning. An honest man is one who does not wrong his fellow men; but a woman who harms another is still considered honest, because for her, honesty is of a special nature. It consists in subscribing to the law of men.

Individual existence is not possible for a young woman. At home, under the protection of her parents, she spends her time waiting for a husband. One single duty therefore absorbs all the rest, and most of the others have only one single view in mind: a young woman must retain her virginity for the man who will marry her. To ensure that this is so, primitive people confine young women, just as they do mature women to ensure their fidelity. Civilization has removed the bars, but moral dictates, indeed, material arrangements, fulfill the same function.

In the French bourgeoisie, a young woman is hardly permitted to leave the house without an escort. Hence her experience of life is limited to her relationship with her parents. The exterior world she knows only through novels, which often must be read in secret. In the middle and working classes, a young woman may go out alone, but she is far from enjoying the same freedom as a young man. Although she is not accompanied to her office or workshop, her time is watched carefully, so she can hardly be free without freeing herself completely. Often, a brother will even keep an eye on his sister, independently of the parents. He satisfies an unbridled sexuality but nevertheless thinks he has a right to reprimand his sister if she steps out of line in the slightest. And far from blaming him, the parents praise him for doing what they judge to be his brotherly duty. Moreover, a young woman, raised for slavery, would hardly know how to take advantage of freedom. She frees herself from the guardianship of the family only to fall under the yoke of a man. [. . .]

Men do everything possible to make women break their rules. In this respect, as in many others, their specific interest opposes that of the group. Marriage, while putting woman under guardianship, also enslaves the man, at least to a certain extent. Therefore, he intends to satisfy his senses largely outside the marriage. Through seduction, guile, intimidation, and sometimes violence, man therefore leads woman into illegitimate love. Conven-

Source: Madeleine Pelletier, "Une seule morale pour les deux sexes," chap. 1 of *L'Emancipation sexuelle de la femme* (Paris, 1911), 1–11. Trans. Lydia Willis and Jennifer Waelti-Walters.

tional morality blames him for this, but real morality excuses and even glorifies him. Since woman is considered not only a person but a commodity, the reputation of the seducer equals that of a happy man who succeeds in life.

But if seducing brings credit, being seduced is, on the contrary, a disgrace. The moral disrepute suffered by the seduced woman is in fact material depreciation. By losing her virginity she falls to the level of a used object; she joins other "tainted women," damaged goods that are hard to market.

Thus, for a young woman, honesty is her virginity. For a mature woman it is fidelity; an honest woman is one who remains faithful to her husband. The barriers society puts up around a young woman to protect her virginity also guard the fidelity of a married woman.

Young women of the bourgeoisie generally marry to free themselves. Married, they do have more freedom, but marital protection, although less rigorous, is nonetheless guardianship, and the wives must still account for their time.

There is no equality in conjugal love. The man possesses and the woman is possessed; what is a right for him is a duty for her. Subservient in her very flesh, she will go so far as to suffer maternity when imposed against her will by the man, the better to confine her to the home. The husband may exercise his rights or abstain, as he pleases. In the case of the latter, the "deserted" wife has no other resource than clandestine adultery. But the woman who refuses brings the brutality of the man upon herself; even illness often does not stop him. How many women do not complain of abominable treatment received from their husbands because, ill or having just given birth, they have tried shirking their "duty"? Married to a man suffering from satyriasis, or sexual perversion, a woman is again supposed to put up with him. Her parents turn a deaf ear to her complaints, saying she belongs to her husband. And religion also abandons her. In the confessor's manuals it is written, apparently, that men may do as they wish with women, even if it endangers their lives.

A married woman is even more strongly urged to transgress sexual morality for the man's benefit. But while adultery is permitted to the husband, if not altogether by law, at least by public sentiment, it is almost a crime for a woman. The man does not really believe he has to be faithful, and opinion makes it a woman's duty to forgive her adulterous husband; she who refuses incurs blame. But the female adulteress is treated as the one chiefly to blame; the husband who forgives her, far from being praised, is ridiculed, and a man who kills his adulterous wife is considered by both jury and public opinion to be exercising his right.

Traditionalists say that this inequality in the attitudes toward the actions of people of the same sex is justified by the prospect of having a child.

Indeed, a man is fiercely proud of becoming a father. If he has any founded or unfounded doubts regarding his paternity, he believes he has a right to make life miserable for the child he suspects is not his own. And despite the pity that the public usually has for a child, it excuses such a man. Nevertheless, paternal feeling is far from strong. For the father, the newborn is hardly anything but "a bundle of red flesh," to use the expression of a contemporary journalist. If it is a boy, the man is proud to have reproduced his own sex, the superior sex, and he is flattered if assured the child resembles him. True affection comes only as a result of life together. Paternal pride can just as easily be nothing but possessiveness. A man, sovereign master over his wife, reserves for himself and no one else the right to give her children. For him, foreign paternity seems like robbery committed against him.

By taking even this barbaric viewpoint, the male adulterer should not be any less guilty than the adulteress. If the adulterous husband does not bring a bastard into his household, he brings it into another, unless he is weighing down some poor young girl with the burden of maternity. But present day morality does not take these possibilities into consideration; rather, it believes that man has a right to take what he wants from the female herd. If another man is injured, too bad; he should have kept a better eye on the women who, as wives, sisters, or daughters, are dependent on him: "My cocks have been let loose, watch over your hens."

Thus the reason for having two moralities lies nowhere but in the dependence of women on men. [. . .]

A woman becomes the target of masculine vulgarities in the street. If she is young and pretty, men call her obscene names and offer lewd, filthy propositions. Sometimes they add gestures or slimy touches. A woman disgraced by nature endures jeers as she goes down the street. An ugly man passes by unnoticed, but a woman does not have the right to be ugly. When old, her age is insulted. In England women are given more respect and do not have to suffer such contemptible treatment, but in France custom has in this regard remained what it was in barbarian times. There are police regulations that protect a man from the attentions of hookers, but a woman, no doubt because she is weaker, is left without protection, at the mercy of accosters. She is asked to contribute to street maintenance, but here she is in enemy territory, therefore she hurries.

In the country it is even worse. On city streets a woman runs the risk only of being followed or insulted, whereas in the country the risks are more serious, and so she does not go out. Let us hope that eventually a bit of awareness will seep into men's intelligence and dignity into their character, and women will learn to defend themselves.

A woman can, in a pinch, go to the theater alone when she has the means to pay for an expensive seat, but she must not think of getting one of the cheaper ones. When it comes to consideration for women, the lower classes are inferior to the bourgeoisie.

I certainly expect to be blamed by "honest people" for demanding freedom for women to go to cafés. They will protest that I am claiming the right to debauchery, but I do not care. Going to a café does not mean one is a debauched person or a drunkard. As long as no other place is found where one can see other people, read newspapers, listen to music, or meet people without having to go through the complicated formalities of an invitation, the café serves its purpose. If men are generally better *informed* than women, it is partly because of the cafés, which allow them to come into contact with one another. Women, no matter how intelligent, remain in the inferior position of isolated persons. But clearly the freedom of going to cafés cannot be made into the subject of a law; it is for women themselves to ensure it by rejecting the prejudice that forbids them to go. Certainly it will take time for women to feel at ease in cafés, but only courage can triumph over public hostility. And men are beginning to get used to seeing women go in cafés for refreshment; little by little they will cease to be astonished when they see them meeting as they do themselves. This is the path feminists should take; they would serve the cause much better this way than by installing female "homes" as they do now, which serve only to maintain women in their original timidity.

When women have conquered the right to a political life, their emancipation with regard to custom will occur more rapidly. The special virtues demanded of them will no longer have reason for being, and one will acknowledge the equality of both sexes in love.

Will men suffer from this? On the contrary. In his *Essais,* Montaigne writes that sexual ties would be the fairest of all if the union of minds were added to the physical union.[3]

Presently, the moral law that forces women who want to remain honorable to be chaste condemns young men to venal love. In order to satisfy their senses, intelligent and cultured men are reduced to the company of ignorant and unintelligent women; they must suffer insipid gossip and pretend to be interested in tedious stories. It could only be to the advantage of both sexes if to merit the title of "an honest woman" nothing more were required than fulfilling the social duties of an honest man.

Notes

1. See also Pelletier's *Le Célibat: état supérieur* (Celibacy: A Superior Status). Compare her attitudes to celibacy with those advocated by Tolstoy, discussed by Lacour in part 5.

2. Pelletier maintained an exceptionally candid correspondence, including the discussion of sexual matters, with the radical feminist Arria Ly between 1911 and 1926. These letters survive in the Bouglé Collection at the Bibliothèque Historique de la Ville de Paris. In those letters, Pelletier discusses such subjects as her choice of virginity, her rejection of both heterosexuality and lesbianism, her criticism of actively sexually emancipated feminists (whom she called "demimonde feminists"), and her belief that such issues should not be raised stridently (as Arria Ly and her mother sometimes did) because she believed that feminism would succeed only through the cooperation of the sexes and the inclusion of women who had chosen motherhood. On the subject of lesbianism, for example, she discussed the repeated allegation that she was a lesbian because she often dressed "en homme" (in men's clothing): "The voyage to Lesbos does not tempt me any more than the voyage to Cythera [the Ionian island famed for its temple to Venus]."

3. The French Renaissance essayist, Michel de Montaigne (1533–92), produced three volumes of autobiographical essays. Pelletier is referring to book 3, chapter 3, entitled "On Three Kinds of Relationships."

5

MARRIAGE AND MALE-FEMALE RELATIONS

HUBERTINE AUCLERT

Hubertine Auclert (1848–1914) was one of the young women attracted to the Parisian feminist movement led by Léon Richer and Maria Deraismes in the 1870s.[1] She had been born into a family of prosperous and politically active provincial landowners. After rebelling against her convent education and her family's attempt to keep her in the convent, Auclert took her comfortable inheritance (sufficient for a moderate middle-class life) to Paris. Richer and Deraismes welcomed her, and Auclert quickly became one of the most outspoken activists of the movement.

Auclert broke with Richer and Deraismes because they would not support women's suffrage, which she considered the essential instrument of the emancipation of women (see part 7). She founded her own small group of militants, known initially as *Droit des femmes* (Women's Rights) and later as *Suffrage des femmes* (Women's Suffrage). While political rights were clearly Auclert's greatest concern, she had quite diverse feminist interests and wrote on hundreds of aspects of complete equality.[2]

One issue on which Auclert held strong opinions was marriage. Napoleon's decree of March 17, 1803, had established his code of the civil law and, in it, the legal inferiority of married women. Eight chapters of that code addressed the laws of marriage; Articles 212–226 formed one such chapter, entitled "The Respective Rights and Duties of the Spouses." These articles, which were read at all French marriage ceremonies, stated such legal principles as "the wife owes obedience to her husband." Auclert had no doubt that such laws made marriage "a perpetual prison" for women, requiring "the annihilation of the personality and the will." She did not denounce the institution of marriage in principle but rejected the form of marriage created by the civil code. "The marriage dreamt of," she wrote, "is an association, in a communion of ideas and feelings, of two beings who possess the same moral and material prerogatives."[3]

Hubertine Auclert lived up to these ideals at a high personal cost. The one man whom she ever loved, a close associate in the feminist movement named Antonin Lévrier, asked her repeatedly to marry him, but she refused. Even when Lévrier's judicial career took him to Tahiti, an anguished Auclert refused to marry. Only when Lévrier learned that he was dying did Auclert join him in a brief marriage in Algeria.[4]

Auclert made her feelings about marriage clear on several occasions. During the celebration of the civil code's centennial in 1904, she tried to burn a copy of the code in a public protest. Earlier, she had used the tactic of attending civil marriage ceremonies (held openly at the Hotel de ville) and urging the newlyweds to reject the code. The following document gives Auclert's newspaper account of such a protest and the legal reaction to her behavior. It is also noteworthy for Auclert's claim to have coined the words "feminism" and "feminists."

Secular Religion

One day I was delegated by a society of freethinkers to speak at a civil marriage. Not having been given any set program, I thought I had *carte blanche,* and after hearing articles 213–214–215–217 of the Civil Code read to the new couple by the mayor, I could not help saying:[5]

> Not to go to Church to have your union blessed is not enough. You must also condemn the text of a law based on the spirit of the Church, which establishes the principle of authority. If you want to be happily wed, treat each other as friends, associates, equals! . . . Do not take into account a law that gravely offends women, treating them as inferior, any more than you did the Canon Law, which urged you to be married in Church.

Source: Hubertine Auclert, various newspaper articles, reprinted in Auclert, *Le Vote des femmes* (Paris, 1908). Trans. Jette Kjaer and Jennifer Waelti-Walters.

Indignant that any corrections should be made to the Code, the Prefect of Seine addressed the following memorandum to the mayors of Paris:

Civil Marriage Bureau

Paris, April 21, 1880

Gentlemen and dear colleagues,

One of our greatest communal concerns has been the maintenance and development of dignity in the civil marriage ceremony.

But, with due respect to the law, it is not enough that the ceremony should take place correctly and in its right and due order. Language that is disrespectful to the law must not be heard in the very place where we come to pay homage to the law.

We want to increase the prestige of civil marriage, yet we allow the legislation by which it is established to be publicly criticized, and this at the very moment when the wedding has taken place . . .

A few days ago, following a civil marriage at the city hall of the tenth district, a person who is much spoken of these days gave a speech. The text itself was unknown to me, but it centered on the inequality between husband and wife, as established by the articles of the Civil Code, these having just previously been read out by the presiding officer.

You grasp, gentlemen and dear colleagues, without my insisting any further, to what extent such occurrences are intolerable.

We have nothing to say about the fact that this person of whom I have spoken develops her ideas at meetings or communicates them to the newspapers. And we do not complain if she transforms them into administrative complaints. Moreover, in demanding to be registered on the electoral lists, in requesting that her part of taxes be eliminated, or in applying for admission onto the recruitment lists, she avails herself, or will avail herself, of a right, and in this there is no inconvenience; competent powers have given or will give a ruling.

But in this case it is completely different. There are no rights, and as for inconvenience, it arises of its own account. Tomorrow we will have someone speaking up supporting ideas opposite to those exposed at the city hall of the tenth district. Then someone else will have a turn; controversies and speeches from different clubs will become common practice in the house of law, transforming it, to the great joy of our enemies, into a place of discord and agitation.

Not everyone has the right to speak at a civil marriage. That should not be forgotten.

The basic condition that constitutes the only real guarantee against unexpected happenings is the continued presence of the presiding officer.

It is important that you should be there and remain until the end, so that, at the first divergence, you can declare the session ended and give orders to clear the room.

Yours faithfully,
F. Hérold
Senator, Prefect of Seine

"The person with whom M. Hérold disagrees," writes *Le Temps*,[6] treating the issue lightly, "is none other than Mlle Hubertine Auclert."

In *Le Mot d'ordre* M. E. Lepelletier writes: "We know it concerns Mlle Hubertine Auclert, who at a civil marriage, instead of confining herself to congratulating the newlyweds on behalf of the organization of the Commission of Freethinkers of the tenth district of which she is a member, apparently spoke on the inequality between husband and wife and criticized the text of the Civil Code, which had just been read out by the presiding officer."

La Justice asks: "What does it matter whether a discourse on the role of women in society is given after a wedding ceremony or not? Has the law been diminished? Has the institution of marriage been affected by these practices? Obviously not."

The furious freethinkers, whom I dared advise to transgress legal dogma, declared that in the future only men would be officiants of the secular faith. Nevertheless, the city halls were momentarily closed to them. It was only two years later that they were allowed to speak in the marriage halls again. At that point, I wrote the following letter to the prefect of Seine, M. Floquet.

Paris, September 4, 1882

Sir,

The newspapers tell me that a freethinker has lectured a newlywed couple in one of Paris's city halls, and I hasten to thank you for lifting the prohibition made by M. Hérold, which was motivated by a short speech that I had made on a similar occasion.

I do not doubt that the freedom of addressing a few words to newly married couples in the city halls, one that I would happily take advantage of, is granted to women as well as men, and *feminists* as well as freethinkers, for it would not be thinkable that freethinkers could go to city hall and criticize the church, on which the spirit of matrimonial laws are based, while *feminists* could not go to the same city hall and criticize the matrimonial laws, based on the spirit of the church.

You, Sir, will not make a distinction between those who attack the cause and those who attack the effect. From the moment advocates of free thought could speak out, supporters of feminism have had the right to speak.

Yours sincerely,
Hubertine Auclert
Director of *La Citoyenne*

In the September 5, 1882, issue of *Le Temps,* the word "feminists" in the letter I wrote to the prefect is emphasized: "Mlle Hubertine Auclert has," they say, "claimed the same rights for the benefit of women, or rather, *feminists*–nice word–as those assumed by freethinkers. Indeed, why do not *feminists* take advantage of these occasions for preaching their particular dogma?"

The words "feminism" and "feminists" have been used ever since.[7]

Notes

1. In addition to the full-length biography of Auclert by Hause, *Hubertine Auclert,* see the discussions of her in Bidelman's *Pariahs Stand Up!* 106–54, and Edith Taïeb's preface to her edition of Auclert's articles, *La Citoyenne: Articlesde 1881 à 1891,* 7–53.

2. For the range of Auclert's feminist thought, see appendix 1 in Hause, *Hubertine Auclert,* 221–36, which gives the titles of her 171 signed articles in *La Citoyenne* (1881–91), her 413 signed articles in *Le Radical* (1896–1909), and 120 other articles. These essays constitute a small encyclopedia of the feminist concerns of the belle époque.

3. See Hause, *Hubertine Auclert,* esp. 94.

4. Auclert kept an intimate diary that recorded her feelings on these subjects; see Hause, *Hubertine Auclert.*

5. The text of these articles, in force between 1803 and 1942, read:

"Article 213: It is the husband's duty to protect his wife, the wife's duty to obey her husband.

"Article 214: The wife is obliged to live with her husband and to follow him wherever he thinks it advisable to live. The husband is obliged to welcome her and to provide her with all the necessities of life, according to her right and status.

"Article 215: The wife cannot appear in court without the permission of her husband, even though she be a public merchant or have a separate estate. . . .

"Article 217: The wife, even under a separation of property agreement [*séparation des biens*], cannot, without the collaboration of her husband or his written consent, give, transfer, mortgage, or acquire [property] whether it be free or subject to payment." Translation by Steven C. Hause.

6. *Le Temps* was the detailed, gray "newspaper of record" in late nineteenth-century France, comparable to the *Times* of London. It was moderately liberal republican in tone.

7. For Auclert's claim to have coined these terms, see the discussion in the introduction; Karen Offen, "On the Origins of the Words" (or the French version, in *Revue d'histoire moderne et contemporaine*); and Hause, *Hubertine Auclert*, 90–91.

LÉOPOLD LACOUR

Léopold Lacour (1854–1939) graduated brilliantly from the *Ecole normale supérieure,* the training ground of the French academic elite during the Third Republic.[1] He then spent several years teaching history in a succession of provincial posts and finally at the highly regarded Lycée Saint-Louis in Paris. Lacour later abandoned teaching to devote himself full time to a career of letters. He wrote plays and a variety of criticism, sociology, and history.

Lacour, an ardent socialist and feminist, chiefly developed his social analysis in *Humanisme intégral,* published in 1896. His feminism was not a mildly sympathetic feminism but a vigorous body of thought that won the praise of his contemporaries in the women's movement. Harlor, for example, wrote that "Léopold Lacour did not enter the tournament just to demand a modification of our laws and customs; but rather . . . a total enrichment of the female individual, the right to life of the highest order and the duty to raise herself to that."[2] His writings have recently won praise for pioneering the historical consideration of feminism.[3]

Humanisme intégral is a treatise of social morality and psychobiological philosophy whose main theme is to unite the two sexes in harmony, strength, and equality. It is a dense work of elaborate arguments that are difficult to excerpt. The following opening portions of the book give glimpses of what Harlor saw in his male feminism, of his commitment to the emancipation of women, and of his central belief that the future of successful male-female relationships was predicated on this emancipation.

Integral Humanism

In recent times, Tolstoy only, in his *Kreutzer Sonata*, strong in his own un-compromising Christianity against the flesh, has dared bring down the heaviness of *sin* on man.[4]

We shall come across this major work in the following two chapters. But we are already made aware of it as we consider these two broad views:

1. A Christianity that holds the chaste celibate as its ideal cannot consider marriage, if it is followed by sexual involvement, as anything but a "fall."

2. Within marriage itself, woman is bonded through love. She is an in-strument of pleasure for the man, whom she has no doubt made an effort to seduce, and can set herself to enslaving, depressing, and degrading by intox-icating him with pleasure or by demanding her price in various currencies (honor, fortune, intelligence, etc.). But man, being the master, remains the guiltier of the two.

This non-Biblical and non-Catholic viewpoint, by which the great writer distinguishes himself from the Church Fathers, even contradicting St. Paul, turns to feminine advantage the all-too-true idea of an eternal struggle be-tween the sexes.

"Despite everything," Tolstoy declares, "the essential point has not changed. Woman is still an object of sensuality and she knows it. This is like slavery, for slavery is nothing but the exploitation of some people's work for the enjoyment of others." Further on: "She is always the humiliated and cor-rupt slave, and man always remains the debauched master." Still further: "Observe that animals mate only to reproduce their species, whereas the ig-noble king of nature mates at all times. And as if that were not enough, he raises this monkey pastime into an ideal! In the name of love—this filthiness—*he kills half the human race*. In the name of his own pleasure, he makes woman, who ought to be his helpmate in the progress of humanity toward freedom, not a help but an enemy."

Strong words of tremendous significance.

It goes without saying that, not being a Christian, I will set aside the *hu-manist* condemnation of physical love. But love must be free for *every human being, not an economic or lawful restraint*. Physical love that is forced is called prostitution, in marriage as elsewhere. That said, and I will insist on it in several places, I commend the thesis:

Source: Léopold Lacour, *Humanisme intégral* (Paris, 1896), 13–14, 18–21. Trans. Jette Kjaer and Jennifer Waelti-Walters.

Woman is man's enemy, but that is man's fault.

Being corrupted, she is capable of corruption and certainly does corrupt (that is her only means of action in her servitude, and that is how this slave-queen often rules). But who, if not man, wanted and still wants her so, for his own enjoyment? [. . .]

This is humanity's worst misfortune until now (except in the United States, which is a privileged land for women, and to a certain extent in England, where the work of emancipation is making good progress). Yes, it is most unfortunate that not only did man have to make his way alone through the rough paths of civilization, but with every step he had his natural ally, his partner by divine right, against him. And for this he has only himself to blame.

For centuries there would have been much greater justice and much less misery on this planet—there would have been many fewer wars—had woman been promoted by Christianity to the dignity that we are starting to claim for her today: that of being equal to man.

All of the great, social evils that have tormented us, from the economic struggle to European militarism, we really owe to the persistent battle of the sexes. I will prove it.

It is sufficient to have established briefly in these introductory pages that this battle—bemoaned by poets, novelists, and playwrights and complained of by worldly men, the middle classes, the workers, even the peasants, when they suffer because of it, which is often—is man's fault; that it remains necessarily *man's crime;* that he wanted it, and still wants it, because of an aberration of pride aggravated by a keen sensuality. Now, I repeat, it is as various as human life itself; for it is a social crime, as well as being intellectual, sentimental, and sexual. (If it has always been that way it has become even more so in our contemporary society, in which the working woman finds herself in conflict with the working man, the female doctor with the male doctor, etc. And all this as a result of economic laws that woman cannot be blamed for and that she would help man destroy if he could understand that his interests are not separate from her's, the two sexes being neither more nor less victim of these laws.)

I should add that despite the violation of rights caused by men and this whole system of injustice to which, through miraculous endurance and energetic reaction, woman has not succumbed, she was never entirely the enemy, but rather very often she was *still a friend: a tender, devoted, extraordinarily good, compassionate, and noble creature,* man's rival in heroism and his superior in love and charity.

Human history is so horrible; humanity, in the past and present, so ugly; and the battle of the sexes so dreadful that we evoke with delight these pure, and sometimes sublime, images.

Woman, the greatest victim of all time, *oppressed, even by the most oppressed, and still more so in the suffering classes,* has throughout the centuries, in all classes, been the highest image of Moral Good.

There have always been women, everywhere, who have loved with their entire being, who have been wholly love. They have made a religion of sacrifice; a lasting vertigo, I would gladly write. There have been daughters who were marvels of piety; mothers who cannot be praised fittingly enough by words in any language; heroic wives who are truly saints; tender, motherly sisters of passionate goodness. You also, who are extending yourselves beyond the family, beyond the love of one or several human beings, have embraced the whole of humanity with your fervent love, trembling with exhilaration, hope, or pity for just causes. If the dust of all such loving women could be stirred up, their revered ashes would tell us their numbers and they would strike the universe with admiration and, I hope, fill men with repentance!

Notes

1. For the *Ecole normale supérieure* and its role during the Third Republic, see Robert J. Smith, *The Ecole normale supérieure and the Third Republic* (Albany, 1982); Jean-Noël Luc and Alain Barbé, *Des Normaliens: Histoire de l'Ecole normale supérieure de Saint-Cloud* (Paris, 1982); and Hubert Bourgin, *L'Ecole normale et la politique, de Jaurès à Léon Blum* (Paris, 1938).

2. Harlor, "Léopold Lacour," in *Les Célébrités d'aujourd'hui* (Paris, 1911).

3. Klejman and Rochefort credit Eliska Vincent with creating *"le féminisme historique,"* but they state that "Léopold Lacour is without a doubt the first to undertake an historian's examination of feminism" (*L'Egalité en marche* 118).

4. Count Leo Tolstoy (1828–1910) wrote *The Kreutzer Sonata,* a novel of startling social criticism, late in life to dramatize the mystical form of primitive Christian moralism he had developed. It is the story of a Russian artistocrat, Vasila Pozdnishev, who confesses the murder of his wife in a fit of insane jealousy. The point of the story was to attack the idea that sexual relations were a healthy part of life. Even sexual relations within marriage (and indeed marriage itself), Tolstoy contended, are wrong for true Christians.

LOUISE-MARIE COMPAIN

The novel that established Compain's career, *L'Un vers l'autre,* focuses on the subject of marriage.[1] It opens on the eve of Laure Prevel's marriage to Henri Deborda, when she suddenly realizes that she is going to promise to obey him. She is hastily reassured by the people around her that this is traditional but that the vow no longer has any significance. Gradually, however, Laure realizes that Henri does not see her as his equal.

The excerpts presented here show trouble beginning when Laure arranges to go once a week to a choir for working girls without consulting her husband first. Henri supports women's independence, but not for his wife. A little later, she is pregnant, and he takes it upon himself to say (without telling her) that she will not go to the choir anymore. Laure becomes furious; they quarrel; she leaves and subsequently miscarries. The translation given here also includes Laure's reflections on the power relations within her marriage, her realization of how Henri uses lovemaking to his own ends, her explanation of their situation to her father and stepmother, and her confrontation with Henri when he comes to fetch her back.

Later sections of *L'Un vers l'autre* show Henri spending time with his tyrannical father and coming to understand Laure's complaint better. While Laure is studying and teaching at the normal school (see part 2), Henri becomes lonely and has time for reflection. These experiences make it possible for Henri and Laure to reunite at the end of the novel, starting a new marriage with better understanding of each other, of love, and of partnership. This conclusion led Compain to use both characters in her next novel, *L'Opprobre* (The Disgrace [1905]).

On Equality and Marriage

Although she was sorry to find her husband more selfish than she had realized, upon seeing him so annoyed, she said:

"If you wish, I will go only once every fortnight. Nevertheless, I shall find it difficult, Henri. It is not that I am already getting attached to the new job, but I would not like to think our happiness together is making us egoists. Can you really not spare me an hour a week? You know you make me terribly happy, but I too need to lead a useful life."

He was touched by the tenderness in her voice, the look she gave him, and felt ashamed of his own selfishness. Without replying, he gently squeezed the yielding arm leaning against his.

"Besides," Laure added affectionately, "I won't do anything without your consent."

"I should think not," he replied, the tone of his voice becoming suddenly dry again.

She felt hurt and regretted her gentleness. However, since they had arrived in front of their house and Henri was leaving her for a moment to fetch some books, she withheld the answer that came to her lips and instead said smilingly:

"See you later; don't be gone too long."

But once inside, while changing into an elegant housedress, she wondered why her husband, who spent such long hours away from her, in his classroom or at his desk, did not welcome the idea that she devote some time to work he praised himself. Ah, no doubt it was because of his love for her that he wanted her always by his side. And wasn't he the source of her joy; living for him, remaining close by him even when, engrossed in his intellectual work, he seemed to forget her very presence? She had promised herself not to be jealous of his manly occupation and kept her word; but why wasn't she also allowed access to the world around her? Why wasn't she permitted to give this surplus of energy and love that she drew from their common affection to others, especially the poor? A vague feeling of fear overcame her, a fear that at the bottom of their hearts a secret misunderstanding lay hidden, a difference in the way they loved one another. In Henri's love for her she had come up against something unknown and perhaps even hostile. She could still hear her husband's voice when, out of love, she had been

Source: Louise-Marie Compain, *L'Un vers l'autre* (Paris, 1903), 56–58, 94–95, 102–05, 109–11, 116, 121, 151–52. Trans. Jette Kjaer and Jennifer Waelti-Walters.

ready to subordinate her wish to his. Dryly he had accepted her surrender, as though she owed it to him. She recalled her fears that last evening before her marriage. And yet Henri hadn't at all been her master in any way then, but just an infatuated and passionate lover. She was ashamed of the confused thoughts that troubled her. She knew he had always been fiercely jealous of her independence. No doubt false pride led her to see her friend as dominating and masterful, which he hardly was. His only fault was loving his darling Laure too much. It was she who was wrong. Stirred up by excessive love, her sensitivity and imagination had joined to create illusions out of the almost imperceptible. Quickly she finished dressing, made tea, and when her husband returned ran to greet him with a kiss. [. . .]

But when these first moments of respite had passed, all possibility of medical complications over, they found themselves alone again with their shattered hopes. They felt that the already existing crack in their love had widened, and neither knew the words that could bridge it. Henri was the more resentful of the two. Being more anxious for happiness, he could not accept that his paternal dream had collapsed, and out of his pain came a belief that his wife was totally responsible for what had happened. He blamed her for the worry she had caused him, or rather, he bore ill will against what he called her pride and resolved to master it. This contradiction irritated his instinct to dominate, and, in the name of their future happiness together, he justified wanting to stifle that tendency in Laure, a tendency that he felt was solely responsible for having disturbed the sweetness of their union.

It was not long before Laure noticed that, far from regretting the way his behavior had hurt her and led to such bitter consequences, her husband persisted in his former manner toward her. She guessed Henri's thoughts with all the more certainty since a weakened physical condition had sharpened her nervous sensitivity, but at the same time it had drained her willpower and she suffered without renewed protest. She did not protest when Henri put aside some of the books sent from the library, saying, "These are not for you: you are not to read them." He also gave their maid instructions not to send anyone up for several days, although Laure had expressed a desire to receive calls. And it was he who decided the days she would get up and the time she should go back to bed again. He was aware that these minor acts arose not out of a feeling of reciprocal power that comes with a certainty of love but from a need to assert the preeminence of his will. He would open Laure's mail and read the letters aloud to her, but those addressed to him he kept for himself. Among these minor gestures—for the things that prompted them were minor—this was the only one Laure did not accept. One morning when her husband brought in a letter from her father and was preparing to read it, she stopped him. Taking the already unsealed envelope, she said calmly:

"I think I can relieve you of this service now."

But otherwise, saddened and astonished, she let him do as he pleased. Above all, she was sorry to feel her adoration and esteem for her husband lessening. Had he been different, had he only shown some regret for what had caused their present sorrow, she would have confessed her own fault and asked that they forget each other's wrongs. But she feared too greatly that if she spoke thus from her heart, expressing her regret, he would take it as a first victory, a prelude to those he counted on winning in the ongoing struggle between them. [. . .]

When he had finished reading, he said:

"Hm, your cousin has made herself Professor of Feminism."

"I don't think that's anything to make fun of," she replied dryly.

"Well, I'm not joking. I'm simply making an observation."

"If you call a mother a feminist because she has foresight and takes care of her children's souls while claiming her half of the power and responsibility in their education, then all mothers must be feminists."

"Rarely is a woman capable of guiding her son's education," he said, in that contemptuous tone of voice which exasperated Laure. "And before condemning Avilard we still have to hear his side of it. If he notices his son resists being taught at home and he estimates that, despite its disadvantages, secondary school is in fact better because Madeleine's education is making him soft, that is his right. The responsibility for the future lies with him. Anyway, I'm not trying to make a case for Avilard. He may be wrong. Having a liver complaint, his behavior may be dictated purely by egotism and a concern for his own peace and quiet."

"So in that case Madeleine must subject herself to the will of a capricious human being who is also ill? His judgment may be false, yet he is the master? And she, the mother, must be quiet and yield while her child's morality is at stake?"

"Of course she won't yield. She's exercising her own means of action. She'll bother him about it to such an extent that he gives in, poor man, you can be sure of that!"

"That is what's so humiliating! She is allowed to wear her husband down, but not to intervene like a human being endowed with reason."

"Bah! Your sex has never been known to be privileged with reason. You have other charms."

"Oh," she said indignantly. "What a strange way you men have of combining love and contempt!"

"Who's speaking of contempt? Each sex has its own qualities. Yours is strong enough that you willingly leave to us matters that concern more the intellect than beauty and the heart. It is a fact that, as a result of their education and contact with the outside world, men acquire a more exact knowledge of life. Hence it is only fair that the law acknowledge the father and husband as having the power to direct."

"I am most pleased to hear you agreeing with Avilard; that clarifies for me your feelings on the subject."

"I couldn't care less about Avilard," he continued heatedly, "and neither could you. But what you want to know, don't you, is whether or not I accept all the responsibilities and power of a father and husband! Well then, I wouldn't be coward enough to say no."

"So," she questioned, growing increasingly calm in order to rise above the emotion gaining on her, "according to you I won't be able to raise the children I bring into this world?"

"And you call that reasoning?" he said, getting up exasperated. "My dear girl, get yourself some schooling. You will raise your children, but not alone, obviously! And I shall know how to make the necessary decisions concerning them."

"Against me, even?"

"Against you, if necessary."

"Even if your decisions should break my heart?"

"Do you think me a brute? Am I not allowed to assert my rights without your drawing ridiculous conclusions from them? All I am saying is that if you think you can make me neglect my future responsibilities, you are mistaken."

"Thus, for example, since you are not religious you will no doubt refuse our children any sort of religious instruction."

"Perhaps."

"And if it is my wish that they be taught these things?"

"We shall see. It all depends on the circumstances, on the intelligence of the pastor to whom we must entrust the children. My answer is neither yes nor no."

"But on all serious issues you reserve the right to say yes or no."

"Of course. Not only it is my right, it is my duty as head of the household. Anyway, this discussion is absurd. Because of your pride, the child that was to have been born did not even form in your womb."

It was her turn to get up.

"I thought," she said, "you had felt your part of the responsibility in the accident that occurred. You do not seem very eager to claim it, though the fault was not mine alone. But today it is a relief to think the child was not born, since he would not have belonged to me. No, I no longer wish to be a mother. And it would only have been fair to have warned me of the conditions you intended to impose on me. Had you spoken on the eve of our wedding as you did just now, I should not have married you."

Then, appalled by her own words and covering her face with her hands, she murmured: "Oh! How awful it is to say that to you."

"Yes," he went on, "it is awful how pride drives you to denying your maternal duty and your love . . . for you know you love me."

She wrung her hands, then dully, as if the avowal had been drawn out of her by some mysterious force, she said:

"Yes, I love you."

"And what you just said doesn't make you blush?"

"Blush? Yes, for loving you, maybe." [. . .]

What was this latent contempt that, weighing heavily on her sex, also fell on her? Had she been of a less idealistic nature she would not have suffered from the ills that were merely a possibility, but her constitution was such that she suffered as much from a thought as from its realization. She felt that even if, more often than not, Henri yielded to her advice and influence, she could not bear the existence of an inequality between them that he would be sure to use to his practical advantage. She could no longer deceive herself. She had found herself a master. Didn't he already consider that she belonged entirely to him? She was his in virtue not of a constantly renewed consent but of a past contract. "I have promised to help and protect you, and you have promised to obey me," he had told her one day. To help and protect her? Was she, like a child, so desperately in need of help and protection? Could she not also have used her brain to earn a living? And was her present occupation, that of making a home for the man of her choice, managing his household, providing him with the strength he needed in the outside world, conceiving and raising his children, inferior work, then, the work of a human being who had no opinions or rights?

No sooner had she opened her eyes and seen the life that had previously been hidden by virgin innocence than she saw woman as subject to man. Right from those women condemned by shameful customs to selling their bodies to lawful women crowned with royalty, who, in reality, were nothing but slaves. And as for the woman bound to a man purely by love, her situation was no more enviable; for, subjected to the same duties as a wife, society had no more respect for her. And all in the name of some social convention or other, established by men to make marriage, that disguised slavery, look enviable.

Seeing all this, she felt humiliated in her sex and her own person. Only one woman had ever appeared emancipated to her, despite her ties to a man. She was the director of the Normal School. Was it necessary, then, to be employed, that is, economically independent, to act according to one's conscience? The thought struck Laure and quietly germinated in her mind, together with her growing revolt. What did it matter that facts, though yet hardly serious and still repairable, had testified to the presence of a dominating mind in her husband? After being married for five months, had circumstances brought more serious events than the death of their unformed infant (and wasn't that enough)? Her observation, that the attitude that oppressed her sex was alive in her husband, was enough to make her revolt against him.

And yet she loved him, and (as she dared admit to herself in times of self-examination) there even lived a second woman in her, an accomplice to man, who loved servitude. When they were first in love she had ignored this presence, for her husband was just a lover to whom she abandoned herself. But then one day the serf started awakening from her lethargy. That was when Henri, after having humiliated his wife, made her forget the offence with his disturbing kisses. Since then, with each accepted caress the slave was aroused, though Laure's heart rose up in rebellion. And now the slave lived; it was she who gave in to Henri's words of passion when he showed disregard for women. It was she again who put on all her finery to please him; who accepted, as an offering of love, the flowers and kisses that paid for her submission. So, since she was made like that, so that one look, one word from her husband overcame her rightful revolt, why did she not submit to man's authority? Then she would have been at peace with herself. Which of the two women arguing inside her would triumph? She who wanted freedom, or she who desired subjection? In the midst of this struggle an idea came to her: why didn't she cut the bonds of her servitude, why didn't she try to recover her complete dignity by pulling away from a life that would swallow her up? But quickly she brushed these thoughts aside. To cause her beloved any pain seemed a wicked temptation. Yet, other wives had left their husbands, even after only a few months of marriage. But these were husbands who were unfaithful, who mistreated them, a voice in her answered, a voice that echoed that of society. But a husband who loves you! To leave a husband who wants only to be the master would be insane, and no one would approve of it. [. . .]

"I understand, Henri. My love has become a sign of subservience to you, therefore I am leaving and returning home to my father." [. . .]

"My husband does not consider me his equal and thus denies me the right to control my own life and manage my children. His dogma is that I am radically inferior. This judgment, which I feel hanging over me whatever I do, is causing me too much pain. That is why I have broken the ties that bound me to him." [. . .]

"Will you love me well enough to treat me as your equal?"

"My equal?! Aren't you the joy of my life? Do I reflect upon these vain and childish acts of yours? I love you and I'm yours. I'm asking you to be mine also."

"And tomorrow you will treat me as an inferior again! You will say you adore me and then deny me my most sacred rights. No, be sincere, I beg you. You know . . . you know," she repeated, this time fixing her blue eyes on her husband without fear. These eyes, once so clear, were today clouded with anguish. "You know why I fled from you. And no matter what you may say, you also know that I love you. But even more, I cherish our love and want it to be elevated and noble. I am willing to return to you, but can you promise me that all your pride and unfair contempt are gone? Can you make me the solemn promise that this thing I have read in your eyes will never be there again . . . that you hate it as I do, and finally, that I shall never have to blush for loving you? If you can promise me that, if you can swear that your domineering love will give way to this higher love that I have glimpsed but haven't felt fully with you, I will follow you this instant. But take care, for if you deceive me now, you will kill my love for you. In a word, do you want us to learn together how to love each other differently than in the past?"

"I don't know what you mean. The past was completely happy before you spoiled it with your pride. I love you, you say you love me, let us be happy with what we've got."

"I no longer want to be enslaved by this love."

"What you are saying is nonsense."

"Henri, for the last time, are you offering to love me as you did yesterday?"

After a moment of tragic hesitation between his male instinct and his love, he said distinctly: "Yes."

"Adieu, then" she said as she stood up.

Note

1. See the introduction to Compain in part 2 and part 3, above.

COLETTE YVER

Colette Yver (1874–1953) was the literary pseudonym of Antoinette de Bergevin, later Mme Auguste Huzard. Her family prided itself on its Breton origins, but her father was from Martinique and her mother from Guadeloupe. De Bergevin grew up in France with a precocious interest in literature and later claimed that she had dictated her first novel at the age of six to her thirteen-year-old brother. Whatever the truth of that claim, she did publish a successful children's novel at the age of seventeen.

Yver's first major novel, *Les Cervelines* (The Brainy Ones), appeared in 1903, when she was twenty-nine. The manuscript was read by Auguste Huzard, an editor for the publishing house of Juven, and he later claimed to have married her because of it. While this was probably just a glib compliment, one must wonder about Huzard's motives: the novel examines a brilliant and successful woman and a man who proposes to her, only to try immediately to persuade her to give up all manifestations of intelligence and independence, for love of him. After a trial week of doing housework, she refuses.

In 1907, Colette Yver was awarded the "Vie Heureuse" (Femina) Prize for her novel *Princesses de science* (Princesses of Science), and she subsequently became a member of the Femina Jury. In later years she worked for the Catholic church and for the sick, devoting her writing to religious subjects. Her early novels, however, were quite subversive. They challenged accepted attitudes about male-female relationships and especially about marriage. Nonetheless, all of Yver's heroines after Marceline in *Les Cervelines* accept the societal norm: they give up their own careers to become their husbands' assistants and thus save their marriages. Yver's novels show clearly how such a choice was forced on women by the social pressures of the era and how unfair such a choice is. The following excerpt comes from a novel about women doctors and the state of the medical profession. It shows the double standard for women and for men, and it depicts the permanent tension women feel between career and marriage.

Double Standard: Student or Woman?

"You are speaking that way, Thérèse, because this state of affection is new and unfamiliar to you. You are still too much *student* to be completely *woman*. Little by little love will kill the student in you, and when your feminine soul blossoms, then you will finally understand why I demand that you should give yourself absolutely, without any reservations or ulterior motives. What is more, you will desire and thirst to do so, like a real woman!"

"A real woman? But I am a real woman, I think, and fully so, since I have gained all the intellectuality I could. A half-woman is the one whose brain stays atrophied. And you wish me to belittle myself to that condition? I truly wonder what you could be thinking of, my poor Guéméné!"

"Do you really want to know what I think? Fine. I am a man looking for a companion with whom to share my life, for that is the law, and I need a home and someone to keep this home. Gladly will I slave away all day, paying house calls, auscultating hearts, getting old asthmatics to spit, delivering babies, palpating newborns, and certifying deaths. But on one condition: that once this wearisome part of life that we call a profession is over, I have a pleasant house and a friend to come home to. I want this friend—and perhaps I am being selfish, but I am a man, and a normal one—I want her all to myself. I will not share my wife with everyone else . . . Ha, ha, ha, the doctor's husband, that would be charming indeed!"

He had stood up, pushing his chair back violently, and now he was walking feverishly around the tiny laboratory. All of a sudden, he seized Thérèse by the wrist:

"I am losing you, I can feel I am losing you! Stay, Thérèse . . . I love you

Source: Colette Yver, *Princesses de science* (Paris, 1907), 12–18. Trans. Jette Kjaer and Jennifer Waelti-Walters. Reproduced by permission of the Société des Gens de Lettres de France.

. . . forgive my violence. I have dreamed of such happiness close to you in the traditional intimacy of married life. Do not tell me that it is bourgeois and old-fashioned: the happiness I wish for is timeless because it is healthy and natural. Women were meant to stay at home. We would not be happy, Thérèse, if you had a practice and went around the clinics and hospitals; if the family became a hindrance to you instead of your goal. We mustn't waste our lives or make our home blindly. I appear full of prejudice to you, don't I? Nevertheless, I am no retrograde. I want women to be liberated, lucid, and thoughtful. I am not aware of how my love for you came about. Maybe it grew out of my great admiration for you. In any case, the intellectual equality that shall exist between us seems to me to constitute the best element of our happiness. I like your clear thinking and I am proud of it, but I ask that I be the only one to enjoy it."

Her slightly hardened features and limpid, cold eyes having returned to their usual expression, Mlle Herlinge was ardently contemplating her defense. Softening somewhat the tone of revolt that caused her voice to tremble, she went on:

"Why do you demand of me my whole life, when you would be very careful not to give me yours? I'll explain. Wouldn't you consider my claims excessive—and with good reason—if I demanded that you abandon your career as a token of your love for me? Yet I am a doctor like you; we have studied the same things, and I possess the same diplomas as you do. You are a doctor of medicine, I will be one shortly . . . What difference do you see between us?"

"I see a big difference: the passion that you hide in vain below your calm exterior, the covetousness that the medical profession excites in you. The souls of cerebral women like you, although serene, know nothing but this ardor, but you yourselves are devoured by it . . . and so it must be! Without this violent thirst for science and diplomas—sometimes only diplomas— would we be seeing you transforming yourselves into exceptional beings, exhausting yourselves with studies that exceed your strength, confronting a difficult life, leaving fine traditions, going against the stream of conventions and habit again, with a vigor that is more than masculine? . . . How small is our zeal compared to yours! The career toward which such a vivid 'taste' must necessarily lead you offers itself naturally to young men, and they are plentiful. They can take but a secondary interest in their courses—a walk in the Latin Quarter, several stops at the pubs, have quickly enlightened us in this respect—and become, by force of circumstance, very presentable doctors. In short, men give the necessary time and interest to this profession, as to all others, out of obligation and duty, but they keep to themselves their true personality, which is not completely absorbed by their work. On the contrary, women, with their qualities, aptitudes, weaknesses, sensitivities, and affections, lose themselves completely . . . Look, at my first autopsy, as soon as the lancet had pierced the thorax of the corpse, a soft thud on the stone was heard: yours truly had fainted and collapsed like a rag doll. Among my fellow students, many have confessed to having had the same experience, and there are few young students who, at the sight of a human being cut up, have not felt at first a deep sensation of horror. That passes, thank God! . . . Now, I saw you dissect when you started at the Charity. Your hands were steady enough, and you proudly answered my question with: 'I have never flinched before a corpse! . . .' It is a fact that you women are generally composed enough to withstand this macabre scene, and I have noticed that few female students were indisposed in the amphitheater. Thus, although nervous, delicate, and sensitive, infinitely more so than we men, you remain impassive, ignoring the physical repugnance at seeing this foul-smelling slaughter, so strongly are you possessed by your desire to see, to know, and finally, to become a doctor . . . And Thérèse, are you astonished if, at the thought of your becoming my wife, I am alarmed at knowing this sovereign, distorting, and blinding passion is present in your soul?"

Mademoiselle Herlinge, saddened and thoughtful, replied:

"It won't prevent me from loving you well, Guémené."

He answered:

"I would like to be loved by a wife who has given herself completely to her husband, who can comfort, calm, console, or amuse him and who is always there, Thérèse, always . . . The tradition of wives of the past is good, true, and natural. Everything that expels women from the home is bad. Or else, we would have to replace the old marriage theory by some formula or other of heterosexual companionship . . . "

She interrupted him:

"This formula happens to be very beautiful to my mind, Guémené. Don't you find it commendable and useful to unite two equal beings, friends and lovers at once, and solve the misunderstandings in marriage that until now have derived from intellectual disproportion, through learning and the identical functions of men and women? . . . I don't think you are about to deny the equality of the spouses?"

"No, not their equality, but their similarity, Thérèse. I am not saying women are inferior; I find them different. And although all your female-doctor efforts tend to change you into young men in petticoats, by your attitudes, your ideas, even with your science, you remain of another nature than we. A thousand secret tendencies make you dissimilar to those you are copying."

Mademoiselle Herlinge was quietly growing indignant. A scrupulous attention to her dress, of which only a severe bodice of gray silk could be seen underneath her white coat, belied any ridiculous tendency toward masculinization. She sincerely denied the superiority of men but felt vaguely that they had preciser minds, firmer wills, and bolder ideas. Men and women were equal in intelligence and morally of the same worth. But he attributed the highest speculations of the brain and possible genius to men, while recognizing above all the emotional and sentimental superiority of women. But in speaking of female students as "young men in petticoats," he had at least been unfair to this one.

"We are not little schoolgirls," she continued.

"That doesn't make you any less women with an eternal function to perform. The great feminine vocation calls all of you with the same strength; young, naïve women, or learned and reasonable ones. And you have the same dedication, the same nurturing instincts in your blood, Thérèse; nature made you women before you chose to become doctors!"

"Oh! How well you have inherited from your Breton stock that intolerable respect for routine, my poor Guéméné! Well, agreed! Let us leave women in the kitchen or with their needlework, and let us, above all, bolt the door so they stay at home where they belong. But tell me, what will you do with the vast army of girls without dowries, stuck in this home that you won't permit them to leave, and where you know very well, however, that suitors won't come to claim the honor of looking after them? They will quite simply die of starvation, my dear, thanks to your fine theories."

Note

1. For more on Yver, see Waelti-Walters, *Feminist Novelists*, 107–18.

6

ISSUES OF
MATERNITY

MARCELLE TINAYRE

In part 2, Marcelle Tinayre depicts an ideal education for women. A young woman, Hellé, recalls her "second birth," when "books expanded my universe." Tinayre set that description in a novel about the psychology of love, *Hellé* (1899), and her subsequent novels further explored that theme.[1]

The novel that set Tinayre's reputation and led to her being nominated for the Legion of Honor appeared in 1905. *La Rebelle* (The Rebel) is the story of Josanne Valentin, who works for a woman's magazine, *Woman's World*. At the beginning of the novel, she has a sick husband and a little boy who, unbeknownst to anyone, is the son of her lover, Maurice Nattier. In brief, the novel tells of Josanne's husband dying, her lover marrying someone else, and her finding a new love. Josanne becomes friends with, and then falls in love with, a feminist sociologist whose book she has reviewed for her magazine. Noël Delysle, however, has difficulty putting his theories into practice when he learns that Maurice has fathered Josanne's son. Most of the novel is a study of Noël's struggle with jealousy and Josanne's steadfast claim to her right to have loved. It is a very interesting example of a man seeking to change in order to live well with the woman he loves.

La Rebelle also contains several sections that reveal much about attitudes and behavior in 1905. The first of the following scenes takes place at the Blue Villa, a home for unmarried mothers. Josanne and her colleague, Mlle Bon, are visiting there to prepare an article for *Women's World*. Tinayre's description gives a sense of belle époque attitudes to the unmarried mothers in this charitable institution. The second scene shows Josanne musing on the nature of love.

Unmarried Mothers

Blue Villa was a new building. Its walls were too thin, and it seemed like a doll's house, set as it was on a piece of wasteland in lower Auteuil. The garden was new, like the house. In it could be seen countless spindletrees with glossy leaves, four chestnut trees two and a half meters high, and about a hundred stakes that would be trees around 1925.

The architect had been generous with the tiles and shiny bricks for the house, but all in vain: Blue Villa would not be made cheery. It was cold to look at as it stood in the damp wind, stark naked in the stake and rock garden, under the gray sky.

Josanne and Mlle Bon introduced themselves on behalf of *Women's World*. Blue Villa was one of those institutions sponsored by wealthy middle-class ladies that might be spoken of discreetly and decently . . .

The magazine's photographer had already taken some beautiful group pictures of its female founder, directress, and the Committee ladies; of the female doctor, pharmacist, and nurses; and finally, of the female boarders.

"That one there is my triumph!" he had told Foucart. "Not a single one really looks pregnant! . . . I put the fattest and the plainest right at the back, and only the young, nice ones in front . . . Charming!"

Foucart had also asked Josanne to "make the bellies smaller: bear in mind that your article will be read by young girls. They mustn't understand . . ."

Mme Platel, the directress, was still a young woman, serious, mild-mannered, with beautiful, disenchanted eyes; she received Josanne and Mlle Bon in her office. She explained to them the origins of the charity organization and how it operated.

"We take in thirty girls in all stages of pregnancy, and we keep them until the beginning of the first labor pains. Then an ambulance, which we always have ready, conveys them to the Maternity Hospital or Clinic . . . Should an accident occur, our female doctor-midwife looks after them and we have a small nursery all ready . . . We know the name and civil status of our boarders, of course, but they are assured of our discretion; the nurses, and even the supervisors, refer to them by their numbers . . . During their stay, we employ them to do sewing, for which they are fully paid when they leave . . . We also endeavor to lecture them and awaken their maternal instincts. The women from the Committee read to them, give them small lectures . . ."

Source: Marcelle Tinayre, *La Rebelle* (Paris, 1905) 67–76, 209–10. Trans. Jette Kjaer and Jennifer Waelti-Walters. Reproduced by permission of the Société des Gens de Lettres de France.

"That's wonderful," Josanne said, "And the results?"

"Oh, the results! . . . We most certainly have a positive influence on the young women. At the time of their hospitalization they are both morally and physically strengthened. They all declare they will raise their children. But at the Clinic and the Maternity Hospital they are left in the most unfortunate surroundings . . . Other women, the older ones, give them bad advice: 'You are young. You will find someone . . . You mustn't let yourself be burdened with a child . . . I gave all my kids over to the Public Assistance . . .' And the mother who has not yet had time to become truly a mother lets herself be persuaded . . ."

"Often?"

"Too often. They say philanthropists are philanthropists because they are optimists! That's a very naive idea . . . Those people who dedicate themselves to comforting the poor soon learn from their daily experience about the vices, flaws, and ugliness of humanity . . . One must love the unfortunate not because of who they are but despite who they are . . . People who do good must give up their illusions if they wish to persevere in their work. Optimists and enthusiasts, quickly disappointed, get discouraged . . ."

Mlle Bon said regretfully: "Yes, you are right . . . Perhaps we should tire of charity if we weren't sure that it was a way of making restitution, a form of justice . . ."

"These girls you will be seeing," Mme Platel continued, "will astonish you with their carefree air . . . Seduced, jilted, held in contempt, picked up in the street, they are still gay . . . They avoid thinking of the future, the present reassures them. Living together, they become like little girls again, enjoying everything. For a month their thoughts have been occupied with the party we are having for them today . . . This morning one of the girls stopped me on the stairs: 'Is it true we're having sweet buns Ma'm?'–'Yes!'– 'Oh, what luck!' She danced with delight, stomach and all . . . And if you knew her story! A girl of nineteen, plain, redheaded, and pockmarked, who limps and until recently was employed by a wine merchant in Javel . . . they sent her to us bruised, in rags, and almost starving to death. To my first question, she answered: 'The father o' me babby! 'Ow showd ay knaw, 'ow showd ay knaw?' But finally she said, 'Eh, well . . . Ay 'av me suspicions 'bout a certain M'sieur Camille! . . .' "

"Are there many servants among your boarders?" Josanne asked.

"Yes, many . . . young maids, victims of the sixth floor . . . But we also have factory girls, shop-girls, teachers even! . . . Some have remained pure in mind, those who were truly surprised by the man's aggression or who yielded out of love. There are such poignant cases of misfortune! . . . Oh, ladies you must speak and write about it, shout it out loud; it is impossible to pity a woman too much . . . No matter how low she falls, man is almost always responsible for bringing about her descent . . ."

"Why do not talented, well-known women who have a public and who write books do more to defend other women?" said Mlle Bon. "People who belong to High Society and the middle classes hardly read *Women's Support,* and it won't be in *Women's World* that Josanne will be able to express her opinions honestly . . . M. Foucart wants charity to be discreet, unhappiness veiled, and suffering, death even, to retain a 'slight Parisian flavor.' "

Mme Platel suggested visiting the house prior to the party. They went through the white dormitories, the dining hall with its parallel rows of tables, the infirmary, the kitchens, and the large common room where the boarders were waiting.

There were thirty girls seated on straw chairs, like in church. The brown, cotton flannel uniform with its straight top and dark skirt accentuated their disgraceful bodies, and the all-too-white bonnets made their sallow foreheads look dirty . . . Dressed as they were and all lined up, they no longer seemed to be women—only females, a lamentable herd of females . . . In the severe winter light, which is so ruthless to faded faces, it was necessary to look at them for a long time to distinguish any traits of beauty.

"Where's Number Nine?" the directress asked, "I don't see Number Nine . . . She isn't in the infirmary?"

"No, Ma'm," several voices answered, "she's right over there, in the corner . . ."

One of the supervisors called out, "Mme Nine! . . . Nobody's going to eat you, Mme Nine!" All heads turned toward a girl sitting on a small stool in a corner of the room. She had her elbows on her knees, her hands in her hair, and her already advanced stage of pregnancy made her look deformed.

"She didn't want her picture taken! . . . She says she wants to go back upstairs, the party isn't fun . . ."

One of the women started laughing. Another one murmured, "You're difficult! . . . Have you done?"

"Hush," Mme Platel said, "Mme Nine will do as she pleases . . . But M. Bonnafous has arrived, I see. He's out in the garden . . . Come now ladies, quiet please! M. Bonnafous is a celebrity . . . He has performed his tricks in front of Queen Victoria and the Pope! . . . Yes, ladies, he has even made the

Pope laugh! . . . Now, behave properly . . . You would hardly like to offend M. Bonnafous with your chatter . . ."

She pronounced this short speech in a pleasant, soft tone of voice, her sad eyes never altering in their expression. From right to left she went, imposing order and silence. The women shivered with delight when M. Bonnafous appeared on the improvised stage, light as a dancing-master, with his waxed moustache and winning eye. Wearing a frock coat, he looked like the men from fashion illustrations. His voice was suave, his hands, white.

"Follow closely, ladies! . . . Follow closely! . . ." he announced. "With one hand I take the ball, like this . . . And with the other hand, I take my hat. Are you following me, ladies?"

They followed him—he was so handsome! The balls flew by, the cards flipped through his fingers. And from his silk hat, tricolored ribbons and five-franc pieces came out by the dozen . . . The maids and the factory girls, all their sorrows forgotten, gazed with wide eyes and gaping mouths at this M. Bonnafous who had made the Pope laugh!

"They admire him," Josanne said to Mme Platel, "not so much for his talent as for his fine physique . . . They see in him their ideal: the well-set, distinguished gentleman who knows how to 'talk to ladies' . . . Look how their eyes shine in adoration! Each one believes she has rediscovered in M. Bonnafous a feature of the lover who ruined her." She spoke with an irony and bitterness that shocked Mme Platel.

"You are being very hard! True, M. Bonnafous represents a mediocre ideal, but one has the ideal one can. It's very nice to have one at all. The girl who had her 'suspicions' about a M. Camille had no ideal, you may be sure of that . . . Worldly women or common girls, we all cling to the charm of a glance, the sound of a voice, words of tenderness . . . and we think this is true love . . ."

Her beautiful, disillusioned eyes were looking back to memories of long ago. She placed her hand on Josanne's:

"Love's illusion, as you well know, dear Madam . . . for which we suffer, we die . . . Sometimes love, real love, crosses our path and the mirage vanishes . . . but by then it's too late . . . We are old . . . And we have loved only appearances, words, gestures . . ."

"She too! . . ." thought Josanne.

M. Bonnafous no longer seemed so ridiculous to her. Rather, he became a symbol . . . dominating the women, with their enraptured eyes, their childish minds, and their servile hearts . . . And again Josanne rebelled . . . Deep

in her soul she said, "No, not I! . . . I am not like the others." But her conscience protested, "You're lying . . ." This rebel, this emancipated woman,
was like the rest. She had clung to "the charm of a glance, the sound of a
voice, words of tenderness . . ." She had believed, she still believed, that was
true love . . . Yes, when close to Maurice she had been just as weak, just as
cowardly as these girls close to their seducer, be he shop-assistant, office
worker, or clerk with a fine moustache . . . Like these girls, she too had
known the fear of possible motherhood, the terror of certain motherhood.
She had counted the days. She had secretly hoped that nature would be an
accomplice and destroy the unsuspected seed . . . Later, when overcome by
nausea and her belt already pressed tightly against her painful womb, she
had suddenly seen the selfish brute in a man who has been satisfied . . . She
had been forsaken, like these girls. And, less fortunate than these girls, she
had been forced to lie and to deceive . . . Ah! How fiercely she had called
upon death during the agony of her pregnancy, right until the pains of childbirth! . . .

And she had forgiven, she had not stopped loving, she still loved . . .

Why? How? . . . Her love was not a sensual passion, blinding her, yet she
was unable to picture Maurice without feeling a thrill run through her
whole being, her knees becoming weak, her heart missing a beat.

Ah, yes, Mlle Bon was right. We all wish to serve, need to love and to suffer for the one we love, need to obey, need to forgive . . . As long as we love,
we are all helplessly indulgent . . .

She looked at the heavy bodies underneath the brown jackets, the faded
faces under the white bonnets, and she felt very close to those poor women.
She was their sister in suffering, shame, weakness . . . a poor woman . . .

She felt pity, pity for herself, the women around her, and all women pain-
fully giving birth, whose loud cries of motherhood echo throughout the
world every hour of the day and night . . .

The conjuror was juggling now. He unfolded fans and lit candles . . . The
spectators laughed. Some of them secretly examined the lady from the newspaper. She was so white beneath her black toque . . .

Finally M. Bonnafous finished gesticulating. He smiled, bowed, and
seemed to disappear himself . . . Eyes searched for him . . . Wasn't he coming back? . . . No. He had gone, vanished like a beautiful dream.

Tired of sitting, the women got up and surrounded Mlle Bon and Mme
Platel. Some of the supervisors brought baskets with cakes and oranges.
On a table at the end of the room were bowls steaming with hot tea and
chocolate.

"Mme Five! . . . Mme Twenty-two! . . . Over here . . ."

"No, I don't want a bun . . ."

"How about a biscuit? . . ."

". . . I've lost my appetite for ham . . . and sandwiches too . . ."

"It's really a feast today!"

Josanne, sitting in a corner, took notes. Suddenly she felt her chair move. Someone was leaning on it from behind. A voice stammered anxiously:

"Madam, oh please, madam . . . Don't say anything about me."

It was "Mme Nine" who was beseeching her. Perhaps twenty years old, she had a small, pale face covered with freckles, blue eyes, and ashen hair.

"Write about you? And why should I, my dear girl? . . . I don't know you, and even if I did . . ."

"It's just that they told me: 'you mustn't trust journalists . . .' I had a friend once . . . She was in the hospital . . . in Lourcine . . . Well, a journalist came, in connection with an inauguration . . . He spoke to her . . . He seemed all right . . . Well then, afterward he put her name in the paper: 'Ernestine . . .' You know, that isn't very nice . . ."

"You can rest assured. I won't even mention Mme Nine."

"Oh! You are kind!"

Josanne smiled at her naive praise.

"I myself have a little child," she said. "And I understand the sorrows and difficulties of other women because I am a mother. I feel sorry for every single one of them. I would never write a word that could humiliate them . . . On the contrary! . . ."

"Oh, but that's different! . . . You are a respectable lady! . . . You are married! . . ."

Mme Nine looked at the gold wedding ring on Josanne's finger, wondering humbly how a "respectable lady" could compare herself to her, an unmarried mother . . .

Josanne's pale cheeks grew red and hot: "Oh! I . . . I . . . ," she murmured.

The thick swarm of girls buzzed around the cups. Through the tall windows the clear, harsh daylight softened to a bluish hue . . . Perching on a chair, a servant lit the gas lamp, giving everything a new appearance.

"I have twelve vouchers for baby garments to give out . . . to the best behaved!" Mlle Bon was shouting. "And five francs bonus to all those who will nurse their babies."

"I will, ma'm . . ."

"Me too . . ."

"I can't . . . My grandmother is taking the child . . . in Limousin . . ."

"What about you, Mme Nine?" Josanne asked.

"Me? . . . I don't know yet . . . I've got to work . . . And considering the petty life he would have, poor little fellow, I had better . . ."

"Oh! Don't say that!"

The two women looked at each other. What common and heart-breaking drama was told by those faded blue eyes and the drawn mouth!

"I didn't want any children . . . The father left . . . I thought of nothing but him . . . him . . . all the time! And not a penny . . . no work . . . I have nothing to hide. I tried everything . . . everything . . . Some people say that's wrong . . . They should *be* in my place . . ."

Josanne understood—everything! . . . the herb teas recommended by old gossips, the secret visits to the herbalist, the local abortionist . . . everything! . . . She guessed the tremendous courage of the woman fighting against herself, both victim and executioner.

"Poor thing! . . . Poor thing! . . ." she repeated, taking hold of Mme Nine's hand and speaking compassionately and very gently . . . The gas valves whistled . . . They heard the roaring of the stove. Suddenly one of the boarders started to sing, her fresh, frail voice trembling slightly as it drawled . . .

> Let us take short steps, together
> Down the paths of rapture

This ballad, heard for twenty years from thousands and thousands of lips, bellowed in squares, workshops, trains, and under Sunday bowers, retained its hold on popular sentiment . . . For a moment the women collected their thoughts, forgetting the cake and their full cups, and lilacs blossomed in their memories, mingled with the smell of a past love . . .

"Listen, my poor little one," said Josanne, "since you like me and are not afraid, listen to me . . . I do understand you . . . I pity you with all my heart . . ."

"Madam . . ."

"You bear a great sorrow, I see, a great shame . . . And you are especially afraid of the little one who is coming . . . He is in your womb but not yet in your heart . . . You cannot love him yet . . ."

"That's so true, Madam . . . Oh! Madam . . ."

"Do not hide your face . . . I'm talking very gently to you . . . One mustn't feel ashamed, you mustn't feel ashamed . . . It is not a disgrace to love, even when one makes a mistake. It is not disgraceful to have a child outside of wedlock . . . It is disowning the child, abandoning it, that is disgraceful . . . The man, the father, he is the disgraceful one . . ."

The singer was sighing:

O mistress mine, I want to offer you . . .

Outside night had fallen. A tram rumbled, rolling all the sounds into its thundering, which increased, diminished, and was lost in the distance . . .

The women took up the chorus:

O mistress mine!

"We give everything we have to our children," Josanne said, "without asking for anything in return . . . They are our pride and glory, our revenge . . . They can console us for lost love . . ."

Mme Nine lowered her head. She was crying.

"It's too little!" she said, "And it just lets itself be loved . . . And I need someone to love me." [. . .]

Patient, submissive, and attentive, Josanne created around Noël a smooth pattern woven from the habit of love . . . And soon he was hers, as she was his. He loved her with all the desperation of his youth, without reserve, caution, or modesty . . .

And Josanne, with naive wonder, cherished him more and more. No longer was he her friend, he was "her man"—as Tourette had so expressively put it. And she was moved, musing over this new tie that united them, this great and sweet mystery from which they both still drew as much emotion as pleasure.

"A master? . . ."

The word came to Josanne's mind again a few hours later, at Noël's apartment. She was doing her hair up again, sitting in front of a console that supported an old mirror. In the oval frame of the mirror she saw the big brass bed with its shiny knobs, the slippery, yellow silk quilt, Noël, tilted back in an armchair with a cigarette between his lips . . . The golden light filtered in through the corn-colored blinds. On the unbleached linen on the walls, old English prints in brilliant red and sharp greens represented a hunting scene. A harsh aroma of Russian leather, lavender cologne, and Virginia tobacco permeated the masculine room. It was sober, clear, free of knickknacks or frills, and furnished with brass and varnished wood . . .

Josanne liked this room, the furniture, and the smell. She liked the objects handled by Noël, his clothes, and the air he breathed. And looking at him out of the corner of her eye, in the slightly greenish mirror, she thought with delight: "My master! My beloved master! . . . I have only one wish, and that is yours . . . I am but a thing, a very tiny thing in your dear hands. We both want me to be your respected equal in the eyes of the world, in view of your reason and friendship. But the rebel rebelled against an unjust society, not nature; she did not rebel against love's eternal law . . . She does not push away the tender, joyous, noble, and voluntary servitude that, having been consented to, is not humiliating. I like calling you 'my master,' really, because you are strong, clear-sighted, and good; because, although I am able to live alone without your help, it is much more pleasant to live close to you, with your assistance . . . And I even—I'll never admit it!—like being afraid of you—a little, very little!—and to have you in my power sometimes, so weak, like a beautiful wildcat that I have tamed, but that could roar and devour me, were I mean . . ."

"And that doesn't keep me from being a feminist and claiming my right to freedom, justice, and happiness . . . You know very well, my darling, that if I wanted to belong to no one but myself—it was so that I could give myself all the better to you!"

Note

1. See Waelti-Walters, *Feminist Novelists*, 31–53.

LUCIE DELARUE-MARDRUS

Lucie Delarue (1880–1945) was the sixth daughter of a Norman lawyer.[1] In 1900 she married Dr. Mardrus, the French translator of the *1001 Nights;* she left him in 1914. Although she is primarily remembered as a poet, Delarue-Mardrus was also a novelist and a dramatist, in addition to devoting herself to painting, music, and Arabic. She was one of the members of the first jury for the "Vie Heureuse" Prize, which subsequently became the prestigious Prix Fémina. In 1936 she was the first recipient of the Renée Vivien Prize for poetry. She spent much of her life traveling extensively, lecturing in Europe, Brazil, and the United States, but she died in poverty, making a deathbed re-conversion to Catholicism.

Marie, fille-mère (Marie, the Unmarried Mother [1906]) was Lucie Delarue-Mardrus's first novel. In it, she opposes maternal love to sexual passion, suggesting that a woman cannot love both man and child but must choose between them. Marie, a country girl, falls in love with a man who rapes her, becomes pregnant, and must run away to Paris, where she works in terrible conditions. After the birth of her son (Alexandre), she is obliged to allow her brother to raise the child as his own, although the boy always prefers his "Aunt Marie." In the second part of the book, she is courted by a Sicilian who becomes jealous of her affection for the child, whom she has now claimed openly; in his passion for Marie, he kills Alexandre. Marie's suffering, her feelings, and her situation are developed strongly, with technical nicety, in both sections of the novel.

The most interesting parts of the novel today are the description of Marie's rape, her pregnancy, and especially the birth of Alexandre. These passages, which are translated here, juxtapose women's suffering with male control, so that the hierarchy of power in all stages of maternity becomes quite obvious.

From Rape to Birth

The Embrace

Now alone in the pasture, in the gloaming, among the huge haystacks and the hay still lying on the ground like waves, Marie and her lover kiss.

Like Marie, the boy, who has also been stamping down the hay, has wisps of hay in his hair and on his glistening cheeks. Both carry the odor of new-mown hay with them on the whole of their bodies. Enveloped by a mysterious luminosity, they both feel different and closer.

Already breathing heavily against Marie, Budin's son immediately tries to push her down in the hay because his desire cannot wait. Slightly bruised by the hard hands holding her, she laughs like a little girl and thinks this is an amusing game. She resists, turns her head to avoid kisses, then, giving in under a more brutal push, falls backward onto a pile of hay. The boy, following her, lies down beside her. Through the strands of her hair, Marie can see small stars starting to shine timidly in the sky, although the June sunset still lights up the earth as though it is unwilling to disappear. A tender languor overcomes her when she feels her lover's body next to hers. With his face so close to hers, she can see that his blue eyes are just as clouded over as those of the haymakers a little while ago.

A fragrant balminess blows over the young couple, the innocent girl and the boy determined to make love. It is as though the whole of nature were trying to participate in the conception of a new being; the hay offers itself, the shadows conceal, and the fragrance intoxicates.

The potential little boy or girl is thus in the atmosphere and in the complicity of circumstances before it springs forth from the father and is formed within the mother. This may explain the *religiosity* of man, who has always wanted to anthropomorphize nature because he is a product of it as much as of his parents. Animals do not need a special atmosphere to mate.

Source: Lucie Delarue-Mardrus, *Marie, fille-mère* (Paris, 1906), 32–36, 116–33, 134–57, 152–60, 170–71. Trans. Lydia Willis and Jennifer Waelti-Walters. Reproduced by permission of the Société des Gens de Lettres de France.

Now, softly, the young man's hands cover the simple blouse that conceals the small seventeen-year-old breasts, hands that seem to have been shaped on purpose to contain them. Marie is still amused but is puzzled and wants to get up. A commanding arm pushes her back. Marie's heart beats so violently that she can hardly cry out. A lightning revelation shows her the whole drama of love. She understands that man is an animal like other animals and that her gentle lover is going to mount her as she has seen bulls mounting cows in the meadows of her childhood. An immense terror seizes her.

"Let me go! . . . Let me go!" she stutters, her teeth chattering.

She wants to fight back. A hard, clothed shoulder crushes her face. Marie, stifled, brutalized, and reduced to helplessness by terror, suddenly gives a cry more tortured, more indignant, and more terrified than the others. Tears gush from her eyes; her whole body tightens and she braces herself to protest.

The boy is silent, implacable and panting. Marie now cries in impotent rage. Suddenly the shorter and jerkier breathing of her aggressor is added to her muffled moans. Marie is almost quiet, listening to it. A new stupor overcomes her. Is she going mad?

Suddenly the embrace ceases. The boy becomes quiet. The vice is loosened, and Marie, on her back in the disorder of her torn petticoats, is set free. The sunset at the end of the pasture has finally died. Night alone with its many stars reigns over the hay. The boy rises in the shadows.

With a gesture of defeat Marie pulls her dress over her wounded body. A deep pain continues to mortify her innermost parts. Seated in the hay, stupefied, she tries to collect her thoughts. Her blurred eyes look at the night spread before her. She feels her cheeks smeared with tears. Her chignon, half undone, weighs on the side of her temple. A strand of hair falls over her eyes.

After a long time of semi-unconsciousness she pushes back the falling strand of hair, makes an effort, and gets up. [. . .]

Marie at Work

"If only mother could see me! . . . If she could just come suddenly into this old, rat-infested place that they have given me for a room! . . . If only she would open that door! . . ."

Marie, in rapture at this thought, redoubles her sobbing. She stares at the door, which shows faintly in the darkness, as if her mother were about to enter. With what accusing energy would she then tell her all that is being done to her, all the horrors she is forced to listen to, of the despair of having to stay in four small rooms at Billancourt among wicked strangers, and of the discomfort caused by her tightly corseted belly that expands daily! She would tell her of her pain in not seeing the damp meadows, the peaceful cattle, the dry forest in winter; of not hearing the bells of the New Year. She would tell her how she misses the evenings at the farm 'round the candle in its old copper candlestick! . . .

Marie is hypnotized by the door. Her belly, finally liberated from its corset, appears in its maternal fullness, round under the bedsheet. Finally, when she has no more tears left, just as she is about to fall asleep, the door miraculously opens. Marie looks up, panting . . . Her employer appears, a candle in her hand.

Have her experienced eyes finally suspected something? She pounces on Marie before she has time to do anything, pulls back the bedsheet, and discovers the naively obvious pregnancy. Then the coarse voice is raised:

"Ah, ah! . . . I knew it! She's well gone in her pregnancy and she gives herself airs in front of everybody! Honest employers are taken in by her! . . . Such a hussy! Such . . ."

A cascade of insults flows from her mouth. Standing there in her stained silk blouse, she is out of breath, and her painted mouth stutters with anger, while a poisonous look flashes from her mascaraed eyes.

Marie, cowering in terror, tries to hide her offended body. The candle, now standing on the floor, throws great shadows onto the bedsheet. The employer shakes Marie with a furious hand, while the flow of horrible insults continues from her old, rouge-coarsened lips.

"I'm throwing you out," she repeats, fist raised ready to strike.

The other housemaid, the husband, and neighbors have come without knowing why, attracted by the noise. Stifled laughter fills the hallway.

Marie, with chattering teeth and wide-open eyes, dresses as well as she can to leave. While she tries to gather the fair and abundant hair that ripples against the small of her back like a flame, she briefly exposes the floral freshness of her seventeen-year-old body.

Suddenly, her employer has a change of mind, and in a pompous voice, trying to impress the captive audience in the hallway, she cries:

"You don't need to dress, brazen hussy! I shall keep you, out of the goodness of my heart. But you understand that with a belly like yours, you are not worth fifteen francs a month. From now on I shall pay you five francs, and you will accommodate me by squeezing your belly a bit tighter into your dirty corset. My house is respectable, do you understand?"

When Marie falls back onto her bed and looks up at her with the air of a martyred little girl, she adds, while picking up her candle, and with the approval of all those in the murky hallway:

"When you finally feel that your rotten kid is due, you will be so kind as to get out of here and have it somewhere else, is that understood? [. . .]

Anguish

After the lengthy, dark winter, the first signs of spring started to blow over the world and on Billancourt. It was the month of March, and Marie, in spite of the atmosphere of terror and revulsion in her life with her employers and their mean expressions, in spite of the coarseness of the customers who come for drinks and the muted hatred of the other servant, in spite of the suffering of being every day more and more squeezed into the hypocritical corset, Marie felt in her native simplicity that renewal was near.

Was she not herself like a swollen bud about to open in the sun, now that her pregnancy was nearly at term?

Marie, through physical and moral misery, poor food, and excessive fatigue, has already lost her beautiful Norman coloring, which had faded on her wasted cheeks. It looked more and more as though her face had sunken in, as though her vigor and freshness had been sucked away to profit the little one growing in her womb. She experienced a thousand silent agonies, a thousand sinking feelings. Some nights her teeth chattered with extreme pain. When she combed her beautiful auburn hair, strands of it remained between the teeth of the comb. All along her swollen hips, on her tired thighs, a hundred tiny breaking veins had formed a zig-zagging, ugly blue network on her pure and lovely skin.

Through the new painful and drawn mask that life had imposed on her, she looked out with her eighteen-year-old eyes, which were even bigger now and filled with constant anguish. One could say that her whole soul was now concentrated in their greenish glow.

Thus, through an imperceptible process, begun at the start of her pregnancy, Marie's glorious radiance of applelike "little red miss" has faded.

Is virginity the only condition of beauty for the poor? As soon as they have conceived, they do not know how to prevent their delicate bodies and their tender, fragile coloring from being ruined forever. Rich women know how to take care of themselves and remain flowers in spite of childbirth. A deprived girl cannot help becoming the fruit with its inevitable withering corolla. The rose of her youth fades as quickly as roses in the garden.

The first signs of the new season tormented poor, abandoned Marie. A silent restlessness incited her to wander along the river bank when she went for eggs at Mother Delcourt's. Accustomed by now to her employers' perpetual nasty scenes, she became less afraid of lingering on her errands.

The people of the open air cafés and the fishermen had become well acquainted with her familiar figure. She was greeted here and there as she walked with her head down beside the murky water. La Pipe, the gudgeon-fisherman, the manager of the *Père Lapin,* the manager of the merry-go-round, and the athletes practicing on the trapeze all waved to her. She responded vaguely from far off, lips tightly closed, always unsociable. In the arbors, a piano out of tune, playing a vulgar waltz, added its noise to the hurdy-gurdy of the merry-go-round and the grinding of the cranes unloading coal. Dark smoke, drifting up to the sky from the factories, reminded one of fantastic, swaying trees deformed by the wind.

Not looking at the ugly factories, Marie tried to see only the stand of elms, the island of Billancourt far off in the river, and the tarred barges with their green shutters, gay flowerpots, children with smeared faces, and henhouses perched out over the water. In her somber mood she could not understand the joy of those who laughed while eating a paper cone of french fries or a plate of fresh mussels. What Marie was looking for in this landscape was a patch of fresh grass on which to put her tired feet.

Cars passed by, raising clouds of dust. Marie thought desperately of spring in Normandy, when the invading grass covers everything like green snow. If she could only go back to the days of green pastures, the blissful days of her innocence when she was unaware of her own happiness!

Sometimes, when looking at the heavy barges attached to their busy tugs, which breast the small waves of the Seine with their squat shapes, she read the word *Rouen* on their sides. Then tears blurred her eyes because she knew that Rouen was the capital city of her lost province.

One day, while exploring these poor surroundings, she discovered the cemetery and went in because the grass was high and the light was subdued. It was not an old cemetery. A naive, philosophical caretaker, while waiting for the dead, had sown carrots and radishes in the unoccupied spaces.

Whenever Marie was able to escape, she went on her own into this city of threaded pearls of marble and wrought iron, and although Paris was so full of people, she never met anyone.

No metaphysical concept ever struck her simple mind. She did not think, while parading her pregnant body among the dead, that death is the eternal egg from whose ashes the phoenix of life rises, and that her child was cocooned within her like the corpses in the earth. She did not think that the sons of the dead may be the spirits of their fathers . . .

The only thing she could think of was her own cemetery, the faraway cemetery around the small Norman church at home. Her life was so miserable that she even imagined that it might be better to be under the earth than on it, and she often had the wish to die suddenly so that her sufferings could end.

Then she leaned against a tombstone more overgrown than the others, not realizing that the mystery of birth is as inscrutable as the mystery of death. Her eyes instinctively watched the grass growing in the sunshine, while her head, heavy with nostalgia, weighed on her chest.

It was in the growing darkness of the cemetery, full of this nostalgia, that Marie felt the first pangs of labor.

Since early that morning she had been so anxious, somber and ill at ease that she had dared to go out furtively to see her fresh mortuary grass and find some comfort in a little rest and solitude.

Seated in her favorite corner, she distractedly stroked the small flowers around her. Her vacuous eyes looked at the rows of tombstones. There was still some blue left in the sky. Suddenly Marie felt something horrible. Before she could even make a move to get up, her clothes were drenched and clung to her body, and she realized that she was sitting in a puddle of water mixed with blood. Simultaneously, a tearing pain overwhelmed her.

"It's the child coming . . . " she thought, terrified.

She was amazed that this had happened so quickly. She had counted on eight or ten more days.

Not daring to get up because of her soaked dress, she remained on the spot, her heart pounding and her eyes fixed. The pain deep within her increased and advanced toward the small of her back.

"Am I going to give birth in this cemetery?" . . . she asked herself.

She could see herself prostrate on the grass, delivering her child among the tombs.

"This is impossible! By God, this is impossible," she murmured, clenching her teeth.

Suddenly, like an invisible whip striking the small of her back, a lightning pain tore through her and made her cry out.

Trembling, out of breath, she pulled herself together and closed her eyes, as though trying to understand her pain and prevent it from returning.

The dull pain persisted in the small of her back, seemingly creeping toward her backbone.

"I've got to go . . . got to go . . . ," repeated Marie, gasping for breath.

She made an effort and got up. A feeling of shame and the fear of appearing ridiculous in her soaked dress added to her agitation. Fortunately, night was falling. She crept furtively between the tombs, stopping from time to time, afraid that the searing pain would return.

At the gate of the cemetery she was brought up sharply by a similar pain.

"Ah! . . . ," she cried, in spite of herself. Then, driven by the pain, she started to run, and with the instinct of a beaten animal she avoided places with people, hiding so that she could suffer in peace.

Should she send a cable to Aunt Maltide? That would be impossible with her soiled dress and the sudden pains that made her groan against her will. It would be even more impossible to return to her employers. She had been told to get out when she was about to give birth. Where should she go, then; where should she go?

As it is now completely dark, Marie hurries along the sinister-looking river bank. The lights of Paris glow from afar; the Seine is dark; the red reflection of a sleeping barge undulates on the moving black water like a streak of blood.

Marie runs as though pain were pursuing her, then stops. She undoes her hooks and throws away the murderous corset. She does not know where she is going and for how long she has been walking on the deserted bank in her aimless wanderings. She wants so badly just to lie down, but she is alone in the night, alone in the world. There is no shelter prepared for her anywhere in the world; there is nobody to welcome her, to pity her, to hug her at the time when she is about to endure the greatest human agony.

The expected searing pain returns many times. A cry is forced from her throat. In reaction, she feels so truly unhappy, so alone, that she bursts into tears. But now, as the physical pain continues to increase, her tears stop. She seems made of pain, which cries out against the dark sky. Leaning against a tree, overcome and unable to continue her demented wandering, she slides down onto the earth to roll herself around and scream, as though she is going to give birth in the ditch like a cursed animal.

Then an immense anger rises in her. Raging, she thinks of Budin's son, who is not suffering. She thinks of her father, too, who has unknowingly forced her into exile. She even blames her mother for not being with her. Above all, she hates, ferociously hates the child, that stranger who is even crueler than the others, who tortures her body as it emerges.

For a second in the shadow her fist is poised against life, the unknown and suffering. Just as she is finally ready to give up and fall into despair and horror, a human rag, she suddenly hears a sound in the darkness. What is this thin bleating voice, sounding like a call?

It is Mother Delcourt's goat! Marie looks around her and realizes where she is. She is close to Mother Delcourt's orchard. Two steps ahead is the hovel where the goat is kept. Yes . . . no one will come into the garden this late. Yes . . . no one will see her here; no one will follow her.

Gathering all her energies for one last spurt, Marie enters the garden, pushes open the door of the hovel, and falls onto the straw next to the goat she cannot even see. [. . .]

In the morning, the door opens and Mother Delcourt appears with her apron full of greenstuff for her goat. [. . .]

Now one can see the activity around the girl who is about to give birth. Mother Delcourt's servants, having heard of the event, have all come to the hovel to watch. In spite of the early hour, male and female neighbors are already here chattering away. Two gossips talk about their own deliveries long ago.

"Me, I always gave birth with terrible pains in the small of my back."

"Once it took me fifty hours; I was blocked by the cervical bone . . ."

Words are exchanged. Laughter rises, without reason. Seeing and hearing nothing, Marie screams.

Maltide, informed by telegram, came at eight o'clock in a cab to take her niece away.

She appeared suddenly among the group of onlookers, just as a little woman in a hat was self-assuredly proposing to give Marie an injection.

Maltide glared at her.

"What do you mean, an injection?" she asked.

When it had been explained to her, she crossed her arms and said indignantly, "Not as long as I live. Thank the Lord, when I was still out in the country, I helped deliver more than ten women, who all had beautiful babies. I never saw anyone give them . . ."

The last word was lost among the general laughter. A furious Maltide ran toward her niece as though she was going to slap her. Within a few minutes, helped by two neighbors, she had wrapped her in a blanket and put her into the cab. While the coachman whipped his horse, Marie, pale, weak, eyes half-closed, and mouth open, let herself be carried off toward the faraway hospital. She showed no more interest in her aunt's gestures and mean voice repeating over and over:

"Isn't this shameful, isn't this shameful?" [. . .]

The Birth

Marie gave birth at noon.

When the child emerged, she felt something warm and soft against her legs and the shape of a small foot that touched her, the same little foot that had kicked her ever so lightly during her pregnancy.

Now, lying under her sheet, in a chaos of thoughts, she was trying to remember her coming to the hospital that morning, how she was taken out of the cab, put on a stretcher, and with the funereal impression of having been laid out like a corpse, was carried away, to the heavy rhythm of regular footsteps. She still felt impregnated by the pharmaceutical smell that had overcome her while she was being trundled through the long corridors. As she crossed the threshold, between her uncontrollable groans, she had read with terrified eyes the painful words painted on the door: "Labor Room," words that seemed to synthesize the austere duty of childbirth. At that moment a horrible dizziness had overcome her, as though she were standing at the edge of an abyss.

There were too many things that she had not been able to analyze; she had been in too much of a hurry to suffer! She did not even have the strength to be amazed at seeing three other women lying in three beds at that moment, groaning like her, rolling and biting their fists with tears of rage in their eyes, completely twisted in a furious struggle. She did not recoil when being undressed and bathed, even in front of the men who looked at her nudity. She had felt immediately that these hands and eyes were full of science, chaste and grave, and that their actions would assist her in the hard labor of giving birth. She had been reassured and comforted by the austere figures bent over her and by the complicated names they had given to her condition. A young man with serious eyes talked to her while calling her "my little one." She had felt important in her bed, in spite of the other people, the students and young midwives who were discussing their business without looking at her, with an indifference as total as that of Mother Delcourt's goat. She had even heard a nurse sweeping the hall, singing amid the screamings.

Then suddenly she had heard her own groans above the cry of one of the women giving birth:

"Mother! . . . Oh, mother!"

Like an echo, the two other women had joined in the same desperate chorus: "Mother! . . . ," because such women are susceptible to suggestion, and those who go to the hospital cannot help but imitate one another.

Remembering her own lost mother and afflicted by a sorrow even stronger than her pain, Marie started to sob.

These women who called on their mothers for help, these women whom no one consoled in their agonies in that cold and scientific room, a torture room humming with conversation, were they not Marie's poor sisters?

In four beds standing in the four corners there were four creatures lying among the whiteness of the sheets, four creatures lacerated, disemboweled, and torn by inconceivable suffering. A sort of savage passion expanded their chests full of screams, made them turn their heads of brown or blonde hair and roll their eyes, their feminine eyes, in which pleasure or pain both reflect the majesty of death.

As pathetic as love is the drama of birth, in which the female animal is the prey. The pupils of the "wild animal" grow larger under their lids, and gripping hands tried to stave off suffering.

Here they were impassioned victims of the fatality that weighs on their sex and that even the Holy Scriptures have tried to explain. "In sorrow thou shalt bring forth children," they were told at the beginning. Surely it was necessary from the beginning of time to wrap in a religious formula such a revolting happening!

Here was the woman, her forces failing. Her face was covered with sweat, her nose was pinched, her mouth open; and she screamed for help with all her being.

She did not know that within this hospital full of nature's victims there was a classroom where a professor, with penetrating eyes, possessed by the genius of the organizing male, pontificated. In front of attentive young men seated in an amphitheater, he developed his magnificent thoughts on maternity; in gestures quivering with eloquence, he taught them the great physiological poem that he had created as a result of having watched the agony of women giving birth throughout the long years of his youth. He was exalted. He underlined his words with peremptory gestures. Almost religiously, his voice scanned the word he had found: "rhythm."

He says:

"Nature is admirable, gentlemen!"

He says:

"Know that the woman blossoms completely only after the third lactation."

He says:

"A barren woman is a beautiful, empty jewel-case; she is some sort of monster."

Marie, quartered, disemboweled, bleeding like the others, felt that the natural effort she had made to expel the child's head, which was harder than an enormous stone, had tortured her whole body. She had felt hands penetrating her. They had helped her but also had seemed to be twisting her guts. She had felt all this as a monstrous reality in an unacceptable dream.

Now that the last scream had been heard—she had just given birth, the first woman of the four—she closed her eyes, plunged into indifference, into that admirable feminine forgetfulness that instantaneously follows the horror of giving birth. The nightmare was over, the pupils delivered of their agonized expression, and there was rest . . .

She had just started to enjoy her well-being when a voice exclaimed:

"It's a little boy!"

Marie remained stupefied. Had she really thought of this? Suddenly, after this horrible ordeal, the cause of so much suffering and so much shame, here was somebody, a human being, a person. Up to now, far away from the family that usually prepares the baby's layette, far away from all tender care that surrounds a precious pregnant woman, Marie had thought only of herself, always miserable, reprimanded, and alone.

She had not yet had time to recover from her astonishment when a small, sharp, and unusual cry, the first cry of the child still attached to her, was heard in the hollow of her bed.

With a spontaneous, involuntary movement, Marie sat up. Although quickly pushed back by firm hands, she had glimpsed in the puddle of blood a human frog, moving all its limbs and crying lustily.

"Oh," she cried out . . . "Oh, poor little Jesus! . . ."

She put her hands together. A blissful smile lit up her face. The revealing thunderbolt had struck; the woman's still heaving entrails had reacted; the maternal beast had violently awakened. [. . .]

The Ecstasy

Lying in her hospital bed among other women, she recovered from her delivery and her trials. When some memory of the past horrors or some worry about the bleak future touched her heart, she quickly looked at the small bed where her three-day-old son was sleeping, already pink against his white pillow. [. . .]

Small, humble events flitted through her mind. She thought, with a tender smile:

"Any earlier and he would have been born in the straw like our Good Lord!"

Then, with pride:

"Poor little boy! His tiny hands are quite large. He will be a good worker!"

Then, with anxiety:

"What is Matilde going to say next Thursday when she sees him?"

Her confidence in the future returned with her joy:

"I am going to make a living, for sure! Don't be afraid my little Jesus, my baby! I know how to bring you up as well as anybody else . . ."

Then, trying to see him in the shadow, wearing the same expression, an expression without age or race, the expression of a woman who has created a new being, she tried to find a face in the tiny, chubby features of her newborn.

"This little one is an Avenel . . ." she repeated to herself.

In her vanity as a new mother and her rancor as a jilted mistress, she did not want to remember that Budin's son had contributed to her boy's existence.

Her thoughts continued, her breasts swollen with redoubled tenderness:

"Ah, if mother could only see him! . . ."

Her ideas became confused with vague dreams. Sleep overcame her. She had a last glimpse of the tiny bed and the pointed head of the baby outlined on the pillow. Then, weary, happy, and smiling, she fell softly asleep, her heart full of the typical and magnificent satisfaction of the great and calm sensuality of motherhood. [. . .]

Note

1. For more on Delarue-Mardrus, see Waelti-Walters, *Feminist Novelists,* esp. 56–65.

NELLY ROUSSEL

This volume opened with the text of a 1905 speech by Nelly Roussel providing an overview of French feminism. Roussel, like many of her contemporaries in the women's movement, devoted a large portion of her time to one aspect of emancipation that she considered essential. Just as Hubertine Auclert devoted herself to winning women's suffrage (see part 7), Ghénia Avril de Sainte-Croix spent much of her time combating regulated prostitution (see part 4), or Jeanne Schmahl worked single-mindedly to win a married women's property act, Roussel chiefly concerned herself with neo-Malthusianism.

Neo-Malthusianism was the name used in France for the subject of birth control.[1] The neo-Malthusian movement, which sought to inform the nation about birth control and to make contraceptives readily available, originated in the late nineteenth century. Paul Robin (1837–1912), a teacher and the director of an orphanage, started it in 1889 when he opened a center to provide information and to sell contraceptives. In 1896 Robin created the *Ligue de la régénération humaine* (League of Human Regeneration) and a periodical, *Régénération* (Regeneration), to spread neo-Malthusianism.[2]

Neo-Malthusianism was extremely controversial in belle époque France. The French birth rate had been declining for so long that France's bitter rivals, Germany and Britain, had both surpassed the population of France. This produced a national anxiety about the "depopulation" of France, a subject frequently debated in the Chamber of Deputies and the popular press.[3] Viewed in this context, neo-Malthusianism could be attacked as unpatriotic as well as immoral.

Paul Robin, however, believed that contraception gave women control over their own bodies and that it was therefore a necessary factor in their emancipation. Robin could not convince either neo-Malthusians or feminists of this. He attended the feminist congress of 1896 to seek support for birth control, but the delegates loudly rejected his resolution. Throughout the belle époque, the feminist mainstream continued to oppose neo-Malthusianism. Not surprisingly, there was simply no question for conservative Catholic feminists like the Countess Lecointre, but even the non-Catholic moderates of the CNFF utterly opposed Robin and his program, including birth control as well as abortion. The CNFF employed an eminent feminist physician, Blanche Edwards-Pilliet, to speak against neo-Malthusianism.

Seen in this perspective, women such as Nelly Roussel, Marie Huot, Odette Laguerre, and Gabrielle Petit were exceptionally radical feminists, because their decision to champion neo-Malthusianism separated them even from their feminist friends. Roussel nonetheless did not hesitate to agree with Robin; to her, a woman's control over her own body was "an essential condition of woman's liberation."[4] Her lecture tours of the early twentieth century frequently included talks on this subject, including the following translation of Roussel's 1907 speech entitled "The Freedom of Motherhood."

The Freedom of Motherhood

Until now, unfortunately, as a result of human ignorance, repressive measures have been the first and the most powerful controlling force. And if the population has always struggled to remain at a subsistence level, it is because wars, cataclysms, epidemics, and extreme poverty have come along and mercilessly swept away any excess. That is why men have thought for so long that these horrible scourges were necessary and have treated those who spoke of removing them as utopists or madmen. But modern human beings are more aware, more enlightened, more educated about the laws governing them. They understand, finally, that there is quite a simple way of putting an end to repressive measures, which is to render them useless by substituting other measures, preventive ones; in other words, to limit the birth rate vol-

Source: Nelly Roussel, "La Liberté de la maternité" (1907), published in *Trois conférences* (Paris, 1930), 28–48. Trans. Jette Kjaer and Jennifer Waelti-Walters.

untarily. Let us be wise enough not to create in the first place this over-production, which inevitably has to disappear. Let us substitute for natural selection, which is so painful, so brutal, and the source of nearly all the ills by which humanity is afflicted, an artificial selection that we want and create and that is worthy of the intelligent, civilized beings we are.

I hear you replying: "And what about love? What will happen to love, that powerful yearning of the human soul? Love, source of strength, hope, and joy? What are you going to do about it? Do you intend to conquer it?" Far from it; I don't even want to attack it! I am one of those people who believe that everyone has a right to love, because everyone needs love. But love and procreation are not inseparable; love is self-sufficient; it is its own goal, its own reason for being, its own beauty. Love can remain barren, and that is its imperious duty whenever its natural consequences would be harmful and cause suffering to an individual or community. This is where the whole question lies.

It is easy to conclude from everything I have said up to now that voluntary birth control, in which I see our salvation, is not only a provisional measure imposed as a result of present difficulties, but it is one we can dispense with the day we have become better organized. Controlling the birth rate is an urgent and permanent need, and it is an indispensable condition for happiness on Earth. If men want to live in peace as free and good citizens, without wars or masters, *it is absolutely essential that abundance should reign*. It is essential that everyone should have, not only what is necessary, but superfluity and luxury also, so that no one is tempted to reduce another's share in order to increase his own, which he judges insufficient. And the future city of our dreams, that great and just city of peace and harmony, can exist only to the extent that consumers are in equal proportion to the amount consumed. This balance must no longer be established as it was, as it still is today, by the underhand or violent death of superfluous individuals, but by the *nonexistence* of those who *would be* superfluous.

Do not delude yourselves, you reformers and revolutionaries; the social question is one not only of distribution but of production and consumption. And while I do not propose birth control as a universal panacea that alone must solve all our human ills, I am not afraid of affirming that without it all remedies are condemned beforehand to remain inefficient, or at least insufficient.

At no time, in no country, and under no form of social organization will unlimited fecundity ever be possible. For always and everywhere, the suppression of preventive measures will have immediate and fatal consequences: the reappearance of repressive measures; that is, all the calamities we deplore and are working toward eliminating.

But what is the use of expanding on this? What is the use of pausing to demonstrate that fecundity without limits or rules, blind obedience to the reproductive instinct, could never be possible? For, were it *possible,* it would not be *desirable,* and although without inconvenience from a general viewpoint, it remains threatening from a particular one.

The issue we are dealing with is not only—need I say—an economic one. And it is for a woman to uncover the other sides of the problem, those that interest our sex in particular and are therefore all too easily neglected, no doubt.

So, let us assume for a moment that an unexpected growth, an unprecedented growth in our means of subsistence, together with a perfectly equal distribution, momentarily allows the suppression of all measures. Let us suppose for a moment that unrestricted fecundity becomes, at least for a while, *possible.* I have said, and I repeat, it would not be *desirable.*

In their atavistic egoism, maintained and developed by a disgraceful education, men do not reflect enough on the fact that, while freeing the father from the material worries of supporting a family, improved organization would not save the mother from the suffering and dangers of her maternal function. And even under excellent economic conditions, the thought of giving birth unceasingly is not very appealing to our sex. We are persuaded that if both sexes had to give birth in their turn and share the pain of procreation equally, this neo-Malthusian idea would have many fewer adversaries among the male half of the human population. The worst militarists are those who do not serve in the military, and the most ardent repopulators are those who are very certain never to have children themselves. And it is perhaps inappropriate to advise others to expose themselves to danger when one feels sheltered from it oneself.

Oh, I know very well it is common practice to exalt the "joys" of family life. And far be it from me to deny such true, profound, and sweet joys. Several times a mother, I believe I am in a good position to reason about these things. And maybe it is worth mentioning that I do not rank among those who deserve the most pity. And yet, it is maternity that has made family life so pitiful for mothers; for I cannot recall the pain with which my joys were paid, without thinking of all those, alas! who have even more pain, but infinitely less joy.

"The mother" has been much sung and poetized about. To many minds the word evokes the image of a tender and smiling woman, surrounded by pretty children who are sturdy, happy, and affectionate. The picture is charming, but it has one flaw: it lacks a certain realism, and above all, it is incomplete. What we are not shown are the painful and sometimes fatal stages, the rungs of martyrdom that must slowly be climbed before getting there—if one does get there! For all families, unfortunately, do not resemble this delightful group!—What we are not shown are the true physiological states of this idealized maternity. Pregnancy, first of all, with all its discomforts, heavinesses, sudden dislikes, and sometimes physical degeneration, which distances the egoistic male from the poor body, deformed by his handiwork. Secondly, childbirth; that dreadful tragedy that must be lived through to be understood in its unspeakable terror. Thirdly, convalescence; so slow at times, and so difficult for our anemic and nervous city women. Finally, the nights spent by the child's bedside; the worry of every minute, the slavery of every hour. And do you understand how particularly dreadful all this can be when, for some reason, the child in question was not wanted? Or when in her trials, instead of getting support and consolation from a prospective joy, the mother reluctantly undergoes an unexpected maternity that seems a nuisance, perhaps even a catastrophe! Have those who paint enchanting pictures of large families never met women who were worn out and faded before their time from having too many children? Such women resemble less human females than human wrecks, for they no longer have even the strength to make a gesture of revolt by refusing to give their poor, bruised bodies to the brutal and thoughtless males . . . Have they never met mothers who wear a perpetual look of worry and are always bent over their pale, sickly, degenerate child; a child condemned beforehand to every pain because a corrupt, alcoholic, or sick father did not understand he was committing a crime by passing on his miserable life? . . . Have they not seen mothers in mourning, sobbing hopelessly before the empty cradle of one they could perhaps have rescued from death if the overly large number of the rest, all demanding attention at once, had not forced them to reduce the care given to each? . . . Have they never heard of poor girls who have been seduced and abandoned; who, completely alone in their attics, undergo the tortuous suffering without help, aid, or a word of love to console them, without even a comforting squeeze of the hand, while the forgetful seducer, who retained from his adventure only a memory of a moment's pleasure, a memory that is already almost erased, continues to create new victims while quietly enjoying respect in the eyes of the world?

Ah, gentlemen repopulators! If I could show you the letters we, Malthusian militants, receive every day; naive and poignant letters in which so many poor women cry out their distress to us . . . maybe then you would understand the immense sacrifice you demand of women; and maybe—because I do not like to think you are monsters—you would feel tears of pity and remorse rising to your eyes.

A few years ago, a large daily paper made an infinitely suggestive survey entitled "Lots of Children." After seeking the opinions of its readers, and a certain number of famous people, it published the responses as they came in. Among these highly interesting documents, one seemed especially worthy of being retained and preserved. The letter is from an obscure writer from the Vendée. I cannot resist reading it to you; here it is in all its tragic simplicity:

> Lots of children? . . . My poor mother had twelve . . . Every one of her childbirths was horribly painful, and of her twelve children, the noble creature breast-fed eight . . . Four died young; one was hit by a Prussian bullet at twenty-two and died in Loigny; another expired in the arms of his mother at thirty-three.
>
> She herself, following the fatigues of labor and breast-feeding, saw her stomach degenerate; then rheumatism set in, and she could not rest for atrocious neuralgia. Finally she got breast cancer—that horrible nursling—in the breast that had fed eight children. Twice the disease was operated on—what was the use? After a life of inexpressible physical martyrdom, and moral tortures that were even more cruel—always the children!—the death agony began, slowly and implacably. The poor, condemned woman saw death approaching, and in her body, heart, and mind, she suffered until the very end.
>
> During her agony my father tried to soften the abominable torment with loving words and doleful caresses . . . And then, this woman who had always cherished and admired her husband, pushed him away harshly, crying: "Get away, you executioner!"
>
> Oh, dearly beloved mother, holy creature of devotion and sacrifice, sacrificial victim of the narrowness of mad religious principles, forgive him, forgive us!

The author of this letter does not say if her mother was wealthy or poor. But must we know? Suppose she is rich, surrounded by every care, precaution, and comfort that fortune allows; things are still distressing enough to move us so deeply! If, on the contrary, we suppose she is poor, if to all the physical suffering and moral pain we add the anguish of poverty, there is no Inquisition that could invent a more cruel torture for her punishment, nor a religion that could imagine a worse hell, than this mother's existence! And, alas!, to this example I could add many others, for unfortunately, the chapter on maternal pain is endless! I will spare you, and I will spare myself everything I could still say on this subject—but I ask you, what do you think of a husband who, out of weakness, whim, or a desire to accomplish what he believes is a religious or patriotic duty, condemns the unfortunate creature that the odious marriage law has handed over to him without defense to this terrible martyrdom of perpetual childbirth? Without any concern about getting her consent . . . What do you think of men who would certainly not want their bitch or mare to have too many young for fear of hurting them but impose motherhood on their wives every year? . . . It is customary, I know, to admire these "good citizens"; we have seen newspapers of high circulation stamp special medals for them, and serious senators send their congratulations. Well! I, a woman and mother—certain to be speaking on behalf of all women and mothers, and of all men of heart—want to protest loudly; I feel nothing but the deepest contempt for these brutes!

Oh, I know that our repopulators are not short on arguments. I know well that some will answer, "the question lies elsewhere." They don't deny the formidable trial of maternity; they deplore it but can do nothing about it. A woman must suffer and sacrifice herself for her country. . . Sacrifice herself for her country! Do you fully understand the irony for us women in these few words? What! Our homeland really believes it has a right to our devotion? . . . For centuries it has underestimated, neglected, and oppressed us, never repaying us for our troubles except with ingratitude. It has always treated us like beasts of burden or luxurious trinkets. And still today, under the Third Republic and in the land of the Revolution, it relegates us to the rank of lunatics, children, and lawbreakers![5] How dare this country say to us "Be mothers!" when its laws reduce maternity to a purely physiological function, divested of its noble moral prerogatives, and treats the suffering creator as negligible, as not even having to be consulted! The human mother is even lower than the female animal—for whom no "paternity rights" exist to take away her young! They are really going too far! Not only is our refusal to give birth without plan and without limit, to give birth beyond our strength, means, or desires, an act of wisdom, we want it to be given the significance of an act of revolt.[6]

And now we arrive at the heart of the matter. These arguments are, to my eyes, more decisive and powerful than all economic and sociological considerations. Even when given irrefutable proof that Malthus, Stuart Mill, Garnier, and so many others have been wrong in their calculations and conclusions, that restrictions are not necessary and that the earth can nourish an unlimited number of inhabitants,[7] let me go even further. Even though it were demonstrated that it is in the interest of human groups to grow indefinitely, and that we need to grow more rapidly, I would not be swayed. I would continue to say: woman alone is mistress of her body, no matter what, and it is for her and no one else to decide if and when she will be a mother. We are dealing with an individual right here, the most imprescriptible and most sacred of all. But, alas!, as with everything else, power too often prevails over right; and this right has seen every physical, social, and moral force raised against it. As if it were not enough that some oppose it to the "interest of the homeland," while others invoke the "joys of family life," and still others speak of "divine law," religious doctrines make love into a sin for which maternity is the excuse and punishment. There have been socalled "freethinkers" and pretended "libertarians," people who believe neither in God, country, nor family, who bring up, more or less exactly, the very ancient and well-known theories of all religions. They have changed only one word: their God is called "Nature"! And it is in the name of "Nature" and the respect given to her laws that they condemn as "immoral," because it is "against nature," the caution in procreation that ought to be the rule of all civilized couples, or so it seems to me. But these people being far from consistent, you can be sure that this cult of the goddess Nature does not keep them from profiting, unscrupulously, from all the advantages of civilization. Nor does it keep them from resorting to all the resources of science in order to defend themselves against a rainy day, disease, and ills of all sorts that this excellent mother Nature so generously bestows on us. Let us think a bit rationally here. How can wanting to escape from a serious natural function when, for some reason, one does not feel able to fulfill it properly, be less moral than trying to protect oneself from the cold, the rain, the sun, or to prevent and treat disease *wanted by nature?* To combat disease we destroy the millions of germs *created by nature,* whose existence in the eyes of nature is evidently just as necessary and valuable as ours? . . . How could man's conquest over the forces of reproduction be more immoral than surgical operations or medical treatments, than the catchment of springs, canalization of rivers, domestication of mysterious liquids, all of which go against, transform, tame, and master nature? . . . Alas! Very often, nature is not for us the tender mother celebrated by poets but a blind, cruel, and unnatural mother against whom we find ourselves obliged to struggle. The religion of Nature is a return to primitive times, a negation of progress, and a triumph of instinct over reason and intelligence. Civilization is made up of man's conquests over nature. To soften her laws, alleviate her mistakes, tame and direct her unconscious forces, such is the goal of knowledge. And science is what distinguishes us from animals and savages. Knowledge is what we must love, what we must obey. For it is the affirmation of human power, the victory of the mind over force and matter and of will over fate. Science is the gentle and great redeemer that will lead us, step by step, slowly but surely, toward a luminous and splendid future, where, if man throws aside these last hindrances, we shall see, as the poet says: "This worm opens its wings in the heavens."

So let us not listen to those who do not agree with us and who say that sterile love is immoral. Besides, we would have to agree on the meaning of the word "immoral." "Morality," like "duty," is so relative, and varies so greatly with time, country, and circumstances, that maybe we have a right to give it secondary importance only. Morality in China is not the same as here; duty in the Middle Ages was not the same as duty today. And are we not all more or less tempted to declare that ways of seeing and acting that are different from our own are "immoral"? . . . In truth, nothing could be more vague, more inconsistent, more difficult to define than "morality" in the sense we ordinarily hear the word used. And yet, I believe there is one morality, one superior really human morality, that is still ignored. This morality is nothing but the application to our actions of everything that humanity has acquired in the way of knowledge and comprehension, sense of justice, and awareness of responsibility, little by little during the slow evolution that has raised us above the level of the primitive brute. And if there is anything that is absolutely contrary to that morality, it is making a woman pregnant without her formal and absolute consent. Furthermore, it is inflicting existence on a host of poor beings who were neither desired nor desirable and who were not provided with the conditions necessary for living useful and happy lives. Finally, it is behaving, in the twentieth century, as stupidly as caveman did, without reflection or circumspection, without any other guide than animal instinct, and without any concern for the consequences, when accomplishing the most serious of all acts a human being can accomplish. You take a thousand precautions and wisely examine the most ordinary acts of life in detail before accomplishing them; you reflect—and rightly so—before starting a career or investing money, before renting an apartment, buying clothes or some trinket; and you do not think before bringing a new creature into the world?! You put all your attention and care, all your knowledge, into perfecting breeds of animal and understanding the benefits of selection; you want only choice specimens among your sheep, cattle, horses, and dogs. But the only breed for whom you do nothing, the only one that you are totally uninterested in, is the human race, your race! . . . Actually there is nothing more absurd or more blameworthy. But look around you, think of the vast and tragic multitude of those who should not have been born: children of alcoholics, of the "damaged," the tubercular, or simply poverty stricken, the poor little ones who grow up wilting like flowers in cellars or dark, smelly attics, surrounded by shouting, blows, and abuse, or those who drag out their ragged childhood on the cobblestones without supervision or tender care—probably hospital or prison potential. Think of eight-year-old girls, old before reaching womanhood, their arms bent under the weight of the latest little baby that their mother has entrusted to them, not knowing what else to do with it . . . and all that procession of sad little coffins taking back into nothingness those who had hardly left it and who would have been better off staying there. Contemplate all that, I say . . . and maybe then you will understand that the crime of giving life is sometimes much worse than that of killing! . . . and maybe you will also understand that the worst criminals are not so much the poor, thoughtless people who procreate haphazardly like animals, by instinct, but the so-called moralists who knowingly encourage them in order to perpetuate the misery of the people on whom the luxury of the powerful depends.

Notes

1. This name refers to the population theories of the English economist Thomas Malthus (1766–1834). Malthus's fame rests on his *Essay on the Principle of Population* (London, 1798 and 1803), which stated the Malthusian principle: unchecked population tends to grow at more rapid rates than does the means of subsistence. Malthus concluded that "preventive checks" to population (such as moral restraint or birth control) were needed to avoid the catastrophes of "positive checks" (such as disease and war).

2. For neo-Malthusianism during the belle époque, see Angus McLaren, *Sexu-*

ality and Social Order; Francis Ronsin, *La Grève des ventres;* André Armengaud, *Les Français et Malthus* (Paris, 1975); André Béjin, "Néo-malthusianisme, populationisme, et eugénisme en France de 1870 à 1914," in Jacques Dupaquier, et al., eds., *Histoire de la population française* (Paris, 1988), 3:481–96; and several essays in the *Ecole des hautes études'* series *Communications* 44 (1986), especially Jean-Pierre Bardet and Jacques Dupaquier, "Contraception: les Français les premiers, mais pourquoi?" (3–34) and Alain Corbin, "Les Prostituées du XIXe siècle et le 'vaste effort du néant' " (259–75).

3. For the depopulation debate, see Joseph J. Spengler, *France Faces Depopulation* (Durham, 1938); John C. Hunter, "The Problem of the French"; 503; McLaren, *Sexuality and Social Order,* 169–84; and especially, Karen Offen's "Depopulation," which locates the feminist context of the subject.

4. See the discussion of Roussel and Robin in Klejman and Rochefort, *L'Egalité en marche* 326–37.

5. Roussel refers here to the denial of women's right to vote: the insane, the young, and felons were the categories of men who could not vote.

6. [Author's note in the published text: "The facts have proved, since then, that such a 'revolt' is quite useless. What little has been done in favor of mothers: the authorization of paternity suits, the development of maternal mutual societies, and most of all, the passing of the law providing paid leave for parturient women . . . all this due exclusively to this fall of the birth rate that makes our political leaders panic. One does not think of helping, or encouraging the creator, until the day when one starts to fear that she will soon refuse to create—it is true that in all areas, a strike remains the best weapon.]

7. Roussel refers to economists who employed the Malthusian principle (see note 1). John Stuart Mill (1806–73) was well known to feminist audiences for his pioneering essay entitled *The Subjection of Women* (London, 1869), which remains one of the masterpieces of feminist literature. Mill was also an economist, noted for his *Principles of Political Economy* (London, 1848), which went through many editions. There were several noteworthy Garniers in nineteenth century France, including more than one economist, but Roussel is probably referring to Clément-Joseph Garnier (1813–82), who founded the French Society for Political Economy in 1842, published the basic French text on classical economics in 1845, and produced a commentary on Malthus, *Du Principe de la population* (Paris, 1857).

MADELEINE PELLETIER

The most controversial neo-Malthusian idea was that women had the right to a safe and legal abortion. Few feminists accepted this idea in 1900. The CNFF, which had rebuffed Paul Robin on birth control, opposed abortion so strongly that it supported a subsidiary society to fight it: the *Ligue contre le crime d'avortement* (League against the Crime of Abortion).

It is extremely difficult to estimate the number of abortions performed during the belle époque because the practice was illegal. Scholarly guesses range greatly, up to a remarkable high of 900,000 abortions per year. The practice of abortion was certainly common, and the incidence was increasing steadily. In rural France, infanticide (typically by smothering or by exposure) and child abandonment remained sufficiently common to suggest that the abortion rate might have continued to rise significantly.[1]

Only the most radical turn-of-the-century feminists, such as Paule Minck, sought to legalize abortion.[2] Madeleine Pelletier was not the first feminist to take this position, but she became its best-known advocate. Pelletier, after all, was one of the first women physicians in France and held several public medical posts (see part 2). Her advocacy of a right of abortion had an ending so tragic that it seems worthy of Greek drama. In 1939, Pelletier, then sixty-five years old and half-paralyzed, was arrested on a charge of performing abortions. One of the pioneering students of psychiatric medicine, she was incarcerated in the psychiatric hospital of Pertay-Vaucluse, where she died within the year.[3]

Madeleine Pelletier's 1911 book, *L'Emancipation sexuelle de la femme* (see part 5) contained her most vigorous statement of the right of abortion, a chapter entitled "La Maternité doit être libre" (Motherhood Must Be a Free

Choice). She subsequently published this chapter as a separate pamphlet entitled *Le Droit à l'avortement* (The Right to Abortion). A large portion of it is translated here.

The Right to Abortion

I

The natural goal of love is the reproduction of the species. Partisans of final causes say that nature made the sexual act pleasant to encourage people to perpetuate themselves. The evolutionary theory that is currently admitted and that is based on many facts of natural history states that among the species organized by male and female, the ones that have survived are the ones where the sexual union is pleasurable. If species existed where the two sexes had no attraction for each other, they must necessarily have disappeared.

However, if the initial act of reproduction is pleasurable, giving birth is painful and the offspring a burden. Animals that have only a very inferior intelligence reproduce themselves in spite of it, since they are blind slaves of instinct. The human species, much superior to all animal species, sees the natural law as the origin of both the pleasure and the pain but tries to avoid the pain and retain only the pleasure.

The development of sexuality among civilized people is out of all proportion to the need for reproduction. Important though it is to have offspring within marriage, the sexual act occurs infinitely more often than is necessary to procreate even a large family. It is considered a need that has to be satisfied periodically, similar to the need for food and sleep. While sexual urges appear only at certain times of the year in animals, they have become constant in man.

Lovemaking occurs far more frequently outside marriage than within it. Man makes love extensively from puberty to old age, outside of any matrimonial bond, and any thought of reproduction has been completely banished from his career of sexual freedom. When a child is born, it is by accident, and such an accident is deplored.

So long as woman is considered an inferior being one can say that love is reserved for the male sex. The woman is only an instrument that the man

Source: Madeleine Pelletier, *L'Emancipation sexuelle de la femme* (Paris, 1911), 37–58. Trans. Lydia Willis and Jennifer Waelti-Walters.

uses for his pleasure. He consumes her like fruit. The moral position of the woman is raised through marriage and especially through maternity. Although an object, she becomes something of an intellectual and moral companion as well. As mistress of the house and educator of the children her sexual role is forgotten. But outside marriage, without a household and maternity, the woman becomes the instrument of animal passions. She costs little or is very expensive, depending on her social class, and a man can even ruin himself for her, but she remains an object of contempt. She represents the vice that one can raise up to the heights or cover with flowers but that still remains a vice.

However, the woman desires as well as being desired. The sexual instinct also speaks in her, but society does not allow her any means of expressing it. A woman can satisfy her need for love only by accepting matrimonial guardianship, unless she prefers to sell herself, thereby adding degradation to guardianship.

When the woman starts to reflect on her condition and, thanks to the careers open to her, finds it possible to make a living without the help of her family or of a man, she claims the right to love along with all her other rights.

Certainly, there is nothing exalted about physical love. However, exalted or not, a man is entitled to it, so why refuse it to a woman?

Yet, does she who denies the right of love to her sex describe herself as one whom the habit of thought is freeing gradually from accepted prejudices? The law? Not at all. The only barrier that keeps a woman chaste is a moral one, and moral barriers are easily shattered, merely by desiring to do so.

In reality, the stipulations of an unwritten law are not without power. Because public opinion is against it, the practice of free love brings a variety of sorrows for a woman. Men lose respect for her and families close their doors. Nevertheless, women indulge in free love more and more. They prefer to face contempt and satisfy their senses for, even if they have partly achieved economic liberation already, a social life outside the home remains blocked. Places of amusement are not open to a woman alone, or if they are, she receives the kind of welcome that makes her want to leave as quickly as possible. One cannot always work or stay in one's room sewing or reading. So to be able to go out, women who work in factories, in service, in offices, and female students, too, take lovers.

There has been some progress in this respect, and those women who may well be lovers but who are not "kept women" contribute to this evolution.

They do not behave like prostitutes or semiprostitutes. They show a certain dignity in their relationships, and people are starting to appreciate that a woman who has a lover can be "honest," if she lives decently from her income or her work.[4]

Love tends toward equality and is no longer the exclusive property of men; women want to have their share, an active share. The feminine role, although contrary to the masculine role, is not degrading in any respect.

However, there is an obstacle, even more powerful because it is not social but natural, in the path of any woman who wants to satisfy her sexuality unrestrainedly, and that obstacle is a child.

The prospect of a child plunges any woman who has liberated herself through work or education back into the servitudes of the past. How can one talk about equality in love when the man leaves freely once his needs are satisfied, while the woman must assume motherhood? Maternity makes love a real deception for a woman. Through it a woman ceases to be a person conscious of her dignity and falls into the degradation of the seduced. Like an imploring slave she pursues the man who has abandoned her. Vanquished, she begs him for pity.

In the future, when economic emancipation is complete, being a mother will not necessarily be a calamity for the unmarried woman. Pregnancy is unpleasant, giving birth is painful, but then there is the child, who is a source of pleasure. The man remains alone once his passion is satisfied *(coitus, sad animal)*.[5] The woman has the child who, by giving her so many joys, is the reward for her pain. The child has nothing to give; on the contrary, he asks for everything, but by exerting herself for the child the woman gains instead of losing. She feels responsibility for her child. By protecting the child she experiences something akin to virile joys. By watching constantly over the child the woman is blessed by forgetting herself. The many feelings of weakness she dwelt upon previously have taken flight; she is stronger.

Even though the woman's salary may enable her to bring up one or two children, she must not be forced into motherhood, or it may become servitude. The woman alone must decide if and when she wants to be a mother.

II

Voluntary birth control has been practiced for a long time in educated and wealthy circles. If wealthy people have fewer children than poor people it is not because they are less prolific or because they abstain from intercourse. It is because this is what they want.

Nowadays, to the great terror of the conservatives, contraception has spread to the proletariat. The men of this class, less energetic than the rich, generally refuse to make the necessary effort at the right moment to keep their wives from becoming pregnant. The neo-Malthusians have invented all sorts of appliances and products for feminine protection that are now widely sold in union and anarchist circles. Often, such means fail. The working woman uses them badly. The necessity of employing them methodically at the time of each intercourse is her responsibility. If she is neglectful she becomes pregnant. Nevertheless, neo-Malthusian propaganda has been effective. Not only do the elite of union militants have relatively few children, but now the working classes are beginning to have fewer than they used to have. According to statistics published by M. Bertillon, the number of births has greatly diminished during the last few years among the industrial population of the north.[6]

III

Although they have a fairly constant success rate when used carefully, birth control devices are not always reliable. When a woman becomes pregnant, be it through negligence or ignorance, and she refuses motherhood, a second option is open to her: abortion.

Nowadays, abortion is generally practiced in large cities.

Doctors seldom practice it. Pushed by the difficulties of life in a profession that is becoming more and more overcrowded, some of them consent to perform it if the occasion presents itself, to rescue the odd patient here and there; but they do not make much money from abortions because the occasion rarely arises.[7]

Midwives do more abortions. Patients are less embarrassed to tell them of their predicament. Less qualified than doctors and having a more familiar approach, they make the public more comfortable.

Besides, persons without diplomas find a lucrative occupation in abortions. Anybody can learn the technique, since it is generally not difficult.

Nowadays, a number of women have learned how to cure themselves of their "lateness."

The means are varied: introduction of various objects and injections of soapy water, etc.

Occasionally, abortion is dangerous, but only because it is forbidden. The operation required is one of the most benign. If Article 317 were to be abolished and doctors authorized to terminate pregnancies upon request before the end of the third month,[8] there would hardly ever be any accidents.[9] In rare cases of complications a uterine curettage openly practiced would save almost all patients. The danger comes from the ignorance of the practitioners. [. . .]

Sometimes accidents are due just as much to negligence as to lack of cleanliness. In certain working-class families, when a woman succeeds in terminating her pregnancy herself, no precautions are taken. So women have abortions two or three times a year, with dirty instruments. Naturally, endometritis and salpingitis are common. One should never forget that abortion is only a stopgap.

There are cases when grave accidents occur immediately. The douching cannula may be dirty, but it has the advantage of being soft. This is not the case with curtain rods, knitting needles, hatpins, corkscrews, and pokers, which women sometimes use to abort themselves. When they act so imprudently they face lethal peritonitis.

Abortion is no longer the exceptional event it used to be. One can say that it is the rule in all classes of society. Nowadays, a young woman of the bourgeoisie who "makes a mistake" and becomes pregnant no longer considers suicide; she thinks of getting an abortion. Most of the time her parents do not notice anything. As the young woman has at least a room of her own, she hides her suffering and gets rid of the bloodstained cloths. If the pain becomes too severe, the young woman confesses everything to her mother. At first the mother gets very angry, but she calms down as she realizes that it is in her own as well as in her daughter's interest not to say anything. The family doctor is called in. He diagnoses a hemorrhage caused by anemia, prescribes some rest, and the father himself is duped.

In the world of office workers, servants, and factory girls, it is usually the lover who proposes abortion to the mistress pregnant by his effort. He pays the required price, which is his way of making "reparation." Previously, he had only the choice between "cowardly" abandonment and recognition of the child. Abandonment carried no risk, since paternity claims were illegal. Thus, many seducers followed this course without scruple. It is true that there was always the parting scene with its supplications, tears, and threats, but a man could always sneak off. For those afflicted by conscience and afraid of a woman's cries of vengeance, there were always ways of casting doubt upon the paternity of the child, and such doubt, as we know, always profited the accused. The few good, honest young men who were not prepared to cause tears followed another road. They adopted the child and married the mother, but this was followed by many disappointments. To their detriment, they often experienced how little truth there is in the proverb that says that virtue is always rewarded. [...] Many young men who yielded to an ideal of justice and goodness have been compelled to renounce the brilliant careers they might have had, given their potential, because they were held back by the mediocrity of their marriage.

Abortion allows lovers to show generosity at little cost. Therefore, they insist that their mistresses agree to it. I have loved you. You have loved me. Thus speaks the young bourgeois to the young worker. We have spent pleasant moments together. It is true that I made you pregnant, but I am paying for your abortion and we are quits.

The woman would prefer to have the child, to keep the man and to try to lead him to marriage, or at least obtain financial assistance from him for many years. But the lover insists, and the woman yields, in the end, fearing that she might have the burden without any financial support.

Abortion is not limited to illegitimate love. Married people practice it constantly. Sometimes it is the first pregnancy that is interrupted. It has come too soon; the spouses would like to have a few good years and enjoy life. Children are postponed. Most of the time one resorts to abortion only at the third or fourth pregnancy. The first child was anticipated with pleasure; the second accepted, and to the third one resigned oneself, but the fourth was absolutely refused. The civil servant, the employee, and the well-to-do small merchant insist on giving their children a good education. If possible, they want their descendants to reach ranks superior or at least equal to their own. Only in exceptional cases does the elite worker share this concern for education, but he wants to be relatively well off. In his book dealing with the decline in population, M. Bertillon states that a large number of children is not a cause of poverty.[10] This is an error. Simple arithmetic shows that one needs less money to feed three people than to feed six, and observation of the working-class milieu shows relative well-being where fecundity is limited and poverty everywhere where families are large. [...] This is not only a question of arithmetic. Voluntary restriction is not the only reason for well-being, and prolificacy is not the only reason for poverty. Well-being and restriction both derive from qualities of forethought and order. It is because one is provident that one limits the number of one's children. The same kind of forethought is applied in the administration of the home. Because of this quality one enjoys a relative well-being that is augmented by restrictions of the number of children. Prolificacy, in itself a cause of poverty, is the consequence of disorder and negligence, which are further causes of poverty.[11]

It is therefore mainly for economic reasons that both the middle classes and the poor classes resort to abortion. It is usually decided by common agreement in the interests of the couple. Occasionally, the woman of the working class assumes the responsibility alone. The husband, stupefied by alcohol, would not care about having a large family, but the woman, who is sober and more sensible, does not want to increase her already heavy burden. Besides, there is nothing attractive about being pregnant. Thus, she inquires about means "to get rid of it" as she puts it, and most of the time she is successful.

Thanks to abortion some situations that used to end in tragedy have become fairly simple. [. . .]

These dramas of pregnancy are banal in their frequency. One woman commits suicide to escape dishonor, another kills her child, yet another, a young worker, a young maid, or a farm worker, driven away by her master, falls into prostitution. Thanks to abortion, such terrible outcomes happen less often. They will not happen at all once the law has ceased to make abortion a crime and grants every woman the right to be a mother only when she chooses.

IV

Infanticide is a crime. Once a baby is born it must be respected. It is just as wrong to get rid of it as it is to kill an adult. Its very weakness, far from eliminating its rights, must ensure its protection in any civilized country.

A woman who bears a baby is not compelled to bring it up. In raising it she performs a good deed, but she cannot be forced to do so. However, she does not have the right to kill the baby or to harm it. If she does not want to bring it up, her duty is to hand it over to society which will provide food and care for its new member in her place. In defense of their clients, lawyers for child murderers describe the hours of agony that guilty women endure alone in narrow rooms biting their bedsheets for fear of moaning, and then petrified with panic lest the cries of the newborn be heard.

Usually the jury acquits, and rightly so, because the guilt rests with social prejudice that does not allow a woman to be a mother outside of marriage; but when it is a question of infanticide, the verdict must be nothing other than clemency, because, although the crime may be excusable, it remains a crime.

Abortion does not require extenuating circumstances. The woman can admit it freely because it is her right. On a deserted road a woman encounters a vagrant. He pounces on her and rapes her, making her pregnant. Would one dare to insist that she has to go through with such a pregnancy? That would imply that the woman is a thing that any man, however vile, has the right to use and abuse. On the contrary, a woman is a person, equal with man.[12]

When a woman has accepted sexual relations, her right to refuse maternity is less glaringly obvious, but it still exists. Once her baby is born it is a person, but the fetus in the uterus is not. It is part of the mother's body.

I said above that in all justice one cannot force a mother to look after her baby; similarly, one cannot force a woman to shelter and maintain the seed in her womb. Once she ceases to want to support it, she has no other choice but to expel it. One cannot compare a seed with a person who is entitled to life without falling into absurdity. Men, like women, shelter seeds. Can one oblige them not to lose any but use all of them for procreation?

If it is only the fertilized egg that we identify with a person, then the arbitrary nature of the argument is obvious. While one is considered criminal for stopping the fertilized egg in its development, one is not if one makes fertilization impossible; yet in both cases the result is identical: one prevents a human being from being born.

In all logic and justice birth must be considered the criterion for individuality. All those born have a right to social protection; those who are not born do not exist, and the law does not have to deal with them. A pregnant woman is not two persons, she is only one. She has the right to have an abortion, just as she has the right to cut her hair and her nails and to gain or lose weight. Our right over our bodies is absolute since it goes as far as suicide.

Only the timing of the abortion must be insisted upon. This must be done by counseling rather than by punishment, which is always arbitrary and infringes upon the sacred right a person has over herself. An abortion practiced at six months is an ugly operation. Once expelled, the fetus shows signs of life, breathes, moves, cries. It is alive even though only for a few hours, and abortion under these conditions is beginning to look like infanticide. A woman must be sensible enough to know at the beginning of her pregnancy whether or not she wants motherhood.

If abortion were allowed by tacit agreement, the medical profession would practice it within the first trimester. After the third month a woman who is careless enough not to have made up her mind would be refused the intervention of a doctor. She would then have to resort to abortionists, at her own risk and peril.

Some opponents of abortion declare that a woman who has accepted a man has a duty to carry her pregnancy to its term because she must accept the consequences of her pleasure, painful though they be. Basically, this is a religious idea. Christian religions, considering that we are on earth only to suffer, teach that pleasure is always a sin that has pain as its punishment. Many minds, even among those who seem free from all religion, are still imbued with this idea, and many novels and plays are full of it. Nevertheless, life shows us that this idea is false. To suffer pain that can be avoided in the anticipation of some reward somewhere else is pure dream, a dream that gives those obsessed by it a life without any joy.

Notes

1. See Angus McLaren, "Abortion in France," and the works of Rachel Fuchs, notably *Abandoned Children* and *Poor and Pregnant in Paris*. Several of the articles in *Communications* 44 (1986) are helpful: Jacques Dupaquier, "Combien d'avortements en France avant 1914?" (87–106); Agnès Fine, "Savoirs sur le corps et procédés abortifs au XIXe siècle" (137–74); and Richard Lalou, "L'Infanticide devant les tribunaux français, 1825–1910" (175–200).

2. Paule Minck (1839–1901), born Paulina Mekarska, was the daughter of a Polish nationalist exile living in France. She worked as a seamstress in Paris and participated in the republican and feminist movements of the 1860s. Her support of the Commune in 1871 led to her exile, and she returned to France only after the amnesty of the communards. She joined the socialist movement on her return and regularly wrote articles for *La Question sociale,* including an essay entitled "Le Droit à l'avortement," which appeared in the *Almanach de la question sociale* (Paris, 1893). See the volume of her writings compiled by Alain Dalotel.

3. See Gordon's biography of Pelletier, *The Integral Feminist,* chap. 10 ("How Militants Die"), for details of her final years.

4. Author's note in the original text: "This is the thesis of *The Tomboy* by Victor Margueritte."

5. Pelletier is alluding to ancient medical thought. Claudius Galen, a famed Greek

physician (A.D. 130–200), stated that "every animal is sad after coitus except the human female and the rooster."

6. Dr. Jacques Bertillon was a noted statistician who published on many of the subjects of birth: infant mortality, illegitimacy, frequency of twins, and the falling birth rate. See particularly his *La Natalité en France* (Paris, 1891) and *La Dépopulation de la France* (Paris, 1911).

7. [Author's note in the original text: "Abortion is permitted in Russia; tolerated in Germany and Switzerland."]

8. Pelletier is referring here to the French Penal Code. Article 317 was a law of April 1832 that criminalized abortion, both for the woman receiving it and for anyone aiding her. Physicians, surgeons, midwives, pharmacists, or public health officers who aided in an abortion were singled out for imprisonment at hard labor. Instead of being abolished, Article 317 was expanded in July 1920 by a law that forbade the advocacy of abortion (such as Pelletier's chapter translated here) and even outlawed birth control information.

9. [Author's note in later editions of the text: "Before the war (World War I), many doctors supported abortion, which they were going to call embryonexia. The war and the national embargo have been regressive factors."]

10. Pelletier is referring to Bertillon's *Le Problème de la dépopulation*, which went through several editions between 1897 and 1911.

11. Infanticide was a common form of population control from the beginning of European history. It persisted throughout the nineteenth century, especially in rural France. Article 302 of the Napoleonic Penal Code equated infanticide with murder but did not stop it. A study of French court records for the years 1851–1910 has found 10,498 convictions for infanticide and a total of 21,137 convictions of responsibility for the death of newborn infants (lesser charges were brought when direct infanticide could not be proven). The law was amended in 1901 to distinguish infanticide from other murders and to exclude convicted mothers from capital punishment; see Lalou, "L'Infanticide," and the discussion of infanticide in many population studies, especially Fuchs, *Abandoned Children*.

12. Author's note in the original text: "During the war, there was some question of providing hospital abortions for women raped by the Germans."

7

POLITICAL AND CIVIC RIGHTS

HUBERTINE AUCLERT

Hubertine Auclert (see part 5) quit the moderate feminist group of Maria Deraismes and Léon Richer in 1876 to seek the political rights of women. She was not the first French woman to make this demand, or even the first to propose an organization to call for the vote; that honor belongs to Julie Daubié (1824–74), who died before she could organize French suffragism.[1] Auclert created the French women's suffrage movement when she founded *Le Droit des femmes* (Women's Rights) in 1876. Deraismes and Richer still considered suffragism too radical, and they excluded it from the program of the first feminist congress in 1878. They denied Auclert the opportunity to call for political rights at their congress, a fact that she immediately flaunted by publishing her censored speech under the title "The Political Rights of Women—A Question That Is Not Treated at the International Congress of Women."[2]

During the next decade, Auclert championed women's suffrage with remarkable energy and determination. She took her cause to a socialist congress and won their support. She founded a newspaper, *La Citoyenne* (The Citizeness), dedicated to suffrage. She refused to pay her taxes on the grounds that she was denied her rights. She boycotted the census because women did not count. She repeatedly tried to register to vote. She held marches in the streets. She stood as a candidate (illegal) for office. She showered politicians with letters and petitions, the one political right permitted to women. For all her activity, though, no bill for women's suffrage even reached the floor of the Chamber of Deputies.[3]

Hubertine Auclert led the battle for political rights into the twentieth century. She continued public protests while in her sixties, when she even considered the need for violence. Auclert staged her most vehement demonstration during the Parisian municipal elections of 1908, when she marched into a polling place, seized the ballot box, smashed it to the ground, stamped on the ballots, and denounced "unisexual suffrage." This led to her arrest and to her knickname, "the French suffragette."[4]

Auclert wrote an enormous amount, chiefly in the form of newspaper columns. She compiled many of these writings into *Le Vote des femmes* (1908); after Auclert's death, her sister compiled another volume entitled *Les Femmes au gouvernail* (Women at the Helm). The following excerpts come from several passages in *Le Vote des femmes*. They show that despite the years of rejection and frustration, Auclert retained great faith in the democratic process and the progress that truer democracy could create.

The Vote for Women

[Chapter 1:] The Pretense of Universal Suffrage

*Women's suffrage is using all the
intelligence and energy of a nation
for its greater welfare.*

Suffrage is a progress machine that must be put into gear by the willpower of the men and women of this nation if it is to have any effect. But, since it is activated by only a small number of men, it is reduced to powerlessness for lack of driving force.

Before we belittle universal suffrage, let us make it work; for if it is not giving us the promised results, that is because its principle is distorted and its application curtailed.

Just as many modern inventions can function only by combining certain elements, suffrage needs all the female and male energy of our nation to become an evolutionary instrument capable of transforming the social condition.

Source: Hubertine Auclert, *Le Vote des femmes* (Paris, 1908), 3, 5–6, 7–11, 124–30, 131, 216. Trans. Jette Kjaer and Jennifer Waelti-Walters.

For there to be benefit from the excellent institution of suffrage, it must be applied rigorously to the full extent covered by universalization. It is not enough to misinterpret the words of our language or glorify a falsehood, to give a mutilated suffrage the authority and power to encompass all French men and women.

Suffrage will not produce precise results until, practiced by both sexes, it has been broken in and made intentional.

Universal suffrage does not exist at the moment. What does exist is an imaginary suffrage that authorizes only a small minority of the nation to vote. It excludes all women, learned or not. It also excludes a large number of men; those who are in the army or navy, who travel, are tourists, or are deprived of their political rights by law . . .

Should not paper power, like paper money, have currency everywhere?

Suffrage that has been reduced, falsified, and defrauded doesn't give us even the vaguest notion of what true universal suffrage will be.

The votes given out have such little weight, and the electors so little authority, that at every election the candidates that they have rejected—provided they are governmental—are collected by the ministers, who thumb their noses at sovereign electors by hoisting those who have been black-balled to good positions.

If most republican elections produce nothing but fruitless results, and if suffrage collapses under the weight of commitments made in its name, that is because it is fiction and not reality at all, because it is supported by convention instead of drawing its strength from the force of numbers.

With the existing suffrage, restrictive and unnatural as it is, the voter has only the illusion of sovereignty. But with universal suffrage, which encompasses the entire nation, women as well as men, the elector will be given the substance of sovereignty itself.

[Chapter 2:] Born with No Civic Rights

*Possessing paper power makes
it easier to get paper money.*

No man is by his role, no matter how small, excluded from the prerogative of being French and a citizen. So why does a woman's role deprive her of her rights as a Frenchwoman and citizen? Is the perpetuation of the human species and the care given to domestic affairs less important than the attention brought to bear on exercising a profession?

"Of you and me," said Socrates, glorifying housework, "he who is the most industrious and economical shall contribute the most to society."

For each person the task imposed is different. But everyone has the same inherent rights.

Gender does not confer particular prerogatives, given that moral and intellectual qualities are independent of sex. One cannot convince people today that being a man extends his intellectual faculties, while being a woman restricts hers.

One objects to the maternity of the claimants; yet it is no more in conflict with exercising political rights than with exercising a skill or trade.

Maria-Theresa of Austria had sixteen children, which hardly prevented her from being the great Statesperson to whom Austria owed its existence. For her, the Hungarian Lords drew their sabers from their sheaths, crying: "Let us die for our king, Maria Theresa!"[5]

All women, mothers or otherwise, married or not, must exercise their political rights so as to put order into the community and state.

REMAIN WOMEN

Men buck at the idea of women having equal rights! Instead of seeing women as their helpers, enabling them to attain a better quality of life, men seem to think something is going to be taken away from them.

Frenchmen are imploring Frenchwomen not to try to become citizens. They tell them nothing would be gained by universal suffrage and that their superiority lies in remaining enslaved.

Similar language was used by eligible voters on those who didn't get the vote before 1848.[6] The "Remain women!" of today is the equivalent of the "Remain workers!" of yesterday, and it has the same meaning: stay incapable of bettering your condition.

Those women who see the social and economic advantages obtained by the voters, those women who notice that in every country men deprived of suffrage are desperately trying to claim it, are beginning to understand that this paper power, this voting ballot, is just as necessary to them as paper

money. For possessing one makes it easier to get the other. The voter's registration card will make housework pay and include housewives among retired workers.

Frenchwomen cannot stay stripped of their political capacity, which a
deputy rightly calls, "the beginning of capital."

Work is, in effect, assessed according to the condition of the person accomplishing it. Women's work is so belittled and given such a derisory salary
because these women are outside the law; they are slaves whose efforts are
not judged worthy of reward. Let women enter into common political
rights and soon their economic situation will be changed; their work, en-
nobled by citizenship, will receive a lucrative salary.

Women will not escape oppression from their husbands or exploitation
from their employers until they become their equals at the ballot box.

The voter's registration card, of which Frenchwomen are deprived, is a
certificate of honorability that guarantees consideration to the person who
carries it.

In the present state of society, suffrage is the surest guarantee for human
beings not to be wronged or diminished. It is like insurance bought in order
to obtain law and justice. Why should women not enjoy this insurance?

By becoming citizens, Frenchwomen will be able to do their duty even
better, since their role as teachers will extend from human unity to the human community and their motherly concern embrace the entire nation.

Since a woman's person and condition depend on politics that hem her
in from all sides, it is in her own, as well as the general, interest that she
participate in public life and cooperate in the transformation of society.
Thus, she is assured of not being sacrificed in the social structure of the
future.

To quote M. Thiers, whose pretty phrase those who disdain feminine
competition would do well to deserve: "To put this business in order, I need
my women" (Mme Thiers and Mlle Dosne). These words prove that even a
statesman, whom praise could have made proud, recognized women as having particular faculties complementary to his own. If the male and female
parts of every human being seemed indispensable to M. Thiers to fix a difficult, private affair, how much more indispensable is the cooperation of men
and women for well-run public affairs![7]

Women's suffrage is the utilization of the whole, of the nation's intelligence and energy, in order to bring about a greater welfare.

Bringing men and women closer through politics means establishing a beneficial rivalry between the sexes, in the name of progress. [. . .]

[Chapter 23:] Registration on the Electoral Roll

A woman does what a man does—but does it differently.

It is impossible for Frenchwomen who are the most deserving of esteem and consideration to obtain a single voter's registration card, while ex-convicts are sometimes able to collect these attestations of honorability.

Male robbers can vote, while women with integrity are forbidden to do so by civic order.

We have protested against this abnormality for a long time. As early as 1880, in all the districts of Paris, lady members of the "Women's Rights" society demanded that they be registered on the electoral lists.

The mayor of the tenth district justified his refusal to register women in the following letter:

City of Paris
City hall of the tenth *arrondissement*

We, mayor of the tenth district of Paris,

Given the request presented on the 2d of February of this year by Mlle Hubertine Auclert, who wants to obtain her enrollment on the electoral list of the tenth district;

Given the grounds, which have been developed in length and on which this request is based;

Given the electoral laws presently in force, particularly the organic decree of February 2d, 1852, the laws of July 7, 1874, and November 30, 1875;[8]

Considering that since 1789 and until our present day, all electoral laws that have succeeded each other have, without any exception, been interpreted and applied in the sense that they have conferred, and do confer, rights only to men and not women;

Considering that the claim formulated by the claimant to draw an interpretation out of the text of these laws, the result of which would be to create electoral and eligibility rights in favor of women identical

to those that belong to men, from then on constitutes a political innovation, the merit and legal value of which it is not in our competence
to determine;

Considering that consequently it is even less for us to take it upon
ourselves and allow the putting into practice of this claim;

It is hereby ruled that given the present state of legislation, Mlle
Hubertine Auclert's claim is declared inadmissible.

Paris, February 4th, 1880.
Devisme.

The ladies of the "Women's Rights" society had this protestation published by the press everywhere: "We, the undersigned, born of French parents and fulfilling all the duties and obligations that are incumbent on the
French people, have presented ourselves armed with justificatory papers
that establish our identity, majority, and duration of abode to the city hall of
our respective districts, so that we may be enrolled on the electoral register."

We were told that, being women, we could not be registered.

"We appeal to public opinion concerning the injustice that the Republic,
after the other regimes, sanctions by keeping us in bondage."

Although our claim was rejected, we persisted in demanding our electoral registration. [. . .]

Female citizens have demanded their electoral registration in a number of
cities and communities to no avail. Women of the people, working women
who let themselves be guided by sound reasoning, have been demanding
their registration on the lists in different regions for a long time now.

"We had," they say, "read the public notices for the revision of the electoral list, and ignoring that women are not electors, we went in a group to
city hall to request our registration.

"The men there made a good deal of fun of us; we answered that there
was nothing to laugh at, since they had been foolish enough to hinder
women from voting."

Nowadays, when ladies request electoral status the men no longer answer
as they used to: "Horses and cattle will vote before women do." They acknowledge their applications for registration with a receipt.

In suburbs like those in Paris, the applications for electoral registration
by women are recorded on the register.

Those women who possess a receipt for their request and a response from
the committee in charge of judging the protests concerning the election

must guard these papers preciously. These parchments are worth many an-other, since they establish the intellectual superiority that has made women protest against the placing of their sex outside the law.

The law stipulates that all Frenchmen twenty-one years of age are eligible to vote. The term "all Frenchmen" encompasses women when it comes to paying taxes and being subject to law. But when it comes to exercising rights, this word, "Frenchmen," is supposed to designate men only.

Frenchwomen have tried everything; to invalidate not a law that does not exist, but a custom that nullifies them politically. They have gone before all the jurisdictions: before the Council of the Prefecture, the Council of State, and the Supreme Court of Appeal, to demand their electoral right.[9]

The judges of the Supreme Court of Appeal called to their aid the 1791 Constitution in order to stipulate that women should not exercise political rights. The Constitution recognizes the electoral capacity only of people registered on the list of the national guard.

Now, since to be a member of the national guard you had to pay forty francs in taxes, the electoral right was derived from the responsibility of be-ing a taxpayer.

Besides, the 1791 Constitution has been repealed by that of 1848, which the Supreme Court of Appeal has not mentioned, precisely since it favors us. It declares that sovereignty resides in the entirety of the French people [*l'universtalite des français*], that this sovereignty is inalienable, and that no individual nor any fraction of the people can lay claim for themselves to the exercise of it.[10]

The judges of the Supreme Court of Appeal realize that men cannot ap-propriate the rights of women; nevertheless, they have asked us to find a leg-islative text authorizing women to vote.

You show us, your Honors, a legislative text that forbids women to vote. [. . .]

[Chapter 24:] The Price of a Woman's Vote

Under the Republic, which preserves the salic law excluding women from the government,[11] Frenchwomen are forbidden to interfere with the affairs of their country to the extent that a mayor from the Landes region, M. Dubedout, who in 1885 had allowed two women to vote, was given a two hundred franc fine. One hundred francs per woman's vote; that is ex-pensive!

One must not be put out by this method of intimidation. It would suffice that a mayor and municipal council were determined to make a *res publica* out of the *res hominum,* for a solution to the feminine franchise to be found without further delay.[12] [. . .]

[Last Chapter:] The Universalization of Suffrage

In our society, as it works toward transformation,
the person who has no voice on the subject, not
having the right to vote, is missing today and will
be sacrificed tomorrow.

Rich women would be deprived of their fortune and poor women would remain needy if individual ownership became socialized before the female sex became elector and eligible for election. For women who had been stripped of their possessions would not recover in the new society what had been taken from them, given that the positions, jobs, and worthwhile work would belong to the electors alone. Women who remain deprived of their political rights, therefore, risk becoming even more unhappy in the future than they are now.

In order for a social transformation to occur that will profit all of humanity, it is essential that men and women have the right to participate and to benefit from participation.

Only equality in today's society will guarantee women equal treatment to men in tomorrow's society.

Hence, we recognize the importance of putting into practice quickly the political equality of both sexes, as it is written in the law.

The law on the franchise says, in effect: *all Frenchmen* aged twenty-one years are electors . . .

The word "Frenchmen," which includes men and women as taxpayers when it comes to paying taxes, certainly also includes men and women as voters when it comes to exercising the vote.

A commendable equity has enlarged the interpretation of the legislative text of the law on the eligibility for jury service and permitted workers to judge criminals. Why does this equity not enlarge the interpretation of the electoral law as well and permit women to vote?

It is better to admit having interpreted a law badly than to let the legislation of the Republic exclude women as a group, women whom the royal charters before 1789 allowed to participate in politics to some extent.[13]

Upon their arrival on the political scene, women will curb the wasting of public funds and hence make it easier to bring about the desired reforms.

When women, having the same interests as men in the State, are likewise armed with the necessary rights with which to protect and defend themselves and to rise in society, then France, in full possession of its cerebral power, will take on a leading role in the world.

The universalization of suffrage among women will increase the strength of the nation tenfold, accelerate the social evolution, intensify the solicitude of the collectivity toward the individual, and open up an era of happiness for human beings.

Notes

1. For Daubié, see Raymonde Bulger, *Lettres à Julie Victoire Daubié*.

2. For the early era of suffragism, see Hause, *Hubertine Auclert*, 21–46; Bidelman, *Pariahs Stand Up!* 71–105; Moses, *French Feminism*, 212–20; Klejman and Rochefort, *L'Egalité en marche*, 31–56.

3. For the suffrage campaign of the 1880s, see Hause, *Hubertine Auclert*, 47–131; Bidelman, *Pariahs Stand Up!* 106–54; Klejman and Rochefort, *L'Egalité en marche*, 75–82.

4. For the early twentieth-century suffrage campaign, see Hause, *Hubertine Auclert*, 165–219; Hause with Kenney, *Women's Suffrage*, 71–168; Klejman and Rochefort, *L'Egalité en marche*, 262–302. For the demonstrations of 1908, see also Steven C. Hause and Anne R. Kenney, "Women's Suffrage."

5. Maria Theresa (1717–80) succeeded to the throne of the Habsburg dominions when her father, the Emperor Charles VI, died in 1740 without a son. Charles had prepared for that moment by persuading other states to sign a document called the "Pragmatic Sanction," accepting his daughter on the Austrian throne. The ancient Salic Law, which prevented the rule of women monarchs in some countries (such as France) did not block Maria Theresa in Austria, but it prevented her election to succeed her father as the Holy Roman Emperor (the electors chose Maria Theresa's husband). Maria Theresa ruled with considerable success for forty years, and Auclert does not exaggerate her importance.

6. The right to vote, even for adult males, was sharply restricted (chiefly by property and tax qualifications) under the monarchies of 1815–48. Parts of the middle class, most of the peasantry, and all of the working class could not vote. The Second

Republic reintroduced "universal" (manhood) suffrage in 1848. Auclert is correct in asserting that the same arguments used against manhood suffrage were later adapted to oppose women's suffrage.

7. Adolphe Thiers (1797–1877) was a historian and journalist who became one of the most prominent political figures of nineteenth-century France. He served several different regimes, especially Louis Philippe's monarchy of 1830–48, where his posts included the premiership (1836–40). In his seventies, Thiers became one of the central figures in the founding of the Third Republic. He was effectively the president of France (without the title) between 1871 and 1873, when he was instrumental in leading moderate monarchist opinion to accept the reality of republican government.

8. Auclert became a keen student of French electoral law to conduct her legal battles to win the vote. This was a complex subject because France had repeatedly changed forms of government since 1789. The laws Auclert mentions here are a decree of 1852 explaining voting rights under the constitution of the Second Empire (1852–70) and two of the early electoral laws of the Third Republic (1871–1940). The law of 1874 stated the qualifications for voting in municipal elections, and the law of 1875 stated the regulations for the voter registration lists for parliamentary elections. The phraseology of these laws varied, but the wording of the decree of 1852 was typical: "All French citizens of at least twenty-one years of age and in possession of their civil and political rights are eligible to vote." The interpretive battle over such laws typically involved the definition of the word "citizen" and the nature of the denial of civil rights. The courts usually ruled that women were not citizens in this sense because the Napoleonic Code had vested their civil rights in their fathers or their husbands.

9. During her career, Hubertine Auclert tried arguing with each of these appellate bodies, but she never persuaded any of them of her claims. The Council of the Prefecture was a secondary administrative tribunal for local government, with one located in each of the departments of France. The Council of State (*Conseil d'état*) and the Supreme Court of Appeal (*Cour de cassation*) were national institutions whose functions varied under the different constitutions. The Council of State was an advisory body that gave the government ruling on the consistency and interpretation of the laws; the Court of Appeal was the highest appellate court in France.

10. Auclert is citing Chapter 1 Article 1 of the constitution of the Second Republic, promulgated on November 4, 1848.

11. The Salic Law was a compilation of many ancient customs that chiefly functioned as a penal code. It formed part of the early medieval Frankish laws (the *leges barbarorum*) and dates back to the reign of Clovis I (A.D. 466–511). Much of Eu-

rope, including France, inherited the Salic Law from Charlemagne's empire. It had a long history of interpretation to exclude women from inheriting certain property, titles, and rights. It is most often cited, as Auclert does here, as the legal reason why women could not rule as monarchs in many countries.

12. Auclert is making a bilingual play on words here. The Latin (and legal) expression *"res publica"* is the source of the word "republic" in both French and English. It literally meant "public affairs" and was used to mean the state. The word *"publica,"* of course, included women. Auclert uses the Latin expression *"res hominum,"* "the affairs of men," as a clever way to assert that the republic concerns itself only with men.

13. Auclert is correct in asserting that women had (slightly) more political rights under the monarchical Old Regime than they did under the republic. For this earlier period, see Albistur and Armogathe, *Histoire du féminisme français,* vol. 1. The contrasting political rights are summarized in Hause with Kenney, *Women's Suffrage,* 3–5.

NELLY ROUSSEL

The belle époque came to an abrupt end during the summer of 1914. At 3:55 P.M. on August 1, Premier René Viviani responded to an international crisis by ordering the mobilization of the French army. A few hours later, German armies invaded Belgium and Luxembourg, following a plan that would bring them within a few kilometers of Paris by early September. French politics changed abruptly. Virtually every political movement in France (including the feminists') swore support for a "sacred union" and vowed not to resume protests until the Germans had been defeated. "Duty," as Marie Bonnevial put it, "called more loudly than rights."[1]

The catastrophe of 1914 was an especially severe blow to the French women's suffrage campaign, which had reached its apogee in July 1914. The French Union for Women's Suffrage (UFSF) had enrolled 12,000 members, with branches in seventy-five departments of France. Ferdinand Buisson had delivered a committee report to the Chamber of Deputies in favor of women's suffrage, and over forty percent of the chamber had already announced that they would vote for the bill. A new suffrage organization, the *Ligue nationale pour le vote des femmes* (LNVF, the National League for Women's Suffrage), had persuaded many militants to focus on winning the vote. One of the largest newspapers in Europe, *Le Journal,* with a circulation over one million, sponsored a mock election in Paris in which nearly 506,000 women asked for the right to vote. Finally, on July 5, 1914, more than 5,000 women marched in a suffragist parade honoring the Marquis de Condorcet as a pioneer of women's rights—by far the most French women ever to join a feminist demonstration in the streets.[2]

Nelly Roussel was among the militant feminists who decided in the spring of 1914 that it was time to give more of their energies to suffragism. She had previously found the UFSF too timid for her, and she now joined the LNVF, giving lectures to help it attract working-class women to suffragism. She joined the sponsors of the *Journal* poll and worked for a large turnout. As always, Roussel's greatest contribution was her vigorous oratory. She gave her most noted suffrage speech, which is translated here, on March 16, 1914, at *Le Journal's* meeting hall. The title of this speech, "Let Us Create the Female Citizen" [*la Citoyenne*], contained a sad tribute to Hubertine Auclert, who had launched French suffragism a generation earlier with a newspaper entitled *La Citoyenne*. As Roussel spoke, Auclert lay on her deathbed, still talking of her next demonstration. Auclert died three weeks later, four months before the war derailed the suffrage campaign.

Let Us Create the Female Citizen

Gentlemen and Citizens,

Ladies . . . I should like to be able to say, "and citizens," but of course, that would be taking my wishes for reality, since, Ladies, it is precisely with the goal of claiming the title of "citizens" that we are gathered here this evening.

Our claim is not new, by the way. It is almost as old as the word "citizen." Already during the Revolution, during that grand and terrible period when the "Rights of Man" were being drawn up, a few daring women and generous men were trying to give the word "man" the wide and full meaning of "human being," instead of the restricted and inexact sense of "male individual." But their voices remained isolated and misunderstood. Most of the men in '93 showed themselves fiercely masculinist and in matters of rights hardly recognized any for women, excepting that of the scaffold. You know the famous words of Olympe de Gouges: *"Women have the right to mount the scaffold; they must have the right to mount the tribune."*[3] Later, in 1848, despite renewed efforts, the qualifier "universal," applied only to male suffrage, representing the most biting of insults to our sex—putting us, as it did outside

Source: Nelly Roussel, *"Créons la citoyenne"* (1914), in *Trois conférences* (Paris, 1930). Trans. Jette Kjaer and Jennifer Waelti-Walters.

the universe—an insult against which just and free minds have never ceased protesting since.

I do not have enough time to give you here a historical account of feminism in general, and the demands made by the suffragists in particular; to draw your attention to all the admirable and unsuccessful attempts made by our precursors to whom we cannot pay tribute enough. But, if women's suffrage has had its defenders at all times, it has been only a few years since it gave birth, here, to a real movement, which, getting bigger every day with encouraging speed, permits us to have great hopes. Moreover, the circumstances favor us at the moment. And now, at the start of the elections, when all Frenchmen aged twenty-one and over who have not been convicted and lost their rights of citizenship will be called to exercise their prerogatives as citizens, we Frenchwomen judge this to be an excellent opportunity to emphasize strongly the injustice of which we are victims and protest more loudly than ever before: "We want to be citizens!"

We want to be "citizens" the way you are "citizens," Gentlemen, under the same conditions and for exactly the same reasons. We want to be *citizens* like you, because we are *workers* like you, *taxpayers* like you, and *subject to trial* like you. Because like you we contribute to our national prosperity; because like you we have needs to be met and interests to defend; because like you we are subject to regulations, institutions, and laws that you have established alone, and—we should have to be blind not to notice—having established them *without* us, you have also established them *against* us. We want to be citizens because experience has taught us sufficiently that we can expect nothing from any social organization whatsoever to which we do not provide active and direct assistance. We want to be citizens because we believe M. René Viviani was right when he said, "Legislators make laws for those who make the legislators";[4] in other words, *nobody who cannot vote counts in the eyes of the elected*.

Oh! I know perfectly well what they could tell me at this point! They could tell me that once the electoral period, with its flatteries, promises, and lies, is over, the voters themselves do not count for much. And unfortunately, there would be some truth in this. But we must not exaggerate. And we all have reason to believe that if employers alone placed their ballots in the ballot box, the situation of the workers would be even more unfortunate. Besides, and allow me to tell you, Gentlemen, if your elected representatives mock you at times, it is because you want it that way. It is because you do not know how to call them to order and impose your will on them. After all, the voters get the representatives they deserve.

So, and we cannot repeat it often enough, we do not see the civic rights we are claiming as a goal, ideal, or crowning achievement but simply as a way to better our lot, perhaps only slightly, but at least immediately. It is like a combat weapon, the absence of which is so much the more unfortunate for us, as our adversaries have it in their hands and do not hesitate to use it against us. It is enough, to give but one example, to know that the states where women have the vote are the only ones in the world where school-teachers and government employees of both sexes receive equal treatment for equal work. This fact, among many others, is enough for you to understand the reasons why we want these rights.

And when one looks at what is happening in our country, when one sees the outcome of most reforms favoring women, when one knows the time it takes our legislators to enact measures of the most elementary equity and the difficulty we have in extracting the smallest scrap of justice from them, it is impossible not to tell oneself that the presence of female deputies in Parliament, or simply requiring male deputies to account for their mandate to female voters, would perhaps shake up the laziness, the lack of concern, and the egoism of these gentlemen somewhat. And it is the same with little things as with big ones. Whether it be a question of obtaining protection, recommendation, or help from a candidate or an elected official, the single woman who does not vote and who has no voters around her will always be served last—that is, if she is not forgotten altogether.

And even without speaking of laziness, egoism, and lack of concern, as I have just done, should it not be enough just to speak of *incompetence?* Indeed, even with the best intentions in the world, is it not from incompetence that these gentlemen usually err when they pretend to settle our personal affairs without bothering to consult us? Let us be sure, Ladies, that our affairs will never be well taken care of *unless we do it ourselves,* or, at the very least, lend our assistance. It is in the name of this principle that men have instituted so-called universal suffrage for themselves. It is in the name of this same principle that we, in turn, want suffrage to become truly universal.

And yet, Ladies and Gentlemen, I must confess that no matter how interesting the direct material results of female suffrage may be, I myself am counting especially and infinitely more on the indirect results, the moral ones. I know one must not expect anything from laws but what they can give, that is, not a lot; and if female suffrage were concerned only with these laws, I do not say it would be completely useless, but perhaps it would not be worth our while to act this way. But it will change customs and will bring about the best of all revolutions, a moral revolution. Everyone who knows how simpleminded men boast naively of their title of "citizen" will understand how women who become "citizens" will immediately grow in prestige in the eyes of those men. We have told these men, we have told them on every occasion since childhood, that civic rights are an honor and it is a sign of weakness not to have them.

Now, women do not have them! Not more than do lawbreakers and madmen! The men know and see that, socially, women are nothing, women can do nothing, women do not count! And they, who belong to the "sovereign people," become extremely scornful of women. That is why we see them so often, alas too often, abandoning the family home and preferring the conversation of the first person they meet in a bar to that of their life companion and mother of their children and replying, when this companion ventures a timid observation, "Oh, be quiet! You don't know anything about it! Politics don't concern women!" Well, Ladies and Gentlemen, from now on we want politics to concern women, and we want this to be known to women and admitted by men. And we want male and female citizens to discuss things on equal terms, aware that her opinion is worth his and that she must be taken into account.

"A new subject for discord between couples!" they will tell us. Perhaps— although, to be honest, this subject of discord is not new, for not having the vote has never kept women from having or expressing an opinion—but also, and we must not forget this, at times a new subject for *agreement,* for a fuller and more intimate understanding between two human beings who dream of the same ideals and pursue the same goal. And it is an invitation, Gentlemen, to be concerned from now on not just with the physical appearance and dowry but also with the mentality and deepest aspirations of the woman to whom you join yourself for life; an invitation if you are wealthy to look no longer for a pretty, luxurious "trinket" as your future wife, or if you are poor, a docile servant, but for a true companion who, your sister in soul and in mind, will make your union stronger, more harmonious, and more delightful.

And then, finally, it is necessary to mention that the interests of our sex are not the only ones at stake here. We are talking about something infinitely higher still, the question of not thwarting a great, natural law, a law of universal harmony. Men and women are not made to act in isolation or to take refuge behind a wall the other cannot penetrate. And it is crazy to think that a perfect and lasting achievement is possible in any field without the close and continual collaboration of the two essential elements that constitute humanity. Wanting to organize human society without the help of these two elements appears to me as insane, chimerical, and unreasonable as pretending to create a new life without the aid of a father and mother. It is in the name of this principle that we are claiming our place everywhere and that we want, in all things, the official advent of freely blossoming female minds. And all we demand can be summed up in these few words.

If necessary, Ladies and Gentlemen, I could stop right here. I could limit myself to putting forward our reasons and trust you to compare them carefully with those of our adversaries, which no doubt you know all too well. But I cannot resist giving you a quick review of the enemy army and presenting you with the arguments that are used to fight against us.

I begin with an argument I could perhaps ignore completely and on which, in any case, I shall not insist. It revolves around the presentation of women's access to politics as a danger to their grace, beauty, and charm. We have known that argument for a long time, have we not! It is the oldest, most worn-out of all and has served to fight our demands one by one, at all levels and in no matter what connection. Each time women have tried, be it ever so slightly, to leave traditional female occupations, expand their horizons, and spread their influence, the conservatives have risen up before them shouting in the name of beauty: "Now wait a minute!"—without ever having managed to explain to us, by the way, how beauty can be the exclusive prerogative of slaves and in what way it is incompatible with light, justice, and liberty! If I don't want to stop at this argument, it is not just because I consider it particularly stupid, or because it seems to me sufficiently refuted by the fact that the greatest women politicians in history, from Cleopatra to Mme Roland,[5] have almost always been as remarkable for their charms as for their abilities, no—if I don't want to stop at this argument, it is simply because I do not believe the people who put it forward are sincere. When I see the same men who fight against our *rights* in the name of beauty becoming annoyed because a woman recoils before accomplishing a *duty* such as her maternal duty, also in the name of beauty and in order to preserve her charm, I tell myself that this much-vaunted cult of beauty can be nothing but a pretext, a weapon men brandish against us but quickly put back in its sheath when they perceive that we, in our turn, can use it against them. For we must be rational here. If we are truly the fragile and charming "trinkets" before whom you tremble, Gentlemen, the luxurious dolls who have no other function but to cultivate and conserve a beauty that pleases you, then for goodness' sake be logical! Do not ask of us precisely what compromises and makes this beauty fade more than anything else: *numerous pregnancies* and *housework*. Do not be astonished or indignant if we are in complete agreement with you and, glorifying your idol in our turn, declare: no more deforming pregnancies! And no more tiring nursing! No more heavy domestic tasks that ruin our delicate hands, force us to maintain ungainly postures, and wear inelegant clothes! You are right, Gentlemen, beauty first! Beauty above all! Why, then, would it be blameworthy to sacrifice our maternal burdens and domestic drudgery to this beauty, since you find it just, reasonable, and necessary that we sacrifice our interests as working women, our obligations as citizens, and our dignity as human beings for it? . . . Why? . . . If not because antifeminist illogicality and incoherence are infinite and immeasurable! (I say *antifeminist* and not *masculine,* Gentlemen, for I do not want to forget that we have friends among men or that, alas, not all our enemies are recruited from among them.)

And these enemies, of either sex (here I am going to present another of their arguments, one that merits more of our attention, although, in the end, it is neither more serious nor more sound), these enemies show no less coherence or logic, and they certainly show much more injustice, when they invoke against us not only our charms but our *duties* and refuse us rights in the name of these same duties, in the name of what is precisely the most touching attribute of women and the most to be respected, in the name of Motherhood!—Ah, Motherhood! This sacred function that should be our glory is, on the contrary, a source of much humiliation and much resentment. How many doors closed, how many dreams broken, how many aspirations quenched because of and in the name of maternity! One would really believe they are trying to make us hate it, the way they always put it before our eyes like a prison wall, attach it to our legs like a ball and chain, always showing it as the obstacle in the way of our progress, the eternal source of all our miseries and humiliations! If we put forward the claim of providing for our needs ourselves by exercising a profession that suits our tastes and our abilities, keeping our dignity through our independence; if we demand a larger and gentler place in the home where we are the heart of the family, as well as a greater respect for our rights and freedoms; finally, if we aspire to an intellectual life, to gaining access to the noble domains of science and thought, we always come up against the same reply, sometimes covered by rhetorical "flowers," sometimes more blunt: "Return to your children, Ladies." "Nothing must distract you from your natural obligation!" is what educated people say to us. "Go look after your kids!" others tell us. But only the formula changes; the intention remains the same, and the door always shuts . . . unless we put our shoulders to it and give it a push, which luckily does happen now and then. *Because we are mothers* we can be nothing, say nothing, do nothing. Ignorance, powerlessness, humiliation, servitude, misery—that's our fate!—*because we are mothers!* And this maternal role, this terrible and sublime role that would make us queens among the bees, makes us slaves among humans! There is nothing, Gentlemen, nothing in your social organization as disgraceful, nothing as odious or revolting, as that! Oh, we must truly love motherhood to become mothers in spite of everything!

And again, it is *because we are mothers,* of course, that we cannot be citizens. Our adversaries assert that these two things are irreconcilable and that the former would be killed off by the latter. "A mother must devote herself exclusively to her children." Here again we must be reasonable and see things for what they are. Come now! Who would believe that even the best mothers today dedicate themselves so completely to their children? Moreover, who would believe they never do anything else without the children suffering from it in any way? Not to mention those women, and the number grows larger every day, who are forced out of necessity to occupy themselves with other things besides their children—or rather, to take even greater and more complete care of them, since these mothers do not just make the soup but also earn it . . . Not to mention every courageous woman who, with marvellous activity and energy, finds a way of reconciling her maternal duties and domestic labor with the most tedious and time-consuming professional occupations and who manages to do a multiplicity of jobs at once without anyone getting upset, something the bravest men would turn away from. Not to mention those working heroines who, although they presently represent more than half the feminine population, are always forgotten by our adversaries when they speak of women . . . Is it necessary to mention all the other women: the society ladies and their pleasures, the gossips and their stories, the devout and their prayers, all those from whom motherhood doesn't drain all the life, so that temptation leads them to look elsewhere for distractions they are missing? . . . Finally, must I remind you that children grow up and mothers grow old; and must I make you think of all those who, having accomplished their maternal role, could employ their active and clear-minded maturity in other jobs beneficial to society . . . Come now! Who would believe that putting a small piece of paper into a ballot box every two years would turn the lives of these women so completely upside down?

Oh, I am aware that to exercise the right we are demanding involves more than putting a tiny slip of paper into a ballot box every two years—or, at least, I hope female citizens would not be content with that, though, alas, male citizens all too often are. I know that the exercise of civil rights brings with it other duties and obligations. I know one must keep oneself informed about politics, that one must read, take part in discussions, and go to meetings in order to base one's vote on more than impulse. But would this really be so new to women? Even today, are not many of the best, and precisely the busiest of us, interested in social activity, and are they not as well informed as their father, brothers, or husbands? . . . What then, would they need to change in their lives in order to become citizens, these valiant women who already today are accomplishing their duties without exercising their rights? As for the rest, the day when honest housewives or little shopgirls opening the morning paper neglect their serial novel for a moment to pay more attention to politics or issues of concern to workers; when idle women of fashion put aside part of the time previously wasted in frivolous and vain pleasures to go to meetings or instructive lectures . . . I don't really see what husbands, children, or households would have to lose; on the contrary, I see clearly everything they could stand to gain.

And then, finally, Ladies and Gentlemen, we must rid ourselves of this deplorable habit of reasoning differently according to the sex concerned. If we women have family duties, do not men also? And are yours any less serious, less important, or less sacred than ours? If really, as you tell us, exercising our civic right is incompatible with these duties, if it means repudiating them, or at least neglecting them, how dare you, Gentlemen, you who are husbands and fathers, who carry the burden of feeding a family by your job, how dare you take time from this valuable and necessary job to involve yourselves in public life? . . . In order to be good citizens, does that mean you are bad husbands, bad fathers, and also bad workers, who neglect their professional duties for politics? . . . That is not so, Gentlemen, is it? You would not tolerate our speaking to you like that! . . . And it seems to me the right time to recall what Condorcet said: *"Making citizens out of women does not mean tearing them away from their housework any more than it means tearing laborers from their fields or artists from their studios."* The same Condorcet also said: *"Either no human individual has any rights or they all have the same rights; and he who votes against the rights of someone else, of no matter what nationality, religion, color, or sex, has renounced his own from then on!"*[6]

Of course, those arguments that serve to fight against women's franchise are also used against their eligibility to be candidates for elections. Is it necessary to point out to you that in that case the arguments are even more unacceptable? In this case it is no longer all women but just a tiny minority that is in question, because a particular mission is concerned, a mandate that no one is forced to solicit and that those women who for some reason or other are not in the position to fulfill, probably will not solicit. Moreover, the voters are always free not to entrust a mission to any candidate, male or female, who in their opinion does not seem to offer them all the right conditions. There is no reason to suppose that female candidates will fulfill these conditions less often than the males, but there are many reasons to believe that the voters will show themselves infinitely more severe toward them than toward their masculine counterparts, for we are used to greater demands for perfection being laid on women, at least when they aspire to a public position, and to their being considered incapable when they are not superior to men in every way.

And this reflection, Ladies and Gentlemen, brings us quite naturally to the last argument I want to examine. Though not major, but simple and timely, it is, nevertheless, more serious and important than all those that have been devised against us. And we really might tend to believe there is some substance to it, given that our friends themselves, intimidated by it, have sometimes hesitated. But we shall demolish it like the others, for the argument is strong in appearance only.

In the eyes of many of our fellow citizens, the greatest obstacle to obtaining the rights we demand is the *women's inability to use them properly*. There are many possible answers to that. We could answer, first of all, by citing the simple proverb: "Practice makes perfect," which has been translated wonderfully into these terms: "The voter is educated by voting." In effect, I do not really see that it can be otherwise. And an educational system that waits for a child to learn how to write before putting a pen in his hand is strange indeed. Nothing has been done, or practically nothing, to give men instruction in civics as long as they were not citizens. Likewise, nothing will really be done to educate women in civics before they become citizens. Let us not delude ourselves about that, Ladies.

And then, Gentlemen, when you use women's lack of ability to refuse them a right you enjoy, let me tell you, you are proving your pretentiousness yet again. To hear you, one would really think that superior capacities and first-class virtues were required to use one's rights as a citizen! I must say, looking at most of the voters and even many of the elected of your sex . . . I had not noticed! . . . And I wonder what we women could do to add any more incoherence, injustice, or stupidity to the structure you have built. Perhaps you are afraid we would not do better than you, but as for doing any worse, oh no, Gentlemen, no, there are records that cannot be beaten, limits that cannot be surpassed! Only look around you; get rid of these old, empty theories and outdated commonplaces in exchange for living reality. Ask yourselves why all these good housewives you see working every day, so active, ingenious, orderly, and sensible, would not bring all those precious qualities that make them so capable of directing a family to the running of the State. Ask yourselves why the first imbecile to come by, the most illiterate peasant, the most insignificant pen-pusher, the greatest drunken barfly, is judged more worthy of influencing the destiny of his country than the female teacher who raises her children, the female doctor who takes care of her family, and all those eminent women, founders of philanthropic works or defenders of social justice, who use their intelligence and courageous devotion to repair the damage done by "men's laws."

Oh, I realize that *these* women are not all women. I know there are narrow-minded and incapable women as well as men, and that, as with men, these narrow-minded and incapable ones, alas, still make up the majority. I also know that some men, moved by a situation where the least significant men have more influence than the greatest women, but nonetheless too timid to conceive of and desire perfect equality, have proposed the lame reform that would make "citizens" only those "elite" women whose works or diplomas guarantee their capacities. But it is precisely here that, in the name of logic, justice, and social progress, I want to shout: Now hold on! A women's suffrage that excludes women of the proletariat, that immense swarm of manual workers whose bitter struggle does not allow them to get a certificate, diploma, or decoration, who have grown pale from bending over machines rather than over books, whose poor arms have carried more urchins than laurels, but who do not need the vote any less to defend themselves against exploitative employers and husbands who mistreat them, I oppose! Such a suffrage appears to me to be the most revolting and dangerous of comedies!

As for the other half-measure that has been proposed to us, whereby only single, divorced, or widowed women would have political rights, it would be superfluous to say that, to me, this is no more acceptable. I see in it a new injustice toward wives, who are already sufficiently downtrodden, and a new illogicality on the part of a society that praises marriage but makes it a downfall and reserves all benefits for spinsterhood.

And, since we have reached the chapter of restrictions on women's franchise, you will hardly be surprised to hear me protesting especially against what is, more than anything else, the order of the day, and which certain feminists have had the weakness to accept and even approve. I want to talk about the bill that proposes giving only *municipal suffrage* to women.[7] Oh, I certainly do not ignore the arguments of those who support it! Like them, I know perfectly well that municipal suffrage would permit us to do some good. And we are quite ready to do some good. But that is not enough—we want to do a lot of good. And we also want something else. We want to defend our interests, better our situation, modify, and if need be destroy, the laws that humiliate and oppress us. We want to take the place we deserve in the family and society. And only *political* suffrage will give us the means to that end.

Some—as I also know—would answer that the conquest of municipal suffrage is a necessary step; that we must not be too demanding to begin with; that prudence and moderation are conditions that lead to success. Ladies and Gentlemen, my view is completely the opposite: I believe that to obtain a little we must demand a lot. Let us leave prudence, moderation, and expediency to the Members of the Legislature, for pity's sake! They will undertake to practice them quite well enough in our stead; they will take it upon themselves to measure out how much we should be given, judging that it is not for us to determine how much we are asking for in advance. Let us say it loud and clear: we are a few women who are very determined to demand our integral rights at all times and in all places. What we need is our full share, and not simply a bone to gnaw; it is not suffrage for such and such a category of women, or such and such a kind of election; it is not some kind of secondary and inferior suffrage, which might be more humiliating than the present situation; what we need, quite simply, is the only kind of suffrage worthy of France and the Republic, *universal* suffrage, without distinction of class or sex. And you have nothing to fear from this suffrage, Gentlemen. The coming of women into public life can only be a blessing. And if you need more facts than arguments to be convinced, let us look to other countries for the experience we lack. Let us see what women's suffrage has given to countries where it has existed for an appreciable number of years, as in Australia, for instance, or certain States in North America. Let us consult the documents, the official statistics. They will show us that everywhere, *alcoholism, prostitution, and the exploiting of child labor* are the first enemies attacked and defeated by female citizens. And all this, it seems to me, must appear desirable; and only rapacious capitalists and depraved idlers would be grieved by it, as they are grieved over there.

And now, Ladies and Gentlemen, I would not forgive myself if I did not insist upon one last reflection, which by its very nature seems to me to impress particularly those high-minded people with generous feelings. We all have reason to believe that the coming of women into public life will have even more splendid consequences: it will mark the most memorable and blessed step in the history of the world—the most tremendous and decisive step that humanity has ever taken on the path toward happiness; . . . it will be the end of the era of violence and the beginning of peace. When our primordial feelings have not been deformed by a monstrous education, we women are the natural, instinctive, and necessary enemies of this social monstrosity we call war. We, the creators, who know the price of life, and have the sublime mission not only of giving birth to it in pain and danger but also of conserving, developing, and beautifying it, do not want works of death! We do not want fratricidal, criminal, or antihuman struggles that, hidden behind pompous names and clever pretexts, are nothing but the unleashing of primitive savagery, the awakening of the beast that sleeps lightly in the half-civilized soul. A few schemers know how to exploit this beast at the right moment for their own profit, but for the greatest harm of true civilization and eternal progress. We, who have always been enslaved in its name, do not accept the right of might. We do not accept the triumph of brute force over reason, science, work, or beauty. And this we will prove magnificently, the day we can finally oppose it with something other than fruitless tears and useless curses!

No, Gentlemen, once more, you have nothing to fear from women's suffrage, nothing! Not even, and I believe I have to say a few words on this subject before finishing, not even a general upset in politics, a change in direction that strikes panic in certain milieux—those whose members have a nice sinecure in the government that they would not like to lose. The question, "How will women vote and for whom?" has never been asked in my presence. Since it is precisely the right to express their opinions freely that I am claiming here for women, and if it were proven that women's suffrage must change something in politics, I would see that as another reason for demanding this suffrage, since it would prove that our present-day politics are not what the real majority of the country wants. Although, as I say, this question has never been asked in my presence, I know only too well with what insistence it is asked of others not to try answering it. Well, Gentlemen, I am persuaded that women's suffrage will have a noticeable effect on the particular questions of public assistance, hygiene, administration, child protection, and the defense of women's interests, which men have taken much too little interest in until now, reserving the major part of their activities for purely political struggles. And by that I do not mean to say that women will remain outsiders to these struggles but simply that they will only increase the number of fighters in each camp without giving an appreciable advantage to one or the other. There is no reason to suppose that from a political viewpoint women will be less divided among themselves than men. And you are imagining things, you who see women's suffrage as a threat or a hope for the party you belong to and whose interests concern you much more than do those of justice, and not for what it really is, that is, a reform based on logic and principles of our democracy.

However, Gentlemen, if you are not mistaken, if with our newly conquered rights we really have to incline toward such and such a party, tell yourselves that it is most likely that we would give preference to the one that has been most loyal in helping us get the vote. When our hour of victory comes, we will know how to remember those good companions who have given us a brotherly hand during the fight. Do I have to tell you how much I personally hope the Republicans and their freethinkers do not let their adversaries play this role and adopt this attitude? Tell yourselves, Republicans, that the safety of the Republic depends only on itself. The Republic has nothing to fear from us if we know we have everything to expect from it. It has but to lean toward us, and we will rise to meet it. It has only to stretch out its maternal arms, and we will throw ourselves into them with confidence. It has but to be the torch of justice, truth, and liberty in our eyes, and we will go joyfully toward its light. And to it we will bring the treasure of our active tenderness, our maternal perceptiveness, our pity as creatures who suffer and wish to abolish suffering, and our ardor as warriors, still trembling from the conquest of our newly won right. And we will make the Republic grander and more beautiful. We will make the *true* Republic, which shall engrave into people's conscience the sublime words: "Liberty, Equality, Fraternity," words that our present Republic that is all show and lies, your Republic, Gentlemen, has been content, out of irony no doubt, to write on the façade of its monuments.

Notes

1. For feminism and the war, see especially McMillan's *Housewife or Harlot*, 101–88, which originated as a doctoral dissertation on the impact of the war on the social

condition of women. See also Steven C. Hause, "More Minerva Than Mars"; Hause with Kenney, *Women's Suffrage*, 191–211; Klejman and Rochefort, *L'Egalité en marche*, 189–98. The Bonnevial quotation is from *L'Action féminine*, August 1916.

2. For the suffrage campaign of 1914, see Hause with Kenney, *Women's Suffrage*, 169–90.

3. For more on de Gouges and women during the French Revolution, see note 31 to the Brion text in part 3. The quotation is from Article 10 of *The Declaration of the Rights of Women*, which is reprinted in Levy, et al., *Women in Revolutionary Paris*, 87–96.

4. Viviani was not yet premier when Roussel spoke. The government in March 1914 was still Gaston Doumergue's cabinet, in which Viviani held the post of Minister of Education. For more on Viviani, see note 16 to Nelly Roussel in part 1.

5. Marie-Jeanne-Manon Roland (1754–93) was an active participant in the French Revolution with her husband, Jean-Marie Roland de la Platière (1734–93). Mme Roland's salon was a center of the Girondist faction, and she wielded great political power between 1791 and 1792. The Jacobin triumph of 1793, however, led to her imprisonment and execution.

6. Jean-Antoine-Nicolas de Caritat, Marquis de Condorcet (1743–94) produced the most clearly feminist writings of the well-known *philosophes* of eighteenth-century France. He was one of the first writers in any country to call for women's suffrage. Roussel quotes from his "Essai sur l'admission des femmes au droits de cité," which appeared in *Le Journal de la société de* 1789 on July 3, 1790. Condorcet also actively supported the French Revolution, but he too wound up in trouble with the Jacobins and found himself proscribed for Girondism; he killed himself with poison to escape the guillotine.

7. Both the bill before the Chamber of Deputies and the Buisson Report called for women's suffrage only in local elections. This was the common pattern of initial enfranchisement in most of the Western world. Sweden, for example, granted women the municipal suffrage in 1862 but did not give women parliamentary suffrage until 1918. For England, the dates were 1869 (municipal suffrage) and 1918 (parliamentary suffrage). New Zealand was the first state to grant women parliamentary suffrage (1893).

APPENDIXES

APPENDIX ONE

Feminist Periodicals of the Belle Epoque, 1890–1914

Many of these titles are extremely rare and survive only in partial sets or isolated numbers. The best sources are the Bibliothèque Marquerite Durand and the Bouglé Collection of the Bibliothèque historique de la ville de Paris. In both collections, some titles can be found only by searching dossiers on related subjects. Other important sources include the Hélène Brion Collection at the Institut français d'histoire sociale (housed at the Archives nationales), the Jane Misme Collection at the Bibliothèque du Trocadéro, and the Avril de Sainte-Croix Collection at the Musée social.

L'Abeille. (Syndicalist-feminist. Pauline Savari, editor. 1901.)

L'Action féminine. (Organ of the CNFF. Avril de Sainte-Croix, editor. 1909–17.)

L'Action féministe. (Feminist teachers. Jane Méo and Marie Guérin, editors. Nancy: 1908–26.)

L'Action sociale de la femme. (Catholic-feminine. Jeanne Chenu, editor. 1901–23.)

L'Almanach féministe. (UFF annual publication, 1906–08)

L'Avant Courière. (Jeanne Schmahl, editor. Irregular publication 1893-?)

Bulletin. (Organ of *Amélioration.* Feresse-Deraismes, editor. 1894–1910.)

Bulletin. (Organ of *Etudes.* Jeanne Oddo-Deflou, editor. 1898.)

Bulletin. (Organ of the *Ligue d'électeurs pour le suffrage des femmes.* 1911–14.)

Bulletin. (Organ of *Maçonnerie mixte en France.* Georges Martin, editor. 1895–?)

Bulletin. (Organ of the *Société féministe du Havre.* Pauline Rebour, editor. 1909.)

Bulletin. (Organ of the UFF. 1890.)

Bulletin. (Organ of UFSF. Cecile Brunschvicq, editor. 1911–40.)

La Citoyenne. (Suffragist weekly. Hubertine Auclert, editor. 1881–91.)

La Combate féministe. (Militant. Arria Ly, editor. 1913–14.)

Le Cri des femmes. (Feminist. Clotilde Dissard, editor. Amiens: 1914.)

Le Droit des femmes. (Organ of the LFDF. Maria Vérone et al., editors. 1876–.)

L'Echo de la Ligue patriotique des femmes françaises. (Conservative Catholic feminine. 1902.)

L'Egalité. (Irregular pamphlet series. Eliska Vincent, editor. 1904–07.)

L'Entente. (Moderate feminist. Héra Mirtel, editor. 1905–09.)

L'Equité. (Working class-feminist. Marianne Rauze, editor. 1913–16.)

Le Féminisme chrétien. (Catholic feminist monthly. Marie Maugeret, editor. 1896–?)

Le Féminisme intégral. (Madame Remember, editor. 1913–22.)

La Féministe. (Anne de Réal, editor. Nice: 1906–11.)

La Femme. (Protestant-feminine monthly. Sarah Monod et al., editors. 1879–1937.)

La Femme affranchie. (Socialist-feminist. Gabrielle Petit, editor. 1904–30.)

La Femme contemporaine. (Conservative-Catholic, feminine. C. Mano, editor. 1902–21.)

La Femme de demain. (Moderate feminist. Jeanne Oddo-Deflou, editor. 1913–14.)

La Femme de l'avenir. (Socialist-feminist. Astié de Valsayre, editor. 1896–1901.)

La Femme socialiste. (Socialist-feminist. Elisabeth Renaud and Louise Saumoneau, editors. 1901–02, 1912–38.)

La Française. (Weekly newspaper. Jane Misme, editor. 1906–40.)

La Fronde. (Feminist daily newspaper. Marguerite Durand, editor. 1897–1905, 1914, and 1926.)

L'Heure de la femme. (Moderate feminist. Lydie Martial, editor.)

Le Journal des femmes. (Militant feminist. Maria Martin, editor. 1891–1910.)

Jus suffragii. (Moderate suffragist organ of UFSF.)

Le Mouvement féminin. (Moderate feminist. 1913.)

Le Pain. (Catholic. 1900.)

La Rénovation féministe. (Militant. Arria Ly, editor. Toulouse: 1908. Supplement to Adolphe Morel's *La Rénovation morale.*)

La Revue féministe. (Clotilde Dissard, editor. 1895–99.)

Société d'éducation. (Irregular pamphlet series. Odette Laguerre, editor. Lyons: 1900–05.)

Suffragia. (French bulletin of the IWSA. 1910–?)

La Suffragiste. (Militant feminist. Madeleine Pelletier, editor. 1908–19.)

La Travailleuse. (Syndicalist-feminist. 1913–19.)

Les Travailleuses. (Feminist-syndicalist. Marie-Louise Berot-Berger, editor. 1906–19.)

La Vie féminine. (Moderate feminist. Valentine Thomson, editor. 1914–19.)

Other Translations of Feminist Writings from the Belle Epoque (Following the Outline of This Book and Chronological Order)

1. The Situation of Women

Hubertine Auclert on the emancipation of women, from *La Citoyenne* (editorial, 1881), in Hellerstein, Erna O., Leslie P. Hume, and Karen M. Offen (eds.), *Victorian Women* (Stanford: Stanford UP, 1981), 445–46.

Hubertine Auclert's electoral campaign program, from *Le Rappel* (newspaper article, 1885), in Steven C. Hause, *Hubertine Auclert* (New Haven: Yale UP, 1987), 239.

Program of the French League for Women's Rights (circular, 1892), in Patrick K. Bidelman, *Pariahs Stand Up!* (Westport: Greenwood, 1982), 211–13.

Jeanne Schmahl on "The Progress of the Women's Rights Movement in France," from *Forum* (article, 1896), in Susan Groag Bell and Karen M. Offen (eds.), *Women, the Family, and Freedom*, 2 vols. (Stanford: Stanford UP, 1983), 2:100–02.

Marie Maugeret on Catholic feminism, from *La Fronde* (newspaper article, 1897), in Bell and Offen, *Women, the Family, and Freedom*, 2:96–97.

Marcel Prévost on feminism as an affliction and a religion, from *Les Vierges fortes* (novel, 1900), in Bell and Offen, *Women, the Family, and Freedom*, 2:51–56.

Charles Turgeon on the nature of French feminists, from *Le Féminisme français* (book, 1902), in Bell and Offen, *Women, the Family, and Freedom*, 2:50–51.

2. Education

Madame Alfred Fouillée (pseud: G. Bruno) on educating girls in their domestic duties, from *Francinet* (textbook, 1887), in Hellerstein et al., *Victorian Women*, 67–68.

Pauline Kergomard on child abuse, from *Actes du congrès international des oeuvres et institutions féminines* (congress report, 1890), in Eleanor S. Riemer and John C. Fout (eds.), *European Women* (New York: Schocken, 1980), 123–26.

Nelly Roussel on sex education for girls, from *La Fronde* (theater review, 1904), in Bell and Offen, *Women, the Family, and Freedom*, 2:177–79.

Jeanne Crouzet-Benaben on equal secondary education for women, from *La Revue universitaire* (article, 1911), in Bell and Offen, *Women, the Family, and Freedom*, 2:170–71.

Baptiste Roussy on compulsory domestic education for women, from *Education domestique de la femme* (book, 1914), in Bell and Offen, *Women, the Family, and Freedom*, 2: 171–72.

Julliette Sauget on the schooling of a poor peasant girl (memoirs, 1920), in Reimer and Fout, *European Women*, 142–43.

3. Work

Madame Seignobos on shelters for unemployed women (congress report, 1890), in Riemer and Fout, *European Women*, 9–10.

A. Paquet-Mille on the choice of an occupation for young women, from *Nouveau guide pratique des jeunes filles* (book, 1891), in Reimer and Fout, *European Women*, 43–45.

Labor laws regulating the work of women and children (legal statutes, 1892 and 1900), in Mary Lynn Stewart, *Women, Work, and the French State* (Kingston: U of Toronto P, 1989), 203–04.

A rural teacher on the harassment of a working woman, from *Lettres d'institutrices rurales* (survey response, 1897), in Hellerstein et al., *Victorian Women*, 371–73.

Astié de Valsayre (?) on the working day of a shopgirl, from *La Femme de l'avenir* (article, 1897), in Reimer and Fout, *European Women*, 11–12.

Maria Pognon on "protective" limits on women's work, from *La Fronde* (newspaper article, 1899), in Bell and Offen, *Women, the Family, and Freedom*, 2:211–13.

St. Thérèse of Lisieux on the life of a nun (autobiography, 1890s), in Heller-
stein, et al., *Victorian Women*, 107–10.
Julliette Sauget on the life of a domestic servant in Paris (memoirs, 1920), in
Riemer and Fout, *European Women*, 143–44.

4. Prostitution and the Double Standard

The editors found no translations of significant works on this topic.

5. Marriage and Male-Female Relations

Alfred Naquet on the need for divorce legislation, from *Le Divorce* (book,
1881), in Bell and Offen, *Women, the Family, and Freedom*, 2:187–89.
Ernest Legouvé on the importance of marriage as a career, from *Histoire morale des femmes* (book, 1882), in Hellerstein et al., *Victorian Women*, 163.
The French Civil Code on "The Respective Rights and Duties of Husband
and Wife" (legal statutes, 1895), in Hellerstein et al., *Victorian Women*,
162.
Léon Blum on sex education and marriage, from *Du mariage* (book, 1907),
in Bell and Offen, *Women, the Family, and Freedom*, 2:179–80.
Maria Martin on the need for liberalized divorce laws, from *Le Journal des
femmes* (newspaper article, 1907), in Bell and Offen, *Women, the Family,
and Freedom*, 2: 189–90.
Madeleine Pelletier on feminism and the family (undated pamphlet, *Le
Féminisme et la famille*), translated by Marilyn J. Boxer in *French-American Review* 6 (1982): 3–26.

6. Issues of Maternity

Emile Zola on the value of the large family, from *Fruitfulness* (novel, 1899),
in Bell and Offen, *Women, the Family, and Freedom*, 130–32.
Blanche Edwards-Pilliet on the right to maternal leave, from *Congrès inter-
national de la condition et des droits des femmes* (congress report, 1900), in
Bell and Offen, *Women, the Family, and Freedom*, 2:145.
Eugène Brieux on illegitimate pregnancy, from *Maternity* (play, 1903), in
Bell and Offen, *Women, the Family, and Freedom*, 132–34.

Nelly Roussel on mothers as victims, from *La Fronde* (speech, 1904), in Bell and Offen, *Women, the Family, and Freedom,* 134–36.

Madeleine Pelletier on the right of abortion, *Pour l'abrogation de l'article 317: Le Droit de l'avortement* (pamphlet, 1913), translated by Marilyn J. Boxer in *French-American Review* 6 (1982): 3–26.

Juliette Sauget on having an illegitimate child (memoirs, 1920), in Reimer and Fout, *European Women,* 144–45.

7. Political and Civic Rights

Hubertine Auclert, the statutes of the society Women's Suffrage, from *La Citoyenne* (newspaper article, 1883), in Hause, *Hubertine Auclert,* 237–39.

Hubertine Auclert, Statutes of the society Women's Suffrage (circular, 1900), in Hause, *Hubertine Auclert,* 240.

Maria Martin on French suffragism in a European perspective, from *Le Journal des femmes* (newspaper article, 1906), in Bell and Offen, *Women, the Family, and Freedom,* 2:230–31.

Madeleine Pelletier on suffragist tactics, from *La Revue socialiste* (article, 1908), in Bell and Offen, *Women, the Family, and Freedom,* 2:105–06.

Hubertine Auclert, electoral program (circular, 1910), in Hause, *Hubertine Auclert,* 240–41.

The French Union for Women's Suffrage on the arguments in favor of the vote for women (congress report, 1913), in Reimer and Fout, *European Women,* 79–81.

BIBLIOGRAPHY

1. Works by the Generation of the Belle Epoque

Albistur, Maïté, and Daniel Armogathe, eds. *Le Grief des femmes*. Paris, 1978. Vol. 2. of *Anthologie de textes du second empire à nos jours*. 2 vols. Paris, 1978.

Auclert, Hubertine. *L'Argent de la femme*. Paris, 1904.

———. *La Citoyenne; articles de 1881 à 1891*. Ed. by Edith Taieb. Paris, 1982.

———. *Le Droit politique des femmes: question qui n'est pas traitée au congrès international des femmes*. Paris, 1878.

———. *Egalité sociale et politique de la femme et de l'homme: discours prononcé au congrès ouvrier socialiste de Marseille*. Marseille, 1879.

———. *Les Femmes arabes en Algérie*. Paris, 1900.

———. *Les Femmes au gouvernail*. Paris, 1923.

———. *Le Nom de la femme*. Paris, nd.

———. *Le Vote des femmes*. Paris, 1908.

Avril de Sainte-Croix (Mme Ghénia). *Dixième congrès international des femmes: oeuvres et institutions féminines, droit des femmes . . . tenu à Paris le 2 juin 1913. Compte rendu. . .* Paris, 1914.

———. *L'Esclave blanche: discours*. Alençon, 1913.

———. *Le Féminisme*. Paris, 1907.

———. "Les Françaises et le droit du suffrage." *The Englishwoman* 2 (1909).

———. *Une Morale pour les deux sexes*. Paris, 1900.

———. "Une Nouvelle puissance: le CNFF." *La Contemporaine* 10 November 1901.

———. *La Serve: iniquité sociale*. Paris, 1901.

———. *Le Travail des femmes et le demi-temps*. Paris, 1919.

Bérot-Berger, M-L. *La Femme dans le progrès social.* Paris, 1910.

Bertaut, Jules. *La Littérature féminine d'aujourd'hui.* Paris, 1909.

Bethléem, Abbé Jules. *Romans à lire et romans à proscrire.* Lille, 1914.

Blum, Léon. *Du mariage.* Paris, 1907.

Bogelot, Isabelle. *Complément de trente ans de solidarité.* Paris, 1915.

———. *Mémoire sur l'oeuvre des libérées de Saint-Lazare à Paris.* Paris, 1888.

———. *Trente ans de solidarité, 1877–1906.* Paris, 1908.

Bois, Jules. *L'Eve nouvelle.* Paris, 1896.

———. "La Femme nouvelle." *Revue encyclopédique Larousse* 28 November 1896.

Bonnefon, J. de. *La Corbeille des roses ou les dames de lettres.* Paris, 1909.

Bonnefont, G. *Les Parisiennes chez elles.* Paris, 1895–97.

Bonnevial, Marie. "Le Mouvement syndical féminin en France." *Revue de morale sociale* 1901.

Boudin, Marie-Rose. *Réponses à quelques objections contre le vote des femmes.* Montreuil-sous-Bois, nd.

Bouvier, Jeanne. *Mes mémoires: une syndicaliste féministe, 1876–1935.* Paris, 1983.

Bridel, Louis. *Le Droit des femmes et le mariage: études critiques de législation comparée.* Paris, 1893.

———. *La Femme et le droit: étude historique sur la condition des femmes.* Paris, 1884.

———. *Mélanges féministes: questions de droit et de sociologie.* Paris, 1897.

———. *Questions féministes: (1) Les Deux morales (2) Les Droits de la femme et la famille.* Geneva, 1896.

Brion, Hélène. *Encyclopédie féministe.* Manuscript. Bibliothèque Marguerite Durand, Paris.

———. *La Voie féministe.* Ed. Huguette Bouchardeau. Paris, 1978.

Broda, Rodolphe. "Le Mouvement en faveur du vote des femmes." *Documents du progrès* July 1909.

Brunschvicg, Cécile. *Congrès des institutions d'assistance et d'hygiène sociales . . . Compte rendu . . .* Paris, 1921.

———. "Féminisme: le suffrage des femmes en France." *Documents du progrès* 1913.

———. *Le Suffrage des femmes en France.* Leiden, 1938.

Buisson, Ferdinand. "Suffrage des femmes et le Ligue des droits de l'homme." *Les Cahiers des droits de l'homme* 20 March 1920.

———. *Le Vote des femmes.* Paris, 1911.

———. "Le Vote des femmes." *Documents du progrès* 1913.

Capy, Marcelle, and Aline Valette. *Femmes et travail au 19e siècle: enquêtes de La Fronde et La Bataille syndicaliste.* Ed. Evelyne Diebolt and Marie-Hélène Zylberberg-Hoquard. Paris, 1984.

Chéliga, Marya. *Almanach féministe, 1899*. Paris 1899.

———. "L'Evolution du féminisme." *Revue encyclopédique Larousse* November 28, 1896.

———. "Le Féminisme en France." *Revue politique et parlementaire* August 1,1897.

———. "Les Hommes féministes." *Revue encylopédique Larousse* November 28, 1896.

———. "Le Théâtre féministe." *La Revue d'art dramatique* 16 (1901): 649–58.

Clemenceau, George. *La "Justice" du sexe fort*. Paris, 1907.

Clement, Marguerite. *Conférence sur le suffrage des femmes*. Paris, 1912.

Compain, Marie-Louise. *L'Amour de Claire*. Paris, 1912.

———. "Les Conséquences du travail de la femme." *Grande revue* May 1913.

———. *Les Femmes dans les organisations ouvrières*. Paris, 1910.

———. "L'Initiation sociale de la femme." *Grande revue* 1912.

———. *L'Opprobre*. Paris, 1905.

———. *L'Un vers l'autre*. Paris, 1903.

———. *La Vie tragique de Geneviève*. Paris, 1912.

Cone, Ada. "The Feminist Movement in France and its Leaders." *The Humanitarian*, 12 (1898): 5–12.

Crouzet-Benaben, Jeanne. "Une Assemblée des femmes en 1913: Le Congrès international de Paris (2–7)." *Grande revue* July 1913.

Cruppi, Louise. *Comment les Anglaises ont conquis le vote*. Paris, 1919.

Dagan, Henri. "La Femme ouvrière." *Revue blanche* February 1902.

Dawbarn, Charles. "The French Woman and the Vote." *Fortnightly Review* August 1911.

Delarue-Mardrus, Lucie. *L'Acharnée*. Paris, 1910.

———. *Comme tout le monde*. Paris, 1910.

———. *Douce moitié*. Paris, 1913.

———. *L'Inexpérimentée*. Paris, 1913.

———. *Marie, fille-mère*. Paris, 1909.

———. *La Monnaie de singe*. Paris, 1913.

———. *Le Roman de six petites filles*. Paris, 1909.

———. *Tout l'amour*. Paris, 1911.

Deraismes, Maria. *Ce que veulent les femmes: articles et discours*. Ed. Odile Krakovitch. Paris, 1980.

———. *L'Eve dans l'humanité*. Paris, 1891.

———. *Oeuvres complètes*. Paris, 1895.

———. *Société pour l'amélioration du sort de la femme et la revendication de ses droits . . . Rapport*. Paris, 1893.

Dissard, Clotilde. *Opinions féministes*. Paris, 1896.

Du Breuil de Saint-Germain, Jean. *De l'intérêt qu'ont les hommes au suffrage des femmes*. Paris, 1913.

———. *La Misère sociale de la femme et le suffrage*. Suresnes, 1911.

Durand, Marguerite. *Congrès officiel international de la condition et des droits des femmes, Paris 1900: Procès verbaux sommaires*. Paris, 1901.

Durand, Marguerite, and A. Marpi. *La Manière de traiter les femmes comme elles le méritent*. Paris, nd.

Les Ecrits pour et contre: l'éducation sexuelle. [Anonymous compilation including works by Cécile Brunschvicg, Jane Misme, and Marguerite de Witt-Schlumberger, among others.] Paris, 1924.

Faguet, Emile. "L'Abbé féministe." *Revue bleue* 1902.

———. *Le Féminisme*. Paris, 1910.

Ferrer, Madame C.L. *Pourquoi voteraient-elles?* Paris, 1910.

Finot, Jean. *La Charte de la femme*. Paris, 1910.

Flat, P. *Nos femmes de lettres*. Paris, 1908.

Franck, L. *La Femme avocat*. Paris, 1898.

Gachons, Jacques de. "Les Femmes de lettres françaises." *Figaro illustré* February 1910.

Gemahling, Marguerite. "La Femme ouvrière et la maternité." *Action populaire* 1906.

Ghesquière, H. *La Femme et le socialisme*. Lille, 1893.

Gide, Charles. *La Recherche de la paternité*. Lyon, 1905.

Goirand, A. *De la protection et de l'assistance légales des femmes salariées avant et après leur accouchement*. Thesis. Paris, 1906.

Grinberg, Suzanne. *Historique du mouvement suffragiste depuis 1848*. Paris, 1926.

Guilleminot, A. *Femme, enfant, humanité*. Paris, 1896.

Harlor. "L'Education de la volonté de la femme." *Revue socialiste* April 1900.

———. "La Femme dans la théâtre de demain." *Revue d'art dramatique* October 1901.

———. "En relisant Louise Ackermann." *Grande revue* December 1913.

———. *Le Triomphe des vaincus*. Paris, 1908.

———. *Tu es femme*. Paris, 1913.

Haussonville, Comte de. *Salaires et misères de la femme*. Paris, 1900.

Hire, Marie d'Espire de la. "Le Féminisme en France et les sociétés féministes." *Revue des lettres* August 1907.

Joran, Théodore. *Autour du féminisme*. Paris, 1905.

———. *Au coeur du féminisme*. Paris, 1908.

————. *Le Féminisme à l'heure actuelle.* Paris, 1907.

————. *Le Féminisme avant le féminisme.* Paris, 1911.

————. *Les Féministes avant le féminisme.* Paris, 1910.

————. *Le Mensonge du féminisme.* Paris, 1905.

————. *Le Suffrage des femmes.* Paris, 1913.

————. *La Trouée féministe.* Paris, 1909.

Joseph-Renaud, J. *Le Catéchisme féministe: résumé de la doctrine sous forme de réponse aux objections.* Paris, 1910.

Kauffmann, Caroline. *L'Importance de l'éducation physique scientifique combinée avec l'éducation intellectuelle morale.* Paris, 1899.

Kauffmann, Caroline, and Madame (Paule) Mink. *Idées générales sur les travaux du congrès international féministe de Londres en 1899: Rapport . . .* Paris, 1899.

Kenenburg, B. de. *La Femme régénérateur.* Paris, 1899.

Kraemer-Bach, Marcelle. *Les Inégalités légales entre l'homme et la femme.* Paris, nd.

Lacour, Léopold. "La Femme dans le théâtre du XIXe siècle." *Revue d'art dramatique* October 1901.

————. *L'Humanisme intégral.* Paris, 1897.

Laguerre, Odette. *Biographies d'hommes illustres.* Paris, 1890.

————. *L'Enseignement dans la famille. Cours complet d'études pour les jeunes filles.* Paris, 1888–94.

————. "Notes complémentaires." In Charles Gide, *La Recherche de la paternité.* Lyon, 1905.

————. *Qu'est-ce que le féminisme?* Lyon, 1905.

————. *La Protection de l'enfance.* Lyon, 1906.

Laguerre, Odette, and Madeleine Cartier. *Pour la paix. Lectures historiques à l'usage de l'enseignement élémentaire et des écoles normales.* Paris, 1905.

Laloë, Jeanne. "Les Deux féminismes." *Nouvelle revue* May-June 1908.

Lampérière, Anna. *La Femme et son pouvoir.* Paris, 1909.

————. "L'Organisation d'un enseignement supérieur féminin. Rapport à M. le Ministre de l'instruction publique." *Revue de l'enseignement supérieur* 1903.

————. *Le Rôle social de la femme.* Paris, 1898.

Lamy, Etienne. *La Femme de demain.* Paris, 1901.

Lecointre, Comtesse Pierre. *Etat de la question féministe en France en 1907.* Paris, 1907.

Leduc, L. *La Femme avant le parlement.* Paris, 1898.

Lees, Frederic. "The Progress of Woman in France." *The Humanitarian* February 1901.

Lejeal, Gustave. "La Femme devant la loi." *Revue encyclopédique Larousse* November 1896.

Lemaitre, Jules. *Opinions à répandre*. Paris, 1901.

Levray, Mlle. *L'Alcoolisme et le vote des femmes*. Paris, nd.

LFDF. *Cinquante ans de féminisme, 1870–1920*. Paris, 1921.

Loria, A. *Le Féminisme du point de vue sociologique*. Paris, 1907.

Lourbet, G. *Le Problème des sexes*. Paris, 1900.

Manday, A. de. *Le Droit des femmes au travail*. Paris, 1905.

Margueritte, Paul and Victor. *L'Enlarissement du divorce: exposé des motifs et proposition de loi*. Paris, 1902.

———. *Mariage et divorce*. Paris, 1900.

———. *Mariage–divorce–union libre*. Lyon, 1902.

Marquet, Jean. *La Condition légale de la femme au commencement et à la fin du XIXe siècle*. Nimes, 1899.

Martial, Lydie. *Action du féminisme rationnel: union de pensée féminine*. Paris, 1901.

———. *La Femme et la liberté: la femme intégrale*. Paris, 1901.

Martin, Marguerite. *Les Droits de la femme*. Paris, 1912.

Martin, Maria. *Petit almanach féministe*. Paris, 1906–08.

Milhaud, Caroline. *L'Ouvrière en France*. Paris, 1907.

Mink, Paule. *Communarde et féministe (1839–1901). "Les Mouches et les araignées . . ." et autres textes*. Ed. Alain Dalotel. Paris, 1981.

———. "Le Droit à l'avortement." *Almanach de la question sociale*. Paris, 1893.

Mirtel, Héra. "Nous n'aurons pas encore législatrices en France." [sic] *Documents du progrés* July 1910.

Misme, Jane. *Les Dernières obstacles au vote des femmes*. Paris, nd.

———. "La Femme dans le théâtre nouveau." *Revue d'art dramatique* October 1901.

———. "Les Grands figures du féminisme: de Maria Deraismes à Maria Vérone." *Minerva* 12 October 1930.

———. "Les Grands figures du féminisme: Hubertine Auclert." *Minerva* 19 October 1930.

———. "Les Grands figures du féminisme: Jeanne Schmahl." *Minerva* 26 October 1930.

———. "Madame la Duchesse d'Uzès." *Revue bleue* October 1897.

———. *Pour le suffrage des femmes: le féminisme et la politique*. Paris, nd.

Monod, Sarah. *Souvenir de la conférence de Versailles 17 juin 1895*. Dôle, 1895.

Monod, Wilfred. *Masculin et féminin*. Paris, 1902.

Morsier, Emilie de. *La Mission de la femme: discours et fragments*. Paris, 1897.

Naudet, Paul. *Pour la femme: études féministes*. Paris, 1904.

Neera, Anna. *Les Idées d'une femme sur le féminisme*. Paris, 1908.

Oddo-Deflou, Jeanne. *Congrès national des droits civils et du suffrage des femmes*. Paris, 1908.

———. "Le Congrès national des droits civils et du suffrage des femmes tenu . . . 1908." *Liberté d'opinion* 1908.

———. *Le Sexualisme. Critique de la prépondérance et de la mentalité du sexe fort.* Paris, 1906.

Pégard, Marie, ed. *Deuxième congrès international des oeuvres et institutions féminines . . . 1900.* 4 vols. Paris, 1902.

Pelletier, Madeleine. "Admission des femmes à la franc-maçonnerie," *Acacia* May 1905.

———. *L'Ame existe-t-elle?* Paris, nd.

———. *L'Amour et la maternité.* Paris, nd.

———. *Capitalisme et communisme.* Nice, 1926.

———. *Le Célibat: état supérieur.* Caen, nd.

———. *Les Crimes et les châtiments.* Paris, nd.

———. *La Désagrégation de la famille.* Paris, nd.

———. *Le Droit au travail pour la femme.* Paris, nd.

———. *L'Echo de la pensée et la parole intérieure.* Paris, 1904.

———. *L'Education féministe des filles et autres textes.* Ed. Claude Maignien. Paris, 1978.

———. *L'Emancipation sexuelle de la femme.* Paris, 1911.

———. *L'Enseignement et la culture intellectuelle.* Paris, nd.

———. *Le Féminisme et la famille.* Paris, nd.

———. *La Femme en lutte pour ses droits.* Paris, 1908.

———. *La Femme vierge.* Paris, 1933.

———. *Les Femmes, peuvent-elles avoir du génie?* Paris, nd.

———. *La Guerre, est-elle naturelle?* Paris, nd.

———. "L'Idéal maçonique." *Acacia* May 1906.

———. *Idéal d'hier. Dieu, la morale, la patrie.* Paris, 1910.

———. *In anima virili, ou Un Crime scientifique.* Conflans-Sainte Honorine, 1920.

———. *Justice sociale?* Paris, 1913.

———. *Mon voyage aventureux en Russie communiste.* Paris, 1922.

———. *La Morale et la loi.* Paris, nd.

———. *Philosophie sociale: les opinions, les partis, les classes.* Paris, 1912.

———. *Pour l'abrogation de l'article 317: le droit de l'avortement.* Paris, 1913.

———. "La Prétendue infériorité psycho-physiologique des femmes." *La Vie normale* December 1904.

———. "La Question du vote des femmes." *Revue socialiste* 1909.

———. *La Rationalisation sexuelle.* Paris, 1935.

———. *La Religion contre la civilisation et le progrès.* Caen, nd.

——. *Supérieur! Drame des classes sociales en cinq actes.* Conflans, 1923.

——. *La Tactique féministe.* Paris, nd.

——. *Une Vie nouvelle.* Paris, 1932.

Poinsinet, L. *Le Rôle social de la femme.* Paris, 1906.

Poirson, S. *Mon féminisme.* Paris, 1905.

Potonié-Pierre, Eugénie. *Un peu plus tard.* Paris, 1892.

——. *L'Union libre.* Liege, 1902.

Pottecher, Thérèse. "Le Mouvement féministe en France." *Grande revue* February 1910 and January 1911.

Rauze, Marianne. *Féminisme intégral.* Vincennes, nd.

Remember, Madame. *Le Féminisme intégral.* Paris, 1919.

Renaudot, M. *Le Féminisme et les droits publics de la femme.* Niort, 1902.

Reval, Gabrielle. *L'Avenir de nos jeunes filles.* Paris, 1904.

——. *La Bachelière.* Paris, 1910.

——. *La Bachelière en Pologne.* Paris, 1913.

——. *Les Camps-volants de la Riviera.* Paris, 1908.

——. *La Cruche cassée.* Paris, 1904.

——. *Un Lycée de jeunes filles.* Paris, 1901.

——. *Lycéennes.* Paris, 1902.

——. *Notre-Dame des ardents.* Paris, 1903.

——. *Le Royaume du printemps.* Paris, 1913.

——. *Le Ruban de Vénus.* Paris, 1906.

——. *Les Sévriennes.* Paris, 1901.

Richer, Léon. *Le Code des femmes.* Paris, 1883.

——. *La Femme libre.* Paris, 1877.

Roussel, Nelly. *Derniers combats: receuil d'articles et de discours.* Paris, 1932.

——. *Discours prononcé au congrès du travail féminin en 1907.* Paris, nd.

——. *L'Eternelle sacrifiée.* Ed. Daniel Armogathe and Maïté Albistur. Paris, 1979.

——. *Ma forêt.* Paris, 1920.

——. *Par la révolte: scène symbolique.* Paris, c. 1903.

——. *Paroles de combat et d'espoir.* Epone, 1919.

——. *Quelques discours.* Paris, 1907.

——. *Quelques lances rompues pour nos libertés.* Paris, 1910.

——. *Trois conférences: "La Liberté de la maternité [. . .]" "La Femme et la libre pensée [. . .]" "Créons la citoyenne [. . .]"* Paris, 1930.

Rouzade, Léonie. *Les Classes dirigéantes et les travailleurs jugés par une femme.* Nancy, nd.

——. *Développement du programme de la société de l'Union des femmes . . .* Paris, 1880.

———. *La Femme et le peuple.* Paris, 1896.

———. *Petit catéchisme de morale laïque et socialiste.* Meudon, 1895.

Saumoneau, Louise. *Principes et action féministes socialistes.* Paris, nd.

Schirmacher, Kaethe. *Le Féminisme aux Etats-unis, en France, dans la Grande Bretagne, en Suède et en Russie.* Paris, 1898.

———. "Notes sur l'état du féminisme." *Revue de morale sociale* June 1899.

———. "Salaires de femmes." *Revue de morale sociale* December 1899.

———. *Le Travail des femmes en France.* Paris, 1902.

Schmahl, Jeanne. "L'Avenir du mariage." *L'Avant-Courière* 1896.

———. *Economie domestique.* Paris, 1907.

———. "Le Préjugé du sexe." *Nouvelle revue* March 1895.

———. "Progress of the Women's Rights Movement in France." *The Forum* September 1896.

———. "La Question de la femme." *Nouvelle revue* January 1894.

———. *Raisons biologiques et économiques de l'inégalité de la femme dans le travail.* Paris, 1905.

———. "Women's Suffrage in France." *Englishwoman's Review* 1902.

Sembat, Marcel. "L'Accession des femmes aux fonctions publiques." *Documents du progrès* January 1909.

Sertillanges, A. D. *Féminisme et christianisme.* Paris, 1908.

Séverine. *Choix de papiers.* Ed. Evelyne Le Garrec. Paris, 1982.

Société féministe du Havre. *Le Suffrage municipal des femmes.* Havre, 1913.

Terrisse, Marie C. *Notes et impressions à travers le féminisme.* Paris, 1896.

Thiébaux, Charles. "Le Féminisme et les socialistes depuis Saint-Simon jusqu'à nos jours." Diss. Paris, 1906.

Turgeon, Charles. *Le Féminisme français.* 2 vols. Paris, 1902.

Turmann, Max. *Initiatives féminines.* Paris, 1905.

UFSF. *Le Suffrage des femmes en France.* Paris, 1912.

———. *L'Union française et l'Alliance internationale pour le suffrage des femmes.* Paris, 1910.

Uzès, Anne, Duchesse d'. *Souvenirs.* Paris, 1930.

———. *Le Suffrage féminin au point de vue historique.* Meulan, 1914.

Valette, Aline. *Cahier des doléances féminines, 1er mai 1893 . . .* Paris, 1893.

———. *Socialisme et sexualisme.* Paris, 1895.

Vérone, Maria. *Appel à la justice adressé par le CNFF à la Chambre des députés et au Sénat: rapport . . .* Paris, 1909.

———. *La Femme devant la loi autour du monde.* Paris, 1930.

———. *La Femme et la loi.* Paris, 1920.

——. *Pourquoi les femmes veulent voter.* Paris, 1923.

——. *Quatre ans de nationalisme, 1900–1904.* Paris, 1904.

——. *Résultats du suffrage des femmes.* Paris, 1914.

——. *La Situation juridique des enfants naturels.* Paris, 1926.

Vérone, Maria, and Georges Lhermitte. *La Séparation et ses conséquences.* Paris, 1906.

Vérone, Maria, Chrystal MacMillan, and Marie Stritt. *Woman Suffrage in Practice.* London, 1913.

Villermont, Comtesse Marie de. *Le Mouvement féministe: ses causes, son avenir, solution chrétienne.* Paris, 1904.

Vincent, Eliska. *Congrès général des sociétés féministes.* Paris, 1892.

——. *Electorat et éligibilité des femmes aux conseils des prud'hommes.* Autun, 1907.

——. *Rapport à la VIe Conférence of the International Woman Suffrage Alliance, à Stockholm, 1911.* Paris, 1911.

——. *La Répression de la traite blanche et la préservation de la jeune fille: rapport.* Paris, 1905.

Viviani, René. "La Femme." *Grande revue* February 1901.

Witt-Schlumberger, Marguerite de. *Aux jeunes ouvrières.* Paris, 1911.

——. *Les Idées de Mrs. Olive Schreiner sur la femme et le travail.* Paris, nd.

——. *Une Femme aux femmes.* Paris, 1909.

——. "Du rôle de la femme dans l'éducation des garçons." *Revue de morale sociale* September 1900.

——. *Le Rôle des femmes de pasteurs en France pendant la guerre.* Paris, 1916.

——. *Situation international du suffrage des femmes en mars 1918.* Paris, 1918.

Yver, Colette. *La Bergerie.* Paris, 1904.

——. *Les Cervelines.* Paris, 1903.

——. *Un Coin de voile.* Paris, 1912,

——. *Comment s'en vont les reines.* Paris, 1905.

——. *Les Dames du palais.* Paris, 1910.

——. *Le Métier du roi.* Paris, 1911.

——. *Princesses de science.* Paris, 1907.

——. *Les Sables mouvants.* Paris, 1913.

II. Studies of the Woman Question during the Belle Epoque

Albistur, Maïté, and Daniel Armogathe. *Histoire du féminisme français.* 2 vols. Paris: Editions des femmes, 1977.

Aron, Jean-Paul, ed. *Misérable et glorieuse: la femme du XIXe siècle.* Paris: Fayard, 1980.

Bachrach, Susan D. *Dames Employées: The Feminization of Postal Work in Nineteenth Century France.* New York: Haworth, 1984.

Bardèche, Maurice. *Histoire des femmes.* 2 vols. Paris: Stock, 1968.

Bell, Susan Groag, and Karen M. Offen, eds. *Women, the Family and Freedom: The Debate in Documents, 1750–1950.* 2 vols. Stanford: Stanford UP, 1983.

Bellet, Roger, ed. *La Femme au XIXe siècle: Lutte et idéologie.* Lyon, 1978.

Benstock, Shari. *Women of the Left Bank.* Austin: U of Texas P, 1986.

Bidelman, Patrick. "Maria Deraismes, Léon Richer, and the Founding of the French Feminist Movement, 1866–1878." *Third Republic/Troisième République,* 3–4 (1977): 20–73.

———. *Pariahs Stand Up! The Founding of the Liberal Feminist Movement in France, 1858–1889.* Westport, CT: Greenwood, 1982.

———. "The Politics of French Feminism: Léon Richer and the Ligue française pour le droit des femmes, 1882–1891." *Historical Reflections* 3 (1976): 93–120.

Boxer, Marilyn J. "Foyer or Factory: Working Class Women in 19th Century France." *Proceedings of the Western Society for French History* (1975): 192–203.

———. "French Socialism, Feminism, and the Family." *Third Republic/Troisième République,* 3–4 (1977): 128–67.

———. "Protective Legislation and Home Industry: The Marginalization of Women Workers in Late 19th and Early 20th Century France." *Journal of Social History* 20 (1986): 45–65.

———. "Socialism Faces Feminism: The Failure of Synthesis in France, 1879–1914." In Marilyn J. Boxer and Jean H. Quataert, eds., *Socialist Women,* 75–111. New York: Greenwood, 1978.

———. "Socialism Faces Feminism in France, 1879–1913." Diss. Univ. of California–Riverside, 1975.

———. "When Radical and Socialist Women Were Joined: The Extraordinary Failure of Madeleine Pelletier." In Jane Slaughter and Robert Kern, eds., *European Women on the Left: Socialism, Feminism, and the Problems Faced by Political Women,* 57–74. Westport, CT: Greenwood, 1981.

———. "Women in Industrial Homework: The Flower-makers of Paris in the Belle Epoque." *French Historical Studies* 12 (1982).

Bernheimer, Charles. *Figures of Ill Repute: Representing Prostitution in Nineteenth-Century France.* Cambridge, MA: Harvard UP, 1989.

Brault, Eliane. *La Franc-maçonnerie et l'émancipation des femmes.* Paris: Dervy, 1953.

Bulger, Raymonde. *Lettres à Julie Victoire Daubié (1824–1874): la première bachelière de France et son temps.* New York: Peter Lang, 1992.

Charasson, Henriette. "La Littérature féminine." In Eugène Montfort, ed., *Vingt-cinq ans de littérature française.* 2 vols. Paris: Librairie de France, 1925. 2:65–98.

Charles-Roux, E., et al. *Les Femmes et le travail du moyen âge à nos jours.* Paris, 1975.

Clark, Linda L. "The Battle of the Sexes in a Professional Setting: The Introduction of Inspectrices Primaires, 1889–1914." *French Historical Studies* 16 (1989): 96–125.

———. "The Molding of the Citoyenne: The Image of the Female in French Educational Literature, 1880–1914." *Third Republic/Troisième République* 3–4 (1977): 74–103.

———. "Pauline Kergomard: Promoter of the Secularization of Schools and Advocate of Women's Rights," *Proceedings of the Western Society for French History* 17 (1990): 364–72.

———. "The Primary Education of French Girls: Pedagogical Prescriptions and Social Realities, 1880–1940." *History of Education Quarterly* (1981): 411–28.

———. *Schooling the Daughters of Marianne: Textbooks and the Socialization of Girls in Modern French Primary Schools.* Albany: SUNY P, 1983.

———. "The Socialization of Girls in the Primary Schools of the Third Republic." *Journal of Social History* 15 (1982): 685–97.

Cobb, Richard. "The Women of the Commune." In R. C. Cobb, *A Second Identity: Essays on France and French History,* 221–36. Oxford: Oxford UP, 1969.

Collins, Marie and Sylvie Weil-Sayre. *Les Femmes en France.* New York: Scribners, 1974.

Coons, Lorraine. *Women Home Workers in the Parisian Garment Industry, 1860–1915.* New York: Garland, 1991.

Copley, Antony. *Sexual Moralities in Modern France, 1780–1980: New Ideas on the Family, Divorce, and Homosexuality.* London: Routledge, 1989.

Corbin, Alain. *Women for Hire: Prostitution and Sexuality in France after 1850.* Cambridge, MA: Harvard UP, 1990.

Donovan, James M. "Abortion, the Law, and the Juries in France, 1825–1923. *Criminal Justice History* 9 (1988): 157–88.

———. "Infanticide and the Juries in France, 1825–1913. *Journal of Family History* 16 (1991): 157–76.

Dubief, H. "Hélène Brion, 1882–1962." *Mouvement social* 44 (1963): 93–97.

Dufrancatel, C. "Autobiographies de 'Femmes du peuple.'" *Mouvement social* 105 (1978): 147–56.

Evans, Richard J. *The Feminists: Women's Emancipation Movements in Europe, America, and Australasia, 1840–1920.* London: B & N Imports, 1977.

———. "Feminism and Anti-clericalism in France, 1870–1922." *Historical Journal* 25 (1982): 947–52.

Farge, Arlette, et al. *Madame ou mademoiselle: itinéraires de la solitude féminine, 18e–20e siècle.* Paris, 1984.

Fayet-Scribe, Sylvie. *Associations féminines et catholicisme: de la charité à l'action sociale, XIXe–XXe siècle.* Paris: Les Editions ouvrières, 1990.

Frader, Laura L. "La Femme et la famille dans les luttes viticoles de l'Aude, 1903–1913." *Sociologie du sud-est* 21 (1974): 33–54.

Fuchs, Rachel G. *Abandoned Children: Foundlings and Child Welfare in Nineteenth-Century France.* Albany: SUNY P, 1984.

———. "Legislation, Poverty, and Child Abandonment in Nineteenth Century Paris." *Journal of Interdisciplinary History* 18 (1987): 55–80.

———. "Morality and Poverty: Public Welfare for Mothers in Paris, 1870–1900." *French History* 2 (1988): 288–311.

———. *Poor and Pregnant: Strategies for Survival in the Nineteenth Century.* New Brunswick: Rutgers UP, 1992.

Goliber, Sue H. "The Life and Times of Marguerite Durand: A Study in French Feminism." Diss. Kent State U, 1975.

Gordon, Felicia. *The Integral Feminist: Madeleine Pelletier, 1874–1939.* Minneapolis: U of Minnesota P, 1991.

Guibert, Madeleine. *Les Femmes et l'organisation syndicale avant 1914: présentation et commentaires de documents pour une étude du syndicalisme féminin.* Paris: CNRS, 1966.

———. *Les Fonctions des femmes dans l'industrie.* Paris, 1966.

Guibert, Madeleine, N. Lowit, and M-H Zylberberg-Hocquard. *Travail et condition féminine: bibliographie commentée.* Vol. 1. *Avant 1914.* Paris, 1977.

Gullickson, Gay. "*La Pétroleuse:* Representing Revolution." *Feminist Studies* 17 (1991): 241–65.

Harsin, Jill. *Policing Prostitution in 19th Century Paris.* Princeton: Princeton UP, 1985.

Hause, Steven C. "Citizeness of the Republic: Class and Gender Identity in the Feminist Career of Hubertine Auclert." *Proceedings of the Western Society for French History* 12 (1985): 235–43.

———. "The Failure of Feminism of Provincial France, 1890–1920." *Proceedings of the Western Society for French History* 8 (1982): 423–36.

———. *Hubertine Auclert: The French Suffragette.* New Haven, Yale University Press, 1987.

———. "More Minerva than Mars: The French Women's Rights Campaign and the First World War." In Margaret R. Higonnet, et al., eds., *Behind the Lines: Gender and the Two World Wars,* 99–113. New Haven, Yale University Press, 1987.

———. "The Rejection of Women's Suffrage by the French Senate in November 1922: A Statistical Analysis." *Third Republic/Troisième République* 3–4 (1977): 205–37.

————. "Women Who Rallied to the Tricolor: The Effects of World War I on the French Women's Suffrage Movement." *Proceedings of the Western Society for French History* 6 (1979): 371–81.

Hause, Steven C., and Anne R. Kenney. "The Development of the Catholic Women's Suffrage Movement in France, 1896–1922." *Catholic Historical Review* 67 (1981): 11–30.

————. "The Limits of Suffragist Behavior: Legalism and Militancy in France, 1876–1922." *American Historical Review* 86 (1981): 781–806.

————. "Women's Suffrage and the Paris Elections of 1908." *Laurels* 51 (1980): 21–32.

Hause, Steven C., with Anne R. Kenney. *Women's Suffrage and Social Politics in the French Third Republic.* Princeton UP, 1984.

Heinzeley, Hélène. "Le Mouvement socialiste devant les problèmes du féminisme, 1879–1914." Diss. Paris, 1957.

Hellerstein, Erna O., Leslie P. Hume, and Karen M. Offen, eds. *Victorian Women: A Documentary Account of Women's Lives in 19th Century England, France, and the United States.* Stanford: Stanford UP, 1981.

Hilden, Patrica. "Women and the Labour Movement in France, 1869–1914." *Historical Journal* 29 (1986): 809–32.

————. *Working Women and Socialist Politics in France, 1880–1914: A Regional Study.* Oxford: Oxford UP, 1986.

Hunt, Persis C. "Revolutionary Syndicalism and Feminism Among Teachers in France, 1900–1921. Diss. Tufts U, 1975.

————. "Teachers and Workers: Problems of Feminist Organization in the Early Third Republic." *Third Republic/Troisième République* 3–4 (1977): 168–204.

Hunter, John C. "The Problem of the French Birth Rate on the Eve of World War I." *French Historical Studies* 2 (1962): 490–503.

Käppeli, Anne-Marie. *Sublime croisade: ethique et politique du féminisme protestant, 1875–1928.* Geneva: Loe, 1990.

Klejman, Laurence, and Florence Rochefort. *L'Egalité en marche: le féminisme sous la Troisième République.* Paris: Editions des femmes, 1989.

Kriegel, Annie. "Procès de guerre–procès Brion." *Mouvement Social* 44 (1963): 97–99.

Lacache, Bernard. *Séverine.* Paris: Gallimard, 1930.

Larnac, Jean. *Histoire de la littérature féminine en France.* Paris: Kra, 1929.

Le Garrec, Evelyne. *Séverine: une rebelle, 1855–1929.* Paris: Seuil, 1982.

Lesselier, Claudie. "Employées de grands magasins à Paris (avant 1914)." *Mouvement social* 105 (1978): 11–32.

Li Dzeh-Djen. *La Presse féministe en France de 1869 à 1914.* Paris: Rodstein, 1934.

McBride, Theresa. *Domestic Servants in 19th Century France.* New Brunswick: Rutgers, 1973.

———. "French Women and Trade Unionism: The First Hundred Years." In Norbert C. Soldon, ed., *The World of Women's Trade Unionism.* Westport, CT: Greenwood, 1985.

———. "Public Authority and Private Lives: Divorce after the French Revolution." *French Historical Studies* 17 (1992): 747–68.

———. "A Woman's World: Department Stores and the Evolution of Women's Employment, 1870–1920." *French Historical Studies* 10 (1978): 664–83.

McLaren, Angus. "Abortion in France: Women and the Regulation of Family Size, 1800–1914." *French Historical Studies* 10 (1978): 461–85.

———. "Sex and Socialism: The Opposition of the French Left to Birth Control in the 19th Century." *Journal of the History of Ideas* 37 (1976): 475–92.

———. *Sexuality and Social Order: The Debate over the Fertility of Women and Workers in France, 1770–1920.* New York: Holmes & Meier, 1983.

McMillan, James. "The Character of the French Feminist Movement, 1870–1914." In Fédération historique du sud-ouest, ed., *Actes du colloque franco-britannique tenu à Bordeaux du 27 au 30 septembre 1876: Sociétés et groupes sociaux en Aquitaine et en Angleterre.* Bordeaux, 1979.

———. "Clericals, Anticlericals, and the Women's Movement in France under the Third Republic." *Historical Journal* 24 (1981): 361–76.

———. *Housewife or Harlot: The Place of Women in French Society, 1870–1940.* New York: St. Martin, 1981.

Margadant, Jo Burr. *Madame le Professeur: Women Educators in the Third Republic.* Princeton: Princeton UP, 1990.

Martin-Fugier, Anne. *La Bourgeoise.* Paris: Grasset, 1983.

———. "La Fin des nourrices." *Mouvement social* 105 (1978): 11–32.

———. *La Place des bonnes.* Paris: Grasset, 1979.

Mayeur, Françoise. *L'Education des jeunes filles en France au XIXe siècle.* Paris: Hachette, 1979.

———. *L'Enseignement secondaire des jeunes filles sous la Troisième République.* Paris: Fondation nationale des sciences politiques, 1977.

Mitchell, Claudine. "Madeleine Pelletier (1874–1939): The Politics of Sexual Oppression." *Feminist Review* 33 (1989): 72–92.

Moch, Leslie P. "Government Policy and Women's Experience: The Case of Teachers in France." *Feminist Studies* 14 (1988): 301–24.

Moreau, Thérèse. *Le Sang de l'histoire: Michelet et l'idée de la femme au 19e siècle.* Paris, 1982.

Moses, Claire G. *French Feminism in the 19th Century.* Albany: SUNY P, 1984.

———. "Debating the Present, Writing the Past: 'Feminism' in French History and Historiography." *Radical History Review* 52 (1992): 79–94.

Offen, Karen. "Aspects of the Woman Question during the Third Republic." *Third Republic/Troisième République* 3–4 (1977): 1–19.

———. "Defining Feminism: A Comparative Historical Approach." *Signs* 14 (1988): 119–57.

———. "Depopulation, Nationalism and Feminism in Fin-de-siècle France." *American Historical Review* 89 (1984): 648–76.

———. "Ernest Legouvé and the Doctrine of 'Equality in Difference' for Women: A Case Study of Male Feminism in 19th Century French Thought." *Journal of Modern History* 58 (1986): 452–84.

———. "On the Origins of the Words 'Feminist' and 'Feminism.' " *Feminist Issues* 8 (1988).

———. "The Second Sex and the Baccalauréat in Republican France, 1880–1924." *French Historical Studies* 13 (1983): 252–86.

———. "Sur l'origine des mots 'féminisme et féministe.' " *Revue d'histoire moderne et contemporaine* 34 (1987): 492–96.

Pasquier, Marie-Claire, et al. *Stratégies des femmes.* Paris, 1984.

Perillon, Marie C. *Vies de femmes: les travaux et les jours de la femme à la Belle Epoque.* Roanne, 1981.

Perrot, Michelle. "Les Ménagères et la classe ouvrière." In *Les Femmes et la classe ouvrière.* Colloque. Vincennes, 1978.

———. "De la nourrice à l'employée . . . travaux de femmes dans la France du XIXe siècle." *Mouvement social* 105 (1978): 3–10.

———. "Sur l'histoire des femmes en France." *Revue du Nord* July 1981.

———. "Quelques éléments de bibliographie sur l'histoire du travail des femmes en France (principalement au XIXe siècle)" *Mouvement social* 105 (1978): 127–36.

———, ed. *Travaux de femmes dans la France du XIXe siècle,* Special issue of *Mouvement social* 105 (1978).

Phillips, Roderick. *Putting Asunder: A History of Divorce in Western Society.* Cambridge: Cambridge UP, 1988.

Priolland, Nicole, ed. *La Femme au 19e siècle.* Paris, 1983.

Puget, Jean. *La Duchesse d'Uzès.* Uzès, Gard: Peladan, 1972.

Quartararo, Anne T. "The Ecoles normales primaires d'institutrices: A Social History of Women Primary School Teachers in France, 1879–1905." Diss. UCLA, 1982.

Rabaut, Jean. *Féministes à la Belle Epoque.* Paris, 1985.

————. *Histoire des féminismes français*. Paris: Stock, 1978.

————. "1900, Tournant du féminisme français." *Bulletin de la Société d'histoire moderne* 17 (1983).

Rafferty, Frances. "Madame Séverine: Crusading Journalist of the Third Republic." *Contemporary French Civilization* 1 (1977): 185–202.

Rebérioux, Madeleine, Christiane Dufrancatel, and Béatrice Slama. "Hubertine Auclert et la question des femmes à 'l'immortel congrès' (1879)." *Romantisme* 13–14 (1976): 123–42.

Riemer, Eleanor S., and John C. Fout, eds. *European Women: A Documentary History, 1789–1945*. New York: Schocken, 1980.

Ronsin, Francis. *La Grève des ventres: propagande néo-malthusienne et baisse de la natalité française, XIXe-XXe siècles*. Paris: Aubier, 1980.

Sanua, Louli. *Figures féminines, 1900–1939*. Paris: Siboney, 1949.

Sarti, Odile. *The Ligue patriotique des françaises, 1902–1933: A Feminine Response to the Secularization of French Society*. New York: Garland, 1992.

Schnapper, Bernard. "La Séparation de corps de 1837 à 1914: essai de sociologie juridique." *Revue historique* 526 (1978): 454–57.

Scott, Joan C., and Louise Tilly. "Women's Work and the Family in 19th Century Europe." *Comparative Studies in Society and History* 17 (1975): 36–64.

Shaffer, John W. "Family, Class, and Young Women: Occupational Expectations in 19th Century Paris." In Robert Wheaton and Tamara K. Hareven, eds., *Family and Sexuality in French History*, 179–200. Philadelphia: U of Pennsylvania P, 1980.

Smith, Bonnie G. *Ladies of the Leisure Class: The Bourgeoises of Northern France in the Nineteenth Century*. Princeton: Princeton UP, 1981.

Sowerwine, Charles. *Les Femmes et le socialisme*. Paris, 1978.

————. "Le Groupe féministe socialiste: 1899–1902." *Mouvement social* 90 (1975): 87–120.

————. "Madeleine Pelletier (1874–1939): femme, médicin, militante." *L'Information psychiatrique* November 1988.

————. "The Organization of French Socialist Women, 1880–1914." *Historical Reflections* 3 (1976): 3–24.

————. *Sisters or Citizens? Women and Socialism in France since 1876*. Cambridge: Cambridge UP, 1982.

————. "Socialism, Feminism, and Violence: The Analysis of Madeleine Pelletier." *Proceedings of the Western Society for French History* 8 (1980).

————. "Women and the Origins of the French Socialist Party." *Third Republic/ Troisième République* 3–4 (1977): 104–27.

————. "Workers and Women in France before 1914: The Debate over the Couriau Affair." *Journal of Modern History* 55 (1983): 411–44.

Stewart, Mary Lynn. *Women, Work, and the French State: Labour Protection and Social Patriarchy, 1879–1919*. Kingston, ON: U of Toronto P, 1989.

Strumingher, Laura S. "L'Ange de la maison: Mothers and Daughters in 19th Century France." *International Journal of Women's Studies* 2 (1979): 51–61.

Sullerot, Evelyne. *Histoire et sociologie du travail féminin*. Paris: Gonthier, 1968.

————. *La Presse féminine*. Paris: A. Colin, 1963.

Sussman, George. *Selling Mother's Milk: The Wet-Nursing Business in France, 1715–1914*. Urbana: U of Illinois P, 1982.

Thiesse, Anne-Marie. *Le Roman du quotidien: lecteurs et lectures populaires à la Belle Epoque*. Paris, 1984.

Tilly, Louise A. "Structure de l'emploi, travail des femmes et changement démographique dans deux villes industrielles: Anzin et Roubaix, 1872–1906." *Mouvement social* 105 (1978): 33–58.

————. "Women's Collective Action and Feminism in France, 1870–1914." In Louise A. Tilly and Charles Tilly, eds., *Class Conflict and Collective Action*. Beverly Hills: Sage, 1981.

Tilly, Louise, and Joan W. Scott. *Women, Work, and the Family*. New York: Holt, Rinehart and Winston, 1978.

Waelti-Walters, Jennifer. *Feminist Novelists of the Belle Epoque: Love as a Lifestyle*. Bloomington: Indiana UP, 1990.

Weitz, Margaret C. *Femmes: Recent Writings on French Women*. Boston: G. K. Hall, 1985.

Weston, Elizabeth A. *Prostitution in Paris in the Later Nineteenth Century: A Study in Politics and Social Ideology*. Diss. SUNY–Buffalo, 1979.

Wilkins, Wyona H. "The Paris International Feminist Congress of 1896 and Its French Antecedents." *North Dakota Quarterly* 43 (1975): 5–28.

Zylberberg-Hocquard, Marie-Hélène. *Femmes et féminisme dans le mouvement ouvrier français*. Paris: Editions ouvrières, 1981.

————. *Féminisme et syndicalisme en France*. Paris, 1978.

————. "Les Ouvrières d'état (tabacs et allumettes) dans les dernières années du XIXe siècle." *Mouvement social* 105 (1978): 87–108.

Index